PLANNING·ENVI

Series Editors:Yvonne Rydi

The context in which planning operates has changed dramatically in recent years. Economic processes have become increasingly globalized and new spatial patterns of economic activity have emerged. There have been major changes across the globe, not just changing administrations in various countries but also the sweeping away of old ideologies and the tentative emergence of new ones. A new environmental agenda emerged from the Brundtland Report and the Rio Earth Summit prioritizing the goal of sustainable development. The momentum for this has been maintained by continued action at international, national and local levels.

Cities are today faced with new pressures for economic competitiveness, greater accountability and participation, improved quality of life for citizens and global environmental responsibilities. These pressures are often contradictory and create difficult dilemmas for policy-makers, especially in the context of fiscal austerity. New relationships are developing between the levels of state activity and between public and private sectors as different interests respond to the new conditions.

In these changing circumstances, planners, from many backgrounds, in many different organizations, have come to re-evaluate their work. They have had to engage with actors in government, the private sector and non-governmental organizations in discussions over the role of planning in relation to the environment and cities. The intention of the Planning, Environment, Cities series is to explore the changing nature of planning and contribute to the debate about its future.

The series is primarily aimed at students and practitioners of planning and such related professions as estate management, housing and architecture as well as those in politics, public and social administration, geography and urban studies. It comprises both general texts and books designed to make a more particular contribution, in both cases characterized by: an international approach; extensive use of case studies; and emphasis on contemporary relevance and the application of theory to advance planning practice.

PLANNING·ENVIRONMENT·CITIES

Series Editors: Yvonne Rydin and Andrew Thornley

Published

Philip Allmendinger
Planning Theory (2nd edn)

Ruth Fincher and Kurt Iveson
Planning and Diversity in the City: Redistribution, Recognition and Encounter

Cliff Hague, Euan Hague and Carrie Breitbach
Regional and Local Economic Development

Patsy Healey
Collaborative Planning (2nd edn)

Patsy Healey
Making Better Places: The Planning Project in the 21st Century

Ted Kitchen
Skills for Planning Practice

Peter Newman and Andrew Thornley
Planning World Cities (2nd edn)

Michael Oxley
Economics, Planning and Housing

Yvonne Rydin
Urban and Environmental Planning in the UK (2nd edn)

Geoff Vigar, Patsy Healey and Angela Hull with Simin Davoudi
Planning, Governance and Spatial Strategy in Britain

Other titles planned include

Introduction to Planning
Urban Design

Planning, Environment, Cities
Series Standing Order
ISBN 0–333–71703–1 hardback
ISBN 0–333–69346–9 paperback
(*outside North America only*)

You can receive future titles in this series as they are published. To place a standing order please contact your bookseller or, in the case of difficulty, write to us at the address below with your name and address, the title of the series and the ISBN quoted above.

Customer Services Department, Macmillan Distribution Ltd
Houndmills, Basingstoke, Hampshire RG21 6XS, England

Regional and Local Economic Development

Cliff Hague

Euan Hague

Carrie Breitbach

palgrave
macmillan

First published 2011 by
PALGRAVE MACMILLAN

Palgrave Macmillan in the UK is an imprint of Macmillan Publishers Limited,
registered in England, company number 785998, of Houndmills, Basingstoke,
Hampshire RG21 6XS.

Palgrave Macmillan in the US is a division of St Martin's Press LLC,
175 Fifth Avenue, New York, NY 10010.

Palgrave Macmillan is the global academic imprint of the above companies
and has companies and representatives throughout the world.

Palgrave® and Macmillan® are registered trademarks in the United States,
the United Kingdom, Europe and other countries.

ISBN 978–0–230–21382–1   hardback
ISBN 978–0–230–21383–8   paperback

This book is printed on paper suitable for recycling and made from fully
managed and sustained forest sources. Logging, pulping and manufacturing
processes are expected to conform to the environmental regulations of the
country of origin.

A catalogue record for this book is available from the British Library.

A catalog record for this book is available from the Library of Congress.

10   9   8   7   6   5   4   3   2   1
20   19   18   17   16   15   14   13   12   11

Printed and bound in China

7475521

For Irene and Isla

Authors' previous publications

Cliff Hague, *The Development of Planning Thought: A Critical Perspective* (Hutchinson, 1984)

Cliff Hague and Paul Jenkins (eds.), *Place identity, Participation and Planning* (Routledge, 2005)

Cliff Hague, Pat Wakely, Julie Crespin and Chris Jasko, *Making Planning Work: A Guide to Approaches and Skills* (Practical Action, 2006)

Cliff Hague and Will French, *Urban Challenges: Scoping the State of the Commonwealth's Cities* (ComHabitat, 2010)

Euan Hague, Winifred Curran and the Pilsen Alliance, *Contested Chicago – Pilsen and Gentrification/Pilsen y el aburguesamiento: Una lucha para conservar nuestra comunidad* (www.lulu.com, 2008)

Euan Hague, Edward H. Sebesta and Heidi Beirich (ed.), *Neo-Confederacy: A Critical Introduction* (University of Texas, 2008)

Contents

List of Illustrative Material

Figures

Tables

Diagrams

Boxes

Acknowledgements

The authors wish to thank Heriot-Watt University for agreeing to the use of some materials that had been written for a previous distance-learning module entitled 'Place competitiveness and physical infrastructure'. Harry Smith had co-authored some of those materials with Cliff Hague and Harry's agreement for use of them is appreciated. Thanks are also due to Ya Ping Wang of Heriot-Watt University and Dan MacElrevey of the Doo Wop Preservation League for giving us photographs and permission to reproduce them.

We also wish to thank the Series Editors, Yvonne Rydin and Andy Thornley for their support throughout the commissioning and writing process, and for their comments on the first draft of the manuscript. Similarly, an anonymous reviewer provided valuable advice at that stage. Thanks are also due to Steven Kennedy at Palgrave Macmillan for his persistence in seeking to get this book initiated, and to Stephen Wenham for his support throughout the writing.

Faith Kohler diligently checked and collated references and proofread the manuscript; her help was invaluable. DePaul University undergraduate students Michael C. Armstrong, Phillip T. Jones and Darcy Lydum aided us as research assistants. Elisa Addlesperger and others at DePaul's library helped to locate materials. We are grateful to James Tobin of Fado Irish Pub and Fitz Haile of the Creative Coast Alliance for taking the time to speak with Euan Hague. Alec Brownlow, Winifred Curran, Alex Papadopoulos, Michael Hirsh, Igor Vojnovic and Kevin Ward kindly provided copies of their research, as did Elise Achugbue of Social Compact Inc. Victoria Romero and Alejandra Ibañez provided additional material about Pilsen, Chicago, and Beth Nicols, Executive Director of the Milwaukee Downtown Business Improvement District, kindly responded to requests for information. Thanks to Martin

Barr for copy-editing and Victoria Chow for preparing the index. Lastly, Carrie Breitbach would like to acknowledge the support of Chicago State University, particularly the Department of Geography, and Euan Hague thanks DePaul University and its Department of Geography.

1 Introduction

Standing on the Bund, as cargo boats ply to and fro, you look across the Huangpu River to Pudong, and are dazzled by the architectural extravaganza of Shanghai's skyline (see Figure 1.1). The sheer dynamism of this global city's economic development is evident all around. Construction of Pudong only began in 1990. Within a decade it became China's financial centre. With over 15 million people, the rapidly growing Shanghai metropolis is the world's fourth largest city. Starbucks, Pizza Hut and other global names jostle for lucrative sites where once the Red Guards paraded in the cause of Chairman Mao's Cultural Revolution. There are huge shopping malls whose facades are faced with expensive granite. Above them prestigious office blocks dominate the skyline with an architectural flourish.

Figure 1.1   **Shanghai's skyline, China**

1

Bishop Street is a ordinary side street in a slightly shabby part of Chicago. There are three small houses, all built in the late nineteenth century, and all owned by members of a Mexican-American family who first settled in the USA two generations ago. The houses overlook a colourful mural depicting Mexican revolutionaries, Mayan step pyramids, an eagle and cornfields (Figure 1.2). At the centre of the mural is a multigenerational family. On their right, the sinister claws of a hooded figure, surrounded by bags of money, are pulling at people. To the left of the family, people are parading signs saying 'Not for Sale', 'Stop Gentrification' and 'TIF = Ethnic Cleansing'. TIF is Tax Increment Financing, an economic development tool widely used in the USA. It enables income from local taxation to be targeted on projects that are intended to boost private investment into the neighbourhood. To the north of these three houses is a popular, artsy café; to the south, a former manufacturing facility now converted into luxury flats and a private gym. This is Pilsen. It is about 3 miles south-west of Chicago's Loop central business district.

In rural Sweden, 150 miles west of Stockholm, Värmland County works with the slogan 'Sustainable development through the market'.

Figure 1.2 **Detail of the mural *Alto al Desplazamiento Urbano de Pilsen*, by Hector Duarte and others, located on Bishop Street, Chicago, USA**

GreenMarket is one of several initiatives there. Through it, the County promotes environmentally sustainable business practices to the local business community. They show entrepreneurs how to apply lifecycle analyses to product design, so that the full environmental impacts of a product – from production, through its use and disposal – can be seen and managed. There is a green-product development programme for small businesses, backed by a training and technical assistance programme and grants to hire technical consultants to evaluate new ideas (James and Lahti, 2004: 91).

Mumbai, one of India's economic dynamos, is home to five million slum dwellers. Almost half of the slum households get their water from shared standpipes: only 5 per cent have access through individual taps. Roughly three out of every four of the slum households are dependent on public toilets, which in turn are often a health hazard because of poor maintenance and overuse. Despite these conditions, Mumbai remains a magnet for migrants (UN–Habitat, 2006: 26). Community organizations have won a contract to build 211 toilet blocks in slum areas. They were organized through a group of non-governmental organizations (NGOs), including the Indian Alliance of the Society for the Promotion of Area Resource Centres (SPARC) and the National Slum Dwellers Federation. The construction of the individual blocks has been subcontracted to a multitude of small-scale community contractors, many of which would not be in business but for this World Bank-funded programme. In this way new enterprises can be stimulated among the poor, so that slum residents not only gain vital improvements in sanitation, but also new economic opportunities (McLeod and Hughes, 2006: 142).

These snapshots reveal some fundamental aspects of regional and local economic development in today's world. First, the USA and the UK do not have a monopoly of the practice. This is contrary to the impression that might be gained from scanning the academic literature, where, for example, Anglo-American perceptions of good governance tend to underpin the analysis. Second, there is a wide range of very different practices, undertaken by very different agencies. Some key drivers of development are private sector, some public, some are NGOs; global institutions or governments may be involved but there are also actions at neighbourhood level or in rural settings. There is no single correct approach: what works in one place may not work in another. Third, this diversity not only reflects different development and governance contexts, but also different priorities. Is the aim to maximize economic efficiency, or environmentally sustainable development, or poverty alleviation? Does it matter if a development makes some people rich while leaving others in poverty? Fourth, and related to this, expect conflicts. Finally, the process of regional and local economic development is practice led, rather than theoretically predetermined.

The aims of the book

The book builds on these observations. It aims to introduce readers to the policy and practice of regional and local economic development. This statement may sound bland, but it is important, so let us elaborate. There is a growing academic literature in this field. Robust theoretical writings by geographers, political scientists and environmental scientists (among others) offer explanations and interpretations of how and why settlements and regional economies are developing. Students and practitioners should be aware of these ideas. Good theory can enlighten practice, and most practice is implicitly based on some kind of theory.

However, practice is not dependent on theory. Work in a development company, a central or local government agency, or in an NGO is opportunistic and reactive. Pressures of time and limited resources mean that the key question is 'what can be done?', and not 'what does theory tell us to do?'. Theorizing is about explanation or interpretation that is generalized: practice is concerned with specific situations and details. In principle it is appealing to imagine that theory should inform practice and be built on practice. However, in reality the tension between theory and practice is not a result of ignorance or disinterest: it is due to different priorities and different systems of rewards and punishments among different peer groups. In other words, theorists have to produce writings that appeal to other theorists, while practitioners have to deliver results, and the quicker the better!

In aiming to introduce readers to the policy and practice of regional and local economic development, the intention is to structure the book around real examples and initiatives. It means making extensive use of case studies to show approaches to problem solving. Such an approach is open to criticism. Case studies are not necessarily representative. They are only illustrative and cannot be fully evaluative. Nevertheless, case studies are the only means to demonstrate the diversity of practices that exist. By using case studies we are able to provide evidence of the scope and purposes of economic development. Thus we discuss science parks but also schools, innovation hubs but also homeless people, business support but also bars and nightclubs.

The case studies also show that regional and local economic development exists as practice, is led by practice, and learns from practice. It has been recognized for a long time that policy-making typically takes the form of 'disjointed incrementalism' (Lindblom, 1959). Lindblom argued that theory can be unhelpful in policy-making, because it demands a lot of data but also lacks precision for a particular situation. Most policy-making is based on limited information and understanding, rather than being a rigorously rational process. This insight underpins the notion of policy learning, which has been defined as 'a process in which knowledge about policies, administrative arrangements, institutions etc. in one time and/or place is used in the development of policies, administrative arrangements and institutions in another time and/or place' (Dolowitz and Marsh, 1996: 343). Policy learning can take different forms and draw on multiple sources. Our aim in writing this book is that we might contribute to this form of learning for students of and practitioners in economic development.

A further defining feature of the book is that it is international in scope, rather than rooted in any particular national set of organizations, legislation and development processes. Necessarily this means that some rigor and detail is sacrificed. However, we believe that an international perspective brings significant gains. The global reach of the English language means that conventional academic texts privilege writers whose first language is English. One result is that Anglo-American situations and examples tend to be presented as norms which define practice, while there is much less international coverage of what is happening in other parts of the world. Nel and Rogerson (2005) noted that there has been very little writing or research on local economic development in the global South. It is common to speak of 'globalization', but in the USA and UK awareness of what is happening in other countries remains surprisingly limited. The book will show just how vibrant economic development practices are in parts of Asia and Africa, for example. No country has a monopoly on wisdom in this field: we can all learn from others. The practice of regional and local economic development is diverse. When viewed internationally, the sheer opportunism and vitality of practice, with its diverse agents and stakeholders to satisfy, is striking. Our aim is to capture this within the pages of a book. We hope that by bringing together diverse examples and contrasting approaches we can create spillovers and synergies, replicating conditions that are now recognized as motors of innovation in business (see, e.g. De la Mothe and Pacquet, 1998).

While the focus of the book is on policy and practice, it is important to stress that there is a place for theory too. Theory can provide insights and understanding to newcomers and complement experience for those already working in the field. While theory that does not connect with practice can be abstract and confusing, ignorance of theory and a disregard for evidence and testing is a shaky foundation for practice. A reflective, questioning approach to practice can be greatly enriched by exposure to theories that offer explanations and interpretations of the dynamics of regions and of policy interventions. Therefore the book identifies and summarizes relevant academic ideas and findings where they can illuminate or deepen understanding of practice.

Readers are encouraged to explore such theories in more depth by following the signposts provided to original articles and wider debates.

What is regional and local economic development?

The World Bank (2010a) provides a basic definition of Local Economic Development (LED). It says that: 'The purpose of LED is to build up the economic capacity of a local area to improve its economic future and the quality of life for all. It is a process by which public, business and non-governmental partners can work collectively to create better conditions for economic growth and employment generation.' The Bank uses some key words to further specify the nature of LED. These are 'competitiveness', 'sustainable growth' and 'inclusive'. It adds: 'LED is thus about communities continually improving their investment climate and business enabling environment to enhance their competitiveness, retain jobs and improve incomes.'

While the World Bank stresses cooperation and benefits for all, the book will show that LED policies and practices are often contentious. A distinction can be made between approaches that are primarily pro-business and ones that are pro-poor. Nel and Rogerson (2005: 5) for example, suggested that poverty alleviation was much more important in LED work in the global South than in the global North. The aim of the book is to encompass the wide variety of approaches that characterize the practice of LED. Thus both pro-poor and pro-business initiatives are covered.

The World Bank website also has a useful section on the history of LED (World Bank, 2010b). This identifies three phases. First, from the 1960s until the early 1980s, the focus was on provision of hard infrastructure (e.g. roads, dams) and the attraction of mobile manufacturing industry and foreign direct investment, typically through offering grants, loans and tax breaks. The second phase lasted until the mid-1990s and saw the focus move towards the retention and nurturing of local businesses and a more selective targeting of inward investment. To this end the scope of LED expanded to take in things such as the provision of incubators and small business units, new business parks, and also advice and support services to small and medium-sized firms. Then from the late 1990s, in a third phase, the emphasis shifted away from a focus on individual firms and towards enhancing the business environment as a whole. This meant a new emphasis on 'soft' aspects of LED, such as networking, training and skills, and also public–private partnerships. There was a new recognition that the general 'quality of life' which a location can offer is itself an influence on its capacity to attract and hold businesses and key people.

While the idea of three phases is useful and tells a story that can be widely recognized, it is important to remember that these phases are generalizations. For example, in some places public–private partnerships began earlier than the late 1990s. Similarly, provision of hard infrastructure is still a part of today's strategy. In addition, while the World Bank stresses the need for an overall strategy and a holistic approach, it does not follow that the strategy in any particular place will encompass all the items in the World Bank's listing. To work, a strategy has to be rooted in a careful analysis of the particular local situation.

Chapter 2 will look at factors that triggered these shifts. However, we should note that the increase in concern for the environment, and worries about carbon emissions and global climate change are also impacting on LED. While the World Bank talks about 'sustainable growth', it understates the extent to which environmental sustainability has become an aim of LED in the twenty-first century.

What is meant by 'regional' and 'local', and what are the relations between the two? The World Bank (2010a) says that 'the practice of local economic development can be undertaken at different geographic scales'. In this sense, 'local' only really means 'sub-national', and includes initiatives taken by a regional body as well as actions that have a regional impact. Definitions of regions are ambiguous and can change. It is no coincidence that in any one country, different services, such as health care, education or public transit operation, often have different regional boundaries. As urban areas have spread out, travel-to-work distances have increased, and labour and housing markets have become more extensive, and the search for economies of scale and 'critical mass' intensified, so the scale of a region has also tended to stretch.

While market forces tend to be unconstrained by administrative boundaries, public bodies, and particularly local governments, can be blinkered by them, and the focus of officials stops at the city limits. In fact most economic development initiatives will benefit by having a regional dimension. Firms are unlikely to locate, survive or expand in a location purely on the basis of the local qualities of the town. The regional context – the markets it offers, its infrastructure, training institutions and networks of suppliers – is likely to be very important. Some regions straddle national boundaries, and where a regional tier of administration exists, local policy is more likely to work if it is backed by regional policy, and vice versa. Thus the book uses the term 'regional and local' rather than just 'local economic development'.

Governance

As the World Bank's short history of LED implies, taking and implementing decisions in economic development, has become increasingly complex. Where once governments acted in relative isolation, forms of partnership with the private sector and/or civil society organizations have become more significant. The power of governments (national, regional or local) to do things unilaterally has decreased. Indeed in the European Union for example, these layers of government are themselves overlain by a transnational level. Instead of a linear, top-down chain of command, where instructions and funds for investment were passed down, we now see far more complicated arrangements, initiatives from below, funds from several different sources and the involvement of people and agencies sitting outside formal government structures. The term 'governance' captures this more fluid situation for managing economic development. Successful schemes often require an ability to connect and harness actions and policies across different levels of government. This is the idea of multilevel governance.

Governments are rarely unitary or coherent: even in totalitarian states there will be different bureaucratic groupings competing to shape the policy agenda. Governments at all levels have different departments with differing objectives. Understanding the governance context is essential for successful practice – or academic analysis – of regional and local economic development. This means understanding the nuances of interests, power and influence in any given situation. Such awareness is necessary to build coalitions to support initiatives, or at least to neutralize opposition. Sometimes an understanding of the governance context will lead to the recognition that change and innovation is necessary. For example, it may be necessary to challenge existing mindsets, or to set up a new agency with an economic development brief. Gaining such understanding often involves learning on the job – and from mistakes. It involves a mix of political sensitivity and skills in dealing with people. While an element of this is instinctive, there should always be some consideration of the array of agencies and actors whose support can make a difference to a project.

There is a growing academic literature that stresses the importance of institutions. Key texts exploring 'New Institutional Economics' include North (1990) and Bates (1997, 2005), two authors whose work has influenced the development policy of the World Bank (Leys, 1996). North's argument has been that the assumptions of neoclassical economics (perfect competition, perfect information, rational choice, etc.) too often are not realized in practice. To achieve economic development there have to be effective economic organizations, with rules, principles and mindsets. Such institutions create order and reduce uncertainty, and thus enhance the feasibility and profitability of economic activity. Thus, in this theory, the political and legal framework is very important to the pursuit of economic development.

Bates (1997) provides a concrete example of the importance of institutions to economic development in his discussion of the coffee industry in Colombia. He explains how both of the main political parties need the support of the coffee growers to achieve an electoral majority. Thus both the party of the right and the party of the left followed 'pro-coffee' policies, with the result that support for the small coffee farmers became institutionalized in government policy. In turn, policy stability is likely to create business confidence and thus make investment, especially in fixed capital items like buildings and machinery, more likely.

A feature of the practice of local economic development is that often it works through projects – time-limited interventions that have a special budget and usually quite short-term aims. Such projects are often allocated through a competitive process that is organized by a tier of government, and in which other governments at a lower tier, businesses or community organizations bid to take part. In this way higher tiers of government are able to set a policy framework but, in effect, decentralize the implementation of those policies. The rules of bidding and the criteria for evaluation of bids themselves shape attitudes and practices, by providing incentives to the contenders to act in ways consistent with the overall aims of policy. Some authors, for example Andersson (2006), Marsden and Sonnino (2005), High and Nemes (2007), have gone so far as to speak of the 'project state'. This captures the idea that there has been a shift from a 'welfare state' in which governments had a controlling role, to a situation in which governments are coordinators of a range of other agencies. Of course, this does not mean that coordination is always a success. Indeed there can still be tensions between tiers of government and between governments and their partners in the development process.

In summary, the form that regional and local economic development policy and practice takes is both a consequence of systems of governance and also a shaper of such systems. While projects are often a key part of practice, and may well involve multiple partners, there are still situations where strong governments, at whatever scale, can take decisive action to influence economic development, especially where they control land and have significant fiscal powers.

A typology of approaches to policies and practice

Faced with what might seem like a bewildering array of approaches to regional and local economic development, it is useful to have some way of categorizing policies and practices. This can be done by asking two basic questions. The first of these is: do policies prioritize economic efficiency alone, or is environmental sustainability and/ or social cohesion seen as being at least as important? The practice of regional and local economic development is always likely to be shaped by ideologies and political priorities. The distinction between pro-business and pro-poor approaches that seek social cohesion has already been noted. The increasing importance attached to environmental sustainability may also be given high priority by some policy-makers. This question can therefore provide one dimension to a typology, as shown in Diagram 1.1. On the left of the

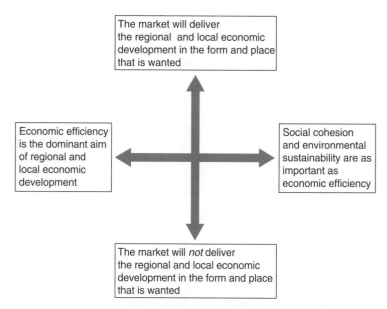

The market will deliver the regional and local economic development in the form and place that is wanted

Economic efficiency is the dominant aim of regional and local economic development

Social cohesion and environmental sustainability are as important as economic efficiency

The market will *not* deliver the regional and local economic development in the form and place that is wanted

Diagram 1.1   **Policy priorities and expectations of market outcomes**

diagram the focus of policy is only on economic outcomes; on the right of the diagram, good environment and social cohesion are believed to be just as important as economic outcomes. Between these two poles are positions where the relative importance of economic as against social and environmental concerns is more mixed. In practice the ends of policies may be blurred, or policies may sit in this 'middle ground' encompassing some combination of business, poverty alleviation and environmental ends. However, a distinction between economic efficiency as the sole aim and economic efficiency balanced against social and environmental aims is a useful way to sort out different approaches to policies and practice.

The second question is whether the policy-makers expect the market to produce the kind of development that they want? For example, will the market produce enough jobs within a particular region, or part of the region? Will the market produce new 'green' industries? In some situations, and for some policy-makers, the expectation will be that the market will deliver the desired economic development. Thus at times and in places where the market is strong, and the resulting development is deemed politically to be desirable, the economic development process is likely to be market led. In contrast, in situations where the market is weak or seen to be failing in some way (e.g. through lack of demand or through supply-side shortfalls such as skill shortages), then policies and practice are likely to be focused on boosting the market, filling gaps left by the market, or even replacing the market by other forms of development. These differences are expressed in the vertical dimension of Diagram 1.1. Market-led approaches are at the top with the degree of action to boost or replace the market increasing towards the bottom.

Using these two basic questions – about policy priorities and market expectations – it is possible to identify four main types of approach. These are shown in Diagram 1.2, and are now described.

Pro-business competition to attract inward investment

This is an approach that aims to take advantage of the economic opportunities offered by market forces to achieve prosperity through economic efficiency. The underlying assumptions are that market competition creates wealth. Places compete with one another to attract and retain mobile inward investment. They market themselves

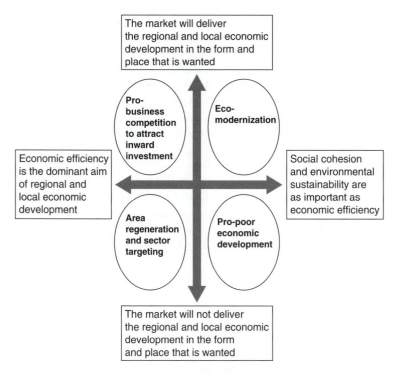

The market will deliver
the regional and local economic
development in the form and
place that is wanted

Pro-
business
competition
to attract
inward
investment

Eco-
modernization

Economic efficiency
is the dominant aim
of regional and
local economic
development

Social cohesion
and environmental
sustainability are
as important as
economic efficiency

Area
regeneration
and sector
targeting

Pro-poor
economic
development

The market will not deliver
the regional and local economic
development in the form
and place that is wanted

Diagram 1.2 **Typology of approaches to policy and practice**

as 'global cities' for example, and seek to lure companies by a mixture of incentives such as cheap loans, favourable fiscal regimes, and provision of sites, factories and other business premises, along with infrastructure such as water supply or new highways. A culture of enterprise is prized and fostered, e.g. through the education system. Regulation of development is likely to be seen in negative terms as 'red tape' and 'bureaucracy', and so is operated with a light touch.

Sector targeting and area regeneration

This also prioritizes economic efficiency and is a pro-business approach, but one that identifies market failure as a fundamental problem. This economic development approach therefore seeks to provide a boost to areas or sectors where the performance of the market can be enhanced, and restored so that it operates efficiently in future. This can involve, for example, a range of interventions to support land and property markets, particularly through the use of gap-financing (e.g. grants for conversion of buildings to new uses) to make marginal and risky schemes commercially viable. Major 'flagship' projects, underwritten by public money, can be a way of rekindling confidence in an area among private investors. Retention of existing businesses is also likely to feature, for example, through forms of support such as business advice services. Similarly, businesses in a declining town centre may look to some economic development initiative to give the area as a whole a facelift and market it better. Where possible, the clustering of related businesses within a particular sector, such as media or biotechnology for example, may be nurtured in the hope of creating additional benefits for the enterprises and the area.

Eco-modernization

The idea of ecological modernization is that new environmentally-friendly technologies and businesses can be the basis for economic development. Thus this approach still has confidence in the capacity of a market economy to deliver desirable development, and therefore it is in the upper half of Diagram 1.2. However, the development that is sought is not only economically efficient but also environmentally sustainable. As Gibbs (2003: 251) observes this can encompass 'a range of responses from "business as usual with a green tinge" to more fundamental reform', and is 'the dominant means of incorporating environmental issues into public and private policy at the present time'. While emphasizing environment, ecological modernization also promises job creation, and thus aspires to deliver economic, environmental and social benefits to an area – a combination often called the 'triple bottom line'. Eco-modernization policies typically seek to encourage new 'green' businesses, such as the manufacture of solar panels. Issues of consumption can also be addressed. One example is 'food miles', the distance that food travels between producer and consumer. Consumption of locally produced food as an alternative to the typical supermarket shopping basket is seen as environmentally desirable, boosting local employment and socially more worthwhile (though there are questions about what the impact might be on agricultural producers in the developing countries whose products travel long distances to the consumers in the rich countries). Because economic efficiency is not the only priority, economic development is expected to meet environmental standards. New technology therefore has an important role to play.

Pro-poor local economic development

This approach is less likely to start from the presumption that market forces will deliver optimal outcomes. Thus it is placed in the bottom half of Diagram 1.2, and because the priority is poverty reduction rather than just economic efficiency, it is on the right-hand side of the diagram. During the 1980s and 1990s international donor and financing agencies such as the World Bank and the International Monetary Fund enforced market liberalization policies on many poorer countries. These typically involved privatizations of state monopolies such as in infrastructure and transport, and full-cost recovery from provision of public services such as health. However, while such measures would fit into the 'pro-business competition' corner in Diagram 1.2, there was also support for a role for NGOs in many aspects of economic development and service delivery, for example in self-help housing provision. Similarly, very depressed towns and regions in deindustrializing countries sought new ways to revive local economies and sustain incomes among residents that conventional market forces seemed to have abandoned. Creation of social enterprises or community-based businesses is an example. Thus there are forms of economic development that seek to be pro-poor. Typically they are people based and start from mobilizing local residents and workers (who may be unemployed or have low incomes). Their prime concern is with protecting and enhancing the livelihoods of these people. Such approaches may well challenge not just the market but also the routine assumptions and policies of officials and public agencies. For example, public policy often sees informal businesses as a problem, since such enterprises are likely to breach many rules and regulations. However, informal businesses can be the main source of income for very poor people.

To explain eco-modernization, Gibbs (2003) refers to the analogy originally used by Huber (1985: 251), who described it as the transformation from 'the dirty and ugly industrial caterpillar' to an 'ecological butterfly'. If we applied such biological metaphors to our other three approaches to regional and local economic development, what kind of animals might symbolize each? Sharks might be appropriate for the 'pro-business competition' approach, because they signify strong, predatory behaviour and a ruthless survival instinct. The mythical bird, the phoenix, which rises from the ashes of a fire, might be the emblem of the area regeneration approach. The phoenix has a colourful plumage and tail: it looks good. It builds a nest that then ignites; fire consumes the bird and its nest, but then a new phoenix arises from the ashes to live again. This image seems to capture the essence of the regeneration approach to economic development. Finally, what might signify the pro-poor approach, with its emphasis often on small-scale and cooperative projects rather that big, pro-business projects and polices? Perhaps ants – social insects that live and work together to support the colony as a whole.

The chapter started with four vignettes, drawn from Shanghai, Chicago, rural Sweden and Mumbai. Each exemplifies one of the four approaches to regional and local economic development. Pudong is the outcome of pro-business policies and practices that prioritize economic efficiency and the attraction of inward investment. The Chinese government and the municipal authorities have played a vital role in this process, but the development is very definitely market led and about international competition. The Chicago case shows the use of TIF as a classic regeneration approach. Again it is pro-business, and certainly seen as such by the residents' organizations protesting against the threat of gentrification. However, the regeneration efforts are necessary because the market is seen as failing to deliver the kind of development that is desired by the policymakers, which is the phoenix-like transformation of the area into more expensive housing, along with wine bars, galleries and other facilities. The Värmland example demonstrates eco-modernization in practice, the ecological butterfly. The work of SPARC and the National Slum Dwellers Federation in organizing the construction of toilets in Mumbai shows what can be achieved through solidarity and cooperative local action. They are the 'ants'.

The forms of governance across these four examples are diverse. The state in China remains extremely powerful, not least because of its ownership of urban land. However, it works closely with private developers and investors. This is a combination that facilitates the delivery of large-scale economic development at regional and local level. In Sweden, there remains the legacy of a long welfare state tradition and a strong concern for the environment. Governments at different scales still play a leading role, and indeed Sweden as a country is seen as a leader in the ideas and practices of eco-modernization. Chicago is renowned for its style of politics, in which the city administration does deals and delivers to its clients and constituents. Locally elected representatives play a key role in fixing the outcomes of policy, liaising between their electors and City Hall, and working with the private sector at a local scale. This can be seen as a form of governance by projects, albeit one with a different character than that demonstrated in the writings by Marsden and Sonnino (2005) or High and Nemes (2007) about rural development in Europe. Similarly, the case from Mumbai describes a multilevel project, connecting an international funding agency, the World Bank, with grass-roots NGOs. In each of the four cases, the practice is closely intertwined with a very specific set of structures and institutions. The challenge then is to learn from many examples, to respect the uniqueness of each, while also searching for some underlying lessons. This is what the book will now try to do.

The structure of the book

Although the emphasis throughout is on policies and practice, the book is divided into two parts. Chapters 2–4 deal with an understanding of the context for regional and local economic development. These chapters build on this opening chapter by explaining how places are changing, economically and in terms of governance. They point readers towards important debates about the drivers of change, and look at how policies and practices have responded to them.

Chapter 2 explores why and how regional and local economies are changing. It looks at traditional forms of regional development policy, which were typically operated by national governments who tried to compensate declining regions by steering jobs to those places. It shows why such policies have given way to new forms of intervention as governments have responded to globalization by creating new ways to attract mobile investment into particular regions. This means introducing some of the debates about the nature of globalization and the restructuring of places and economies. However, in this chapter, as in the rest of the book, we include short case studies to give a sense of issues and responses on the ground.

Chapter 3 looks at place competitiveness and territorial capital. Again some of these notions are contested in the academic literature, so we aim to outline key positions that readers may wish to follow up in more detail. However, again we provide examples from different continents of interventions seeking to draw investment and create jobs. Chapter 4 returns to the theme of governance that was touched upon earlier in this introductory chapter. It looks at why and how new forms of governance such as partnerships shape the economic development process locally and regionally.

The second part of the book (Chapters 5–13) is concerned with the implementation of regional and local economic development. Whereas the first part of the book established key aspects of the competitive and governance environments within which practitioners and policy-makers have to operate, this part looks at the kind of programmes and projects that they are undertaking. Much of local economic development practice developed out of municipal provision of sites and premises for industrial use. Thus Chapter 5 is about land and property. Even in this age of e-business, all economic development depends in some way on having a site to work from. Similarly, business parks and technopoles, which specialize in hi-tech and businesses providing information services, are often key parts of a development strategy: what do we know about them? Similarly, infrastructure and communications, the theme of Chapter 6, have long been recognized as important to regional development, and continue to be so. Businesses need to be connected – to suppliers, customers, their workforce, other businesses and, of course, to energy and water. How do those seeking to stimulate economic development tackle this issue? The environment is now an increasing concern, and so that is the focus of Chapter 7, which looks at how eco-modernization policies can be put into practice to make economic development environmentally sustainable.

While land, buildings, transport connections and a good-quality environment remain important, businesses also need finance, management skills, trained staff and similar 'soft' factors. Thus Chapter 8 is about support for entrepreneurship and business development.

It looks at how traditional businesses and new kinds of businesses, such as social enterprises, can be aided and sustained. In a knowledge economy, attraction and retention of staff is vitally important, and so Chapter 9 looks at housing, housing markets and their relation to labour markets. Indeed as consumption becomes more and more important, so the attractiveness of places takes a more prominent part in economic development. The next two chapters therefore look at practices that seek to capitalize on the dynamism and job growth. Chapter 10 examines retailing, with a focus on food; and leisure, culture and tourism is the subject of Chapter 11. Chapter 12 centres on place marketing and asks how do place branding and place identity contribute to economic development?

Skills and attitudes underpin practice. Many of these skills cut across traditional disciplinary or professional boundaries and will be learned on the job, but awareness of skills needs is a key starting point. Chapter 13 reviews the skills that are needed for practice and returns to the Pilsen neighbourhood of Chicago to reflect a detailed example of local economic development. The final chapter connects the case studies with the classificatory schemes and concepts introduced.

In summary, the book presents some of the important debates in the broad and dynamic field that is regional and local economic development today. It talks about competitiveness, the knowledge economy, the pros and cons of agglomeration, the importance of institutional thickness and networking, among other current concerns. However, the main focus remains on policy responses and practices. In particular the array of case studies should provide a basis for further reflection by the reader, or in classroom discussion. The case studies are intended to inspire ideas and debates, rather than to be pieces of rigorous evaluation already completed. Last but not least, we pose discussion questions and suggest related readings at the end of each chapter. These are intended to help the learning process by provoking thought about, and guiding further research into, the subject matter introduced and reviewed in the preceding chapter. There is rarely a simple answer in economic development. We know some, but not all, of 'what happened', and can only guess at 'what might have happened' had different policies and practices been followed. We hope to engage readers, who can then apply their own learning to the practical challenges of regional and local economic development.

Topic for discussion

Go to the section of the World Bank (2010c) website that deals with local economic development (www.worldbank.org/urban/led). On the basis of what you can find there, what seems to work, what seems not to work, and why?

The site contains a lot of case studies. Look at some of these and try to match them to the four approaches set out in the typology in this introductory chapter.

2 Why and How Are Regional and Local Economies Changing?

A changing economic landscape

Economies have changed and are continuing to change. This is why there is now so much emphasis on regional and local economic development. For most of the world until the closing decades of the twentieth century, a region's economic fate seemed to depend overwhelmingly on natural resources. Coal-mining towns grew on coalfields. Steel mills were built near iron-ore reserves or at places where vast quantities of coal and iron ore could be marshalled. Ports and shipbuilding grew around natural harbours. Market towns prospered serving their agricultural hinterlands. In the humid American south and in Europe's African, Asian and South American colonies there were plantations. Productivity differences between locations, together with protectionist taxation policies against imported goods, sustained this global pattern of production well into the twentieth century.

Today, however, globalization generalizes competition, and many industries have undergone drastic restructuring. Trade barriers have come down, although by no means have they been totally removed by the world's rich countries, and capital is increasingly footloose. Anticipating these processes, Stöhr (1990: 21) argued:

> comparative advantage has shifted with increasing speed between local economies as a result of the exhaustion of local resources, changes in worldwide demand, the emergence of new competitors producing at lower cost, the development of new technologies and organizational forms, and the poor ability of specific locations to provide sufficient

leadership in these change processes or adapt to them fast enough. Absolute advantage, traditionally dependent on locational access to localized resources and markets, has recently become determined primarily by organizational access to the control of capital and innovations.

Globalization is an important but controversial concept. A widely used definition is that by Held *et al.* (1999: 2): the 'widening, deepening and speeding up of worldwide connectedness in all aspects of contemporary social life'. Thus the concept is not purely economic, but includes such phenomena as international migration and changing patterns of government such as the growth of trading blocs such as the EU or ASEAN. Savitch (2002) saw the key components of globalization as being new technology; instant communication that makes information more important than in the past; standardization of products; cross-national integration; but also mutual vulnerability. The 2008 financial crisis illustrated this vulnerability.

There are critics who argue that global economic and political connections have a long history, and that the current fervour is largely driven by ideology, presenting the spread of capitalism as an inevitable and unproblematic process (Harvey, 2000; Hirst and Thompson, 1999). Jenkins *et al.* (2007: 65–6) argued that globalization is exclusive rather than inclusive in nature. They quote data from Hoogvelt (2001) to show that whereas the 'developing world' received 50 per cent of total direct investment up to 1960, by the 1990s 90 per cent of all foreign direct investment went to Western Europe, North America, Japan and nine newly industrializing countries, with just 30 per cent of the world's population.

Our view is that there were indeed significant shifts in the late twentieth century that made the structure of the global economy more international and places more interconnected: the internet, the break-up of the Soviet Union, opening of China, and realization of threats from climate change are some examples. However, we do not see globalization as a uniform process, making everywhere the same. Globalization sets a context, but we see scope for, even the necessity for, action at other scales, particularly local and regional, which can make a difference. Indeed, it is the generalization of competition, which is part of globalization, that has put regional and local economic development on the agenda across much of the globe. Nevertheless, the scope for local action is by no means uniform.

Ideas and policies for regional development

In the early twentieth century, pioneering economic geographers sought to unpick the underlying logic that shaped the location of economic activity. Their focus was on manufacturing industry. They recognized that some locations confer commercial advantages that are likely to be seized by enterprises. The classical example of this kind of 'industrial location theory' was first published by Alfred Weber (1929) in 1909. Weber sought to identify the economically optimum location for a single firm. This 'least cost' location was essentially the product of the transport costs of transporting raw materials to the factory and finished products to the market.

Weber and other analysts of the time recognized that once industry began to grow in one place it made that place more attractive as a location for other industries. For example, component suppliers would be attracted by the market provided by a large manufacturing plant, and their presence would, in turn, help to entice other manufacturers using their products to locate near them. In this way agglomerations would develop, namely interconnected businesses serving each other and located close to one another. A variant on this view was Perroux's (1950) 'growth pole theory' which proposed that the introduction of a leading industry could have a catalytic impact across a whole region.

Such models underpinned the early ventures into regional policy in the industrialized countries. Regional development initiatives often sought to counter 'over-concentration' of industry by dispersing it, steering jobs to regions where there was high unemployment and poverty. In the early 1930s, an international financial crisis created a deep recession in the industrialized economies. Trade slumped, firms shut down, banks crashed and unemployment soared.

The impacts were not spread evenly across all regions within a country. Regions highly dependent on a narrow base of industries were especially hard hit, for example, shipbuilding towns where a high proportion of the male labour force worked in the shipyards. In Britain, the oldest industrial country, the problems faced by traditional industries such as coal mining, shipbuilding and heavy engineering, were compounded by increasing competition from newer, more efficient competitors. The 1940 Barlow Report, a major government study of Britain's industrial population, traced this industrial change with the kind of insights that were new at the time, but would become familiar in many other industrial countries later in the twentieth century. In this study, Barlow ([1940] 1976: 42) observed:

> The fall in the numbers employed in shipbuilding and repairing from approximately 174,000 in 1924 to 133,000 in 1937 was mainly due to a fall in output, which in turn was due to the reduction in international trade and the fall in the export of ships; but it was also associated with technological change in the shipyards and to the growing efficiency of ships.

The geography within Britain of these declining industries was quite pronounced, with concentrations mainly in northern England, south Wales and central Scotland. Even after the economy began to recover in the second half of the 1930s, it was evident that regions that had been especially hard hit were recovering more slowly. In other words there was a problem of regional economic development that was not being resolved simply by the overall improvement in the national economy.

The United Kingdom government responded with the 1934 Special Areas Act designating hard-hit old industrial regions as 'special areas' where public money would be invested in an attempt to revive the economy and create jobs. A key measure was the creation of planned industrial estates such as Team Valley on Tyneside in north-east England. The development of such estates was subsidized by loans from government, with no interest charged for the early period. In this way tenant firms were able to rent specially designed factories that were fully connected to key services and infrastructure (such as electricity, gas, roads, water, etc.), thus avoiding significant capital outlay on buildings. Furthermore, there was typically plenty of space for future expansion – a marked contrast to the normal factory situation in congested urban areas.

The US economy also suffered during the 1930s Depression. The government responded with President F. D. Roosevelt's New Deal. This was mainly a programme of public works and infrastructure development that aimed to create employment while also creating long-term economic assets. Development and management of water resources was probably the main focus of the regional endeavours. The most famous example was the creation of the Tennessee Valley Authority (TVA) in one of the USA's poorest regions in Appalachia. It developed and implemented a programme of creating dams and reservoirs to control floods and generate electricity to provide the power for industrial development. There were major projects in other river basins, for example in California's Central Valley, and the Colombia, Missouri, Arkansas and Red Rivers. What made the TVA special was that it was the only 'authority' in charge of what sought to be a comprehensive development programme. Thus, even more than in the UK, the regional development approach was really a national, top-down strategy, not something being driven in the region itself.

In the Soviet Union (USSR), during the 1930s and 1940s, government policy prioritized industrialization and sought to equalize the distribution of all forms of production between the regions. This policy involved central planning of state investment in almost all sectors of the economy, and often forced migration of labour to meet industrial needs. In particular the Republics within the Union had very little say in matters relating to what were seen as the most important economic sectors (Pallot and Shaw, 1981: 64–5).

As the USSR imposed its political will on much of Central and Eastern Europe after 1945, the same approach to regional economic development was undertaken in those countries. State-owned heavy industry was developed in what had often been 'backward' rural regions. For example, the Lenin steelworks was built at Nova Huta, just outside the university town of Krakow in southern Poland. Its construction features in the 1977 film *Man of Marble* by Andrzej Wajda. The chosen location contradicted almost all the principles in industrial location theory, as the region had neither of the two main natural resources needed for steel making, coal and iron ore. In addition, local demand for the product was relatively small. Furthermore, the air pollution from the site was soon to cause significant problems, exacerbated by its valley-bottom location. However, the aim was to industrialize and proletarianize the region, which was perceived to be less than enthusiastic about the Communist regime. The construction began in 1949, was completed in 1954, and the plant soon became Poland's largest steel producer.

Similarly in China during the period of Mao Zedong's rule, the fundamental aim was a national one – to achieve the shift from an agricultural to an industrial society – that carried with it clear regional development imperatives. The First Five-Year Plan (1953–7) was Soviet-inspired and thus emphasized the location of heavy industry away from the coastal provinces: of 700 projects in the Plan, over two-thirds went to non-coastal locations (Kirby and Cannon, 1989). Liu (1982) argued that considerations of national defence and fear of invasion by enemies arriving by sea also influenced this locational policy.

Elsewhere in Africa and Asia, European powers made little or no attempt to address regional problems in their colonies. Colonial economies typically were based on the production of raw materials and their export for processing in the more industrialized nations. Colonial urban centres were typically ports or military/administrative towns.

In summary, this short and selective review shows that there were some significant differences in approach to regional development between countries between the 1930s and the 1960s. Communist

---

Box 2.1: Regional policy and economic change: Bathgate (Scotland)

Central Scotland boomed in the nineteenth century, based on coal mining, oil shale extraction and iron production. By the 1950s these industries were in decline. Unemployment reached 8 per cent, which was high by national standards. What could be done to create jobs and a more modern economic base? The UK automobile industry was concentrated in the English Midlands, a prosperous region 300 miles south of central Scotland. If part of this modern, growing industry could be transplanted to central Scotland, unemployment there would be reduced.

The UK government's regional policy required firms seeking to expand or locate in an economically strong region to apply for an Industrial Development Certificate (IDC). In 1959 the government refused the British Motor Corporation (BMC) an IDC to expand its plant in the English Midlands. In 1960 BMC announced that it would build a factory at Bathgate in central Scotland to manufacture trucks and tractors. BMC cited the area's good access to road, rail and maritime transportation, labour availability, and the low risk of other local firms poaching trained workers (a problem in the Midlands where demand

→

regimes were extremely directive about the location of industry, and were largely seeking to catch up with the higher industrialization levels that existed in competitor countries. Furthermore, political objectives largely shaped the economic development decisions. In the USA and the UK approaches differed but were more indirect in relation to where industry should go. As much UK and US industry was privately owned, there was more use of incentives to influence the locational decisions of firms. Many Western European governments used a mixture of incentives and regulation to try to even out regional disparities by taking 'work to the workers'.

Rethinking regional policy

By the 1970s and 1980s the increase in global competition created major shifts in regional economies. In particular, production in newly industrializing countries began to undercut the profitability

---

for skilled labour exceeded supply). The new plant was expected to employ 4,000 people and to attract ancillary industries such as those producing vehicle parts, e.g. lights, tyres, and so on.

Success at BMC's Bathgate factory was relatively short-lived. Productivity was lower than at English car factories, mainly because the local labour force was unfamiliar with assembly-line work. Vehicle components had to be transported from England as the ancillary industries did not follow BMC north. In the 1970s the British car industry struggled in the face of growing international competition. Exporting British trucks and tractors became even harder in the early 1980s as international currency exchange rates became less favourable, making Bathgate's products more expensive than similar goods produced in other countries, such as by Mercedes in Brazil.

The Bathgate factory closed in 1986. The industrial estate which had been constructed across the road from the factory for the ancillary industries that were expected but never came, was only one-third occupied. Following the closure, local unemployment reached 22 per cent. Bathgate became a symbol of the failure of a top-down approach to regional economic development based on central government steering companies to locations the firms did not want to go to. (Source: Borrowman, 2000.)

of many long-established industries based in Europe or North America, and triggering deindustrialization. These new challenges highlighted weaknesses in regional policy that sought to steer firms away from locations where firms wanted to be and towards places where politicians would like the factories and jobs to be. There were tensions between the government-prescribed patterns of industrial location and the efficiency of the enterprises themselves.

The example of the use of regional policy to locate a truck and tractor plant at Bathgate, which is described in Box 2.1, shows the failures of this traditional approach of taking 'work to the workers'. With hindsight it is easy to conclude that central Scotland in the 1960s was not an appropriate location for such a plant. It was certainly not a 'least cost' location in terms of transporting raw materials and finished products. The Bathgate example shows that too little attention was paid to market conditions when the decision was taken to develop there. There was certainly a supply of local labour to service BMC's plant, but the labour force lacked the necessary skills. The relative impact of demand from the factory for parts was overestimated, and not sufficient to entice suppliers to relocate from the English Midlands, where most of their customers were. The nature of competition also changed as world markets became more open and competition increased from locations where production of similar goods could be done more cheaply. While its location was not optimal, the plant might well have survived for longer had it not been for these global changes.

There was also a political dimension to the demise of the Bathgate factory. British government policy in the 1980s was much more in favour of letting market forces shape outcomes, rather than government intervention as it had been 20 years earlier. The requirement for expanding firms in growth areas to get an IDC was abandoned. Closure of heavy industry was no longer just a problem of regions that had been in long-term decline. Keeble (1976) showed that industry was declining in all the main conurbations in the UK and that medium-sized towns and relatively rural sub-regions had become the growth centres. This finding confounded the assumptions that had underpinned the UK government's regional policy since the 1930s. These economic, political and geographical challenges to regional policy were by no means unique to the UK. The 1980s saw an international rise in support for neo-liberal economic policies hostile to interventionist policies (see Harvey, 2005). Pressures on state finances made central governments increasingly reluctant and less able to undertake the traditional form of corrective regional policy measures in regions that were underperforming against national indicators of economic development and prosperity.

What was happening and what could public bodies do about it? As central government withdrew from concerns about the inter-regional pattern of economic development, regional and local authorities began to explore ways in which they could sustain jobs and their economies. Development 'from below' seemed to be the only way forward. As well as seeking to attract firms new to an area, it was necessary to retain the firms and labour force already there. As Cooke (1986: 4) argued, 'policy making needs to be sensitive to local specificities'.

Understanding regional and local economic change

From the 1970s onwards there was increasing recognition that a more sophisticated understanding of industrial location was necessary. Krumme (1969) looked at investment decisions of businesses, and how these related to local areas. Such studies of the locational behaviour of firms revealed how complex the decision environment of firms could be. There were national and international influences from suppliers, competitors and governments, as well as regional and local factors including land and physical infrastructure, labour, component suppliers, regional markets, etc. Thus corporate goals and constraints were mediated through the unique characteristics of local places. However, the competitive advantages offered by a particular location were not in themselves seen as sufficient to explain the actions of firms in opening, closing or relocating plants.

A literature began to develop that interpreted the dramatic industrial closures and job losses of the 1970s and 1980s not just as industrial 'change' (implying shifts within an existing pattern) but as industrial 'restructuring' (which suggested more fundamental alterations of key relationships). The argument was that firms were faced with a crisis of profitability. In response they were adopting a variety of strategies, such as closures, reduction of their workforce, introduction of new technology, or relocation to reorganize their operations in significant ways (Massey, 1981; Massey and Meegan, 1982). This process was problematic because capital was tied up in buildings and equipment that were place bound. Furthermore, there was a labour force tied to the place of production that was likely to resist closure and redundancy.

The phrase 'industrial restructuring' typically triggers the image of a deindustrialized urban rustbelt. However, restructuring also affects rural areas and agricultural industries. It is still 're-structuring' because there are fundamental changes, e.g. in how and where production is undertaken, in response to a crisis of profitability.

The restructuring of the cattle raising and meatpacking industry in the Midwest of the USA, which is described in Box 2.2, shows

---

Box 2.2: Restructuring in the US meat industry

In the late nineteenth century, cowboys roamed the US prairies, but the slaughter of animals was done in Midwestern cities such as Chicago, St Louis and Cincinnati where the meat industry was concentrated in the hands of the 'Big Five' meatpackers: Swift, Armour, Morris, Cudahy and Schwarschild & Sulzberger.

By the 1940s, smaller, regional meatpackers were able to make gains, and the industry decentralized. Retail practices changed as supermarkets did their own warehousing and meatpacking. Rising meat consumption kept the Big Five in business, but they had become uncompetitive. In the 1960s nearly all the urban slaughter facilities were closed and over 50,000 employees lost their jobs (Page, 1993). Small diversified farms were well positioned within the US meat industry. In eastern South Dakota, for example, farm output increased by 81% between 1940 and 1953 compared with 31% nationwide: livestock production replaced cash-grain crops as the major source of farm income in the state (Schell, 1968: 355). South Dakota farmers had many options for their cattle. Nearly every town had a small butcher shop which provided

→

that structural economic change is not confined to manufacturing industry or to major cities. The changes in economic geography described in Box 2.2 were driven by the relative competitiveness and shifting patterns of profitability among the various sectors of the industry. The restructuring of the industry resulted in a drastic reconfiguration of the rural economy in states such as South Dakota. Many small towns have lost population and tax revenue since the 1980s, when restructuring in livestock coincided with a national farm crisis. Even when profits in livestock or grain pick up now, the structure of the industries no longer fit with a decentralized small-town geography. This has had social and environmental impacts as well as economic ones. There have been closures and consolidations of rural schools, longer commutes to work for those who live in small towns, and other adjustments that are a consequence of the economic changes.

---

a local market for livestock and food for local consumers. On a larger scale, the state supported four slaughterhouses that employed over 100 people and 6 more that employed between 25 and 100. In 1960, 38 per cent of South Dakota's value added in manufacturing was in meatpacking.

In the 1980s, the meat industry again restructured. The Iowa Beef Packers' (IBP) 'boxed beef revolution' provided shops with vacuum-packed beef instead of partial carcasses. This innovation created enormous gains in shipping and handling efficiencies. IBP used new technologies to 'deskill' the workforce, located its plants in anti-union areas, and employed recent immigrants. Two other companies, ConAgra and Cargill, followed IBP's model and these new 'Big Three' slaughtered and dismembered cattle at increasing speeds: from 175 animals per hour in the early 1980s to 400 per hour in 2000.

Small, decentralized meat production facilities in South Dakota began to close. Unionized workers staged strikes, but by the 1990s both wages and workforces were decimated. In 1960, wages in meatpacking were 15% above the average manufacturing wage in the USA, and by 1990 they had fallen to 20% below this average (Stull and Broadway, 2004: 73). Today, the top four meatpacking companies control about 70% of all cattle slaughter. (Source: Breitbach (2007).)

In other words, while the economic imperatives driving enter-prises are rooted in national or international shifts in prices and competition, their resolution and impacts are intensely local in character. In some places the resistance to disinvestment can be bitter and protracted, elsewhere an accommodation will be arrived at more easily. Much depends on the history, culture, politics and policies of local areas. A substantial programme of research devel-oped that sought to understand the importance of localities in the restructuring process (Cooke, 1989; Bagguley *et al.*, 1990). The nature of the local labour market was recognized as a key factor in shaping the local response. Areas of heavy industry tended to be highly unionized and resistant to change. In contrast local adjust-ment was easier in tertiary and managerial labour markets, not least because in some cases these areas were also centres for new investment and new jobs.

Other authors focused on the characteristics of a local labour force in adapting to changes. Evans and Richardson (1981) argued that a factory closure would have an initial impact on local unem-ployment, since local people will tend to have jobs in the factory: however, the newly unemployed would then begin to look further afield to find new work. Over time the employment rate of com-munities living near to the original closure would improve, and the additional unemployment created by the closure would be absorbed across the urban area as a whole. Cheshire (1979) called this the 'chain interdependence hypothesis', and supported it by arguing that travel to jobs within a city was virtually costless.

This perspective suggests that investment in training and skills, together with the attitudes of the labour force, should be the key to economic development. Getting people back into jobs means removing the obstacles that stand in their way, e.g. lack of child-care may prevent parents of young children from being economi-cally active. Such 'soft', people-focused measures are seen as more important than 'hard' interventions such as the provision of new industrial premises or other forms of physical infrastructure. Simi-larly, the theory implies that programmes need to be targeted at a regional labour market area, rather than a local area.

Thus both research and practice came to realize the significance of connections between geographical scales. Raw materials and geographical access to domestic markets no longer defined the best places to locate a factory. Improvements in telecommunications technology made it easier for firms to operate internationally. They became increasingly 'footloose' and, where labour costs were a substantial element of overall production costs, this meant locating labour-intensive processes in places where labour was cheap and easy to manage.

Company mergers and the growth of services (and particularly financial services) also unravelled many traditional regional economies, creating winners and losers. In general, bigger companies meant that headquarter locations became more economically significant, and this tended to boost cities at the top of global, national and regional hierarchies. The 'division of labour' – who does what work – took on a very spatially differentiated quality globally (see Massey, 1995). Typically the old industrial cities experienced deindustrialization, the 'rust belt' phenomenon, while new production zones developed in some relatively cheap labour locations such as the Asian 'tigers' (e.g. South Korea, Malaysia, Indonesia, and – almost a class of its own – China). Routine service jobs, such as call centres, were also shifted to these countries.

Innovation and the knowledge economy

A startling feature of the period since the 1980s has been the growth of new kinds of knowledge-based industries. Van Doren (1995: 94) talked of 'the rupture of the traditional techno-industrial paradigm'. In other words, the key economic relationships that had underpinned thinking about regional economic development had changed. So why have knowledge and innovation become so important? New technologies and new products give those who can exploit them a competitive advantage; but as time goes by competitors find ways to copy the innovations, and to close the gap. However, globalization has provided opportunities to exploit the advantage created by an innovation on a much wider scale. Prior to the 2008 financial crisis, this 'winner takes all' economy, where the 'first mover' had a huge advantage, generated new possibilities in what has been termed the knowledge economy. In a knowledge economy, know-how, ideas and talented people are the key forces for profitability.

Van Doren's argument is that the traditional economic activity was a linear process linking raw materials through goods into 'well-controlled markets'. There was 'relatively stable growth influenced by short-term adjustments and a steady evolution of production techniques' (1995: 94). In contrast, van Doren proposes that the 'new techno-industrial system' operates on a different paradigm. There is a science–technology–production nexus in which knowledge and relationships are the crucial drivers. Furthermore, uncertainty and economic turbulence are now the norms. This makes more flexible modes of operation necessary, which in turn generate 'new forms of territoriality' (van Doren, 1995: 97), with new interactions between global and local levels.

The key to local economic development within this perspective is an innovative environment linked into networks of innovation. It is this that links competitive places to the new techno-industrial system. In other words, the complexity of the operating environment of modern business means that local economic development seeking to enhance place competitiveness must itself generate networks that integrate the actions of enterprises, research and training institutions, and local authorities.

As noted above, at a global level the real competitive advantage in terms of labour costs is held by Asian countries, perhaps most notably China. Therefore, innovation to improve quality of products and services is particularly important across older economies such as those in Europe and North America. The EU's Third Cohesion Report said that 'In an increasingly knowledge-based economy, innovation holds the key to regional competitiveness' (CEC, 2004b: 8). It stressed that to have a sustainable knowledge-based economy a region must first build a critical mass of workers with a variety of skills.

In a knowledge economy, where innovation is so important, who are the innovators and what does this perspective imply for economic development policies? In a knowledge economy, firms are not tied to a single place for the supply of their raw materials. Coal mines could not move from their coal field, but a company selling software advice can easily relocate if its owners find somewhere else more attractive. Similarly, unskilled labour was relatively immobile, but today's skilled people on whom the knowledge-based enterprises depend, are potentially very footloose. Thus human capital (the people, their skills, experience, attitude, etc.) of a firm or an area is seen as perhaps the most vital asset. The emphasis is strongly on attracting and holding on to talented people.

The creative class

Florida (2002) argued for a new interpretation of societal economic structures that would add a fourth, 'creative' sector, to the traditional division into primary, secondary and tertiary industries. Those engaged in this new sector he called the 'creative class'. These people are flexible and earn their living through their imaginative abilities. They are 'purveyors of creativity', and include:

> scientists and engineers, university professors, poets and novelists, artists, entertainers, actors, designers and architects... non-fiction writers, editors, cultural figures, think-tank researchers, analysts... software programmers or engineers... filmmakers... [and those] who work in a wide range of knowledge-intensive industries such as high-tech sectors, financial services, the legal and health care professions, and business management. (69)

Florida (2005: 36) maintained that members of the creative class seek to reside in locations that offer 'abundant high-quality experiences, an openness to diversity of all kinds, and... the opportunity to validate their identities as creative people'. The result is a 'new geography of creativity' that sees 'concentrations' of creative-class members residing in cities and demanding very different facilities and urban development policies than have been common in postwar USA (2005: 36). He suggested (2002; 2005: 37) that successful local economic development depends on the three Ts: technology, talent and tolerance; Florida subsequently added a fourth T, territorial assets.

It is common to equate globalization with the rise of modern telecommunications technologies and to deduce that people can now do the same work while being physically in almost any location. In this line of thinking, place does not matter much anymore. However, Florida (2005: 28) countered that 'the economy itself – the high-tech, knowledge-based, and creative content industries which drive so much of economic growth – continues to concentrate in specific places'. Furthermore, he asserted that city administrators still pursue economic development by primarily targeting industrial and manufacturing firms with 'financial inducements, incentives, and the like' in an attempt to attract these companies to their regions. In an economy increasingly based on this creative sector, argued Florida, these policies are outdated. Cities instead need to offer incentives to encourage people to invest in research and design (R&D) ventures, recognize that universities offer a central hub for the creative class and encourage their economic activities and, perhaps most of all, put into place policies that will make their urban environments the types of places where the creative class would want to live.

Such policies could range from investment in public transportation facilities to ameliorate the need to commute by car from distant and increasingly sprawling suburbs, to providing a welcoming atmosphere for immigrants and homosexuals. 'A revitalized downtown', Florida (2005: 166) proposed, should be perceived of by city officials 'as an idea generator, and the urban subcenters as incubators' in which lower real estate costs attract creative people to reside and begin to build businesses that rely on creativity. In all of this, Florida (2005: 167) asserted, the 'quality of place is critical'.

Box 2.3: A city for the creative class? Austin, Texas (USA)

Austin, Texas has a population of just over 700,000. The city started the twenty-first century as one of the fastest growing in the USA. Ranking near the top of polls listing the best places to live in the USA, Austin has developed a number of green practices and supposedly sustainable economic development strategies, as well as a vibrant live pop music and art scene which centres around the annual South by Southwest (SXSW) festival which takes place each March and began in 1987 as a musical performance competition. SXSW has expanded annually to include film, internet and other associated cultural productions, hosting conferences, celebrity interviews and hotly tipped performers to such international acclaim that other locations, for example Toronto in Canada, have tried to replicate the formula.

One of the major efforts in Austin was the Smart Growth Initiative which aimed to develop the city economically and demographically in a manner that was sustainable and would attract residents into under-utilized city centre neighbourhoods and generate a local high-technology economy. Operating under the municipal administration

➡

If cities are not attractive to the creative class, they will become losers in this new economy. City policy-makers thus need to recognize that rather than centres for manufacturing, 'the new city is becoming defined more and more as a city of consumption, experiences, lifestyle, and entertainment' (Florida, 2005: 167).

As the example from Austin, Texas, summarized in Box 2.3, shows the policy prescriptions associated with the creative-class thesis are controversial. McCann (2008) alleged that Florida (2002) hinted at the inequalities that were endemic in favouring these relatively affluent workers through urban development policies, but rather elided them. Creative-class initiatives tend to privilege a certain lifestyle and way of living, typically associated with middle- and upper-class people. Peck (2005) outlined critiques of the creative-class thesis. From the political left, it is argued that the policy solutions proposed say little about social inequality, racial or class divisions. The political right contend that using public money for bike paths

that governed from 1997 to 2001 in collaboration with the Chamber of Commerce and other business groups, this initiative sought to 'manage' the city, making it 'liveable' and attractive to younger potential residents.

However, McCann (2008, n.p.) demonstrates that 'inequality... seems to result from Creative Class policies and, thus... creative cities are becoming *less* livable for many'. In Austin at the start of the twenty-first century, the income gap between haves and have-nots was widening, a trend largely repeated throughout the industrialized world. Housing costs increased and neighbourhoods targeted for conversion to creative-class enclaves have gentrified, displacing older and poorer residents. Public employees, such as teachers and fire-fighters, who are often contractually obliged to reside within city limits have found themselves pushed down the residential and income ladders, and low-income groups, who in cities such as Austin tend to be non-white ethnic minorities, saw their neighbourhoods targeted for 'revitalization' and their landlords encouraged by changes in zoning laws to turn rental properties into luxury flats and locations for high-end boutiques, bars and restaurants. (Source: McCann (2008).)

or cleaning up dilapidated buildings to make them attractive as coffee shops and art galleries just perpetuates or even extends government spending.

Peck (2005: 764, 767) explained that the creative-class concept provides:

> a means to intensify and publicly subsidize urban consumption systems for a circulating class of gentrifiers, whose lack of commitment to place and whose weak community ties are perversely celebrated... Uncool cities, it seems, have no-one to blame but themselves, while creative places stand to be rewarded both with economic growth and targeted public spending. Thus, the creativity script works seamlessly with the new urban realpolitik, neo-liberal style... The subordination of social-welfare concerns to economic development imperatives (first, secure economic growth, then wait for the wider social benefits to percolate through) gives way to a form of creative trickle-down; elite-focused creativity strategies leave only supporting roles for the two-thirds of the population languishing in the working and service classes, who get nothing apart from occasional tickets to the circus.

Debates such as this about who gains and who loses from economic development concepts and policies are important. In practical situations economic development policies and practices are likely to be contested. Increasingly, the importance of the social dimension to economic development has become recognized. Lorenzen (2007: 799), for example, wrote that differences in economic development between different regions are increasingly seen as being best understood by looking at their differences in social capital. This means that it is the connections in business life and in civil society that influence how development operates. Lorenzen (2007: 802) sees competitiveness as hinging more on 'the efficiencies of learning' than on 'the efficiencies of production'. Furthermore, even in a world where international migration has become more common, social ties and networks are still typically rooted in a place, such as a school, university, club or village of origin.

Thus, while there have been huge changes in the global economy, and capital has become increasingly mobile, the local and regional aspects of economic development have actually become more, not less important. Similarly, to understand local and regional economies, it is necessary to appreciate, and be sensitive to, their social framework and implications.

Globalization and global challenges

Just as the social and the economic are intimately intertwined, so are political and economic factors. Globalization is not purely an economic process. There have been political shifts that have had global economic significance but also created new challenges and opportunities to local and regional economies. The break-up of the Soviet Union and the lifting of the Iron Curtain is an example. One consequence of this has been the renewal of economic ties around the Baltic Sea, so that the attractive Estonian capital of Tallinn, for example, has now become a major destination for tourists from Scandinavia and points further west. Conversely, the Arctic port of Murmansk, home to the former Soviet Union's trawler fleet and a repair centre for nuclear submarines, suffered badly during the period after 1991, with its population falling from around 500,000 to little more than 300,000, as the perks and disciplines that had sent people there were withdrawn. Oil and gas in the Barents Sea, and the easing of Arctic sea travel consequent on global warming, hold out the possibilities that Murmansk may forge a new future.

Hong Kong is another example of local and regional adjustment to and fashioning of global political and economic change. Hong Kong was occupied by the British in 1841 and became a colony the following year. It was briefly occupied by the Japanese during the Second World War, but then benefited economically after the war as firms and people moved into the British colony after the Communist Party took control of China. In the 1950s, its economic development was characterized by manufacturing of cheap consumer goods such as garments, toys and electronics. However, in the 1970s, as international capital increasingly moved into the Pacific, services, finance and management activities became more important. Crucially the reopening of China to the world in the late 1980s created opportunities for cross-border economic activity. For example, firms based in Hong Kong were able to produce goods in nearby centres in the People's Republic of China, a system known as 'front shop, back factory'. Transport links to China were improved, and a major new international airport was developed. In 1997 Britain handed Hong Kong back to China, where it retains a lot of autonomy under the arrangement known as 'one country, two systems'. Since 1997 Hong Kong has increasingly promoted itself as 'Asia's World City', and as a 'Cyberport' information and telecommunications hub. Other economic development elements in this repositioning of the city include a science park, Chinese medicine port and Disneyland theme park (Newman and Thornley, 2005: 234–7).

Globalization also entails the increased activity of global organizations that shape economic development such as the International Monetary Fund and the World Bank. These imposed neo-liberal macroeconomic policies on many poorer countries during the 1980s and 1990s. After gaining political independence from colonial power, many countries sought to protect their nascent industries through tariffs and to develop manufacturing capacity to substitute imported goods by home-produced ones. The neo-liberal reforms required as a condition for badly needed international loans were known as Structural Adjustment Programmes (SAPs). Typically these involved opening of domestic markets to foreign goods, deregulation, privatization and realignments in public spending and reform of public services. The general effect was to weaken the role of governments in economic planning and development, while at the same time the narrative behind the SAPs was that the main cause of underdevelopment was internal to the country, rather than reflecting unfair international terms of trade and restricted access to markets in the rich countries. While the SAPs were widely criticized, neo-liberalism remains a powerful force shaping international development policy into the twenty-first century.

It is difficult analytically to separate out the impacts of these neo-liberal development mechanisms from the changes that might be attributable to all other aspects of globalization during this period (e.g. the changing international division of labour or the increased exposure of local and regional economies to external shocks). However, in respect of local and regional economic development, two issues need to be highlighted. First, the perception that governments are an obstacle to development has lessened to some extent, and demands for government regulation of economies increased following the 2008 financial crisis. A lot of faith and responsibility has also been placed in civil society organizations, which often have a local or regional focus and a commitment to socially just and ecologically sustainable modes of economic development. Second, there is a widening gap between rich and poor at all scales – between countries and between people within a city. An ethical approach to regional and local economic development needs to engage with this inequality and give priority to poverty alleviation.

Such ethical concerns gained global attention with the publication of the 1987 Brundtland Report and the United Nations Conference on Environment and Development (also known as the Earth Summit) held in Rio de Janeiro in 1992. Brundtland provided the best-known definition of sustainable development: 'development that meets the needs of the present without compromising the ability of future generations to meet their own needs' (World Commission on Environment and Development, 1987: 43). Thus two key ideas were injected into discussions about economic development. The first was that equity is a necessary consideration. Brundtland argued not only for intergenerational equity, but also for giving priority to the needs of the world's poor. The second idea was that environmental limits should sometimes constrain economic activity.

Summary

This chapter has shown how the theories and practices of regional development have changed in response to a changing world. During the middle half of the twentieth century, the focus of academics and practitioners was on manufacturing industry. Policy sought to steer manufacturing jobs to regions with high unemployment or regions thought to be under-industrialized. In terms of the typology in Chapter 1, this approach could be seen as being based on some assumptions behind 'pro-poor local economic development'. State intervention was at least in part driven by concerns for social and economic cohesion within the nation. However, the approach was not that of 'ants'. It was much more top-down and driven by central governments.

Deindustrialization and the rise of neo-liberalism in the closing decades of the twentieth century prompted new ideas and practices. The academic focus both on localities and on globalization recognized the ways that restructuring connections between scales from global to local and the intense mobility of capital. The practice was typified by the SAPs, the withdrawal of state support from the Bathgate factory (Box 2.1), and the fate of those working in the meat production industry in South Dakota (Box 2.2). All these examples fit squarely in the 'pro-business competition to attract inward investment' approach. However, resistance to restructuring also spurred ideas for approaches that would be pro-poor and/or more ecologically sustainable.

The creative-class theory, and associated policy prescriptions (exemplified in Box 2.3), points the way to a phoenix-like regeneration for some cities and neighbourhoods, with city councils or development agencies pump-priming area projects so as to enhance economic efficiency in a knowledge economy. However, the idea of sustainable development that came with the Brundtland Report underpins the practice of regional and local economic development as embracing pro-poor and environmental concerns.

Topics for discussion

Think of a city or region that you know well. How has it changed in the last 10 years? What were the main drivers of the changes? Were they local or global – or both?

Debate the case for and against developing a city so as to appeal to the 'creative class'. What kinds of local development policies could a city pursue to attract members of the 'creative class'?

Related reading

R. Florida (2002) *The Rise of the Creative Class: And How It's Transforming Work*, Leisure, Community and Everyday Life (New York: Basic Books).

J. Peck (2005) 'Struggling with the creative class', *International Journal of Urban and Regional Research*, 29(4), 740–70.

---

3 Place Competitiveness and Territorial Capital

Should we talk about place competitiveness?

It is now commonplace to assert that cities and regions need to be competitive. For example, Gordon (1999: 1001) stated:

> Cities compete in a variety of ways, across market areas of different extents, in conditions which may be more/less stable, and with or without the involvement of territorial agencies. Among the forms of competition, the most significant involve rivalry within product markets, and that for inward investment, the attraction of desirable residents, and contests for funding or events from higher levels of government.

Cheshire (1999: 843) used the term 'territorial competition' which he defined as 'a process through which groups acting on behalf of a regional or sub-regional economy (typically that of a city-region) seek to promote it as a location for economic activity either implicitly or explicitly in competition with other areas'. He argued that such competition focused on the attraction of mobile investment, enhancing the market share achieved by existing local businesses, and generating new businesses and markets. He stressed the local origin and nature of these endeavours. Storper (1997: 20) gave 'place competitiveness' a slightly different slant. It was 'The ability of an (urban) economy to attract and maintain firms with stable or rising market shares in an activity while maintaining or increasing standards of living for those who participate in it.' In other words the concept embraces concern not just for business, but also for residents. However, as Bristow (2005: 289) noted it is still rooted in a 'discourse of firm-based, output-related competition'.

Begg (2002) suggested that globalization altered the nature of competition between places. Thus cities like London, Tokyo,

New York and Paris compete with each other for company head-quarters and similar major business activities, rather than with the other cities in their own country. Boland (2007: 1021) observed that the idea of 'competitive advantage' has become a dominant theme in economic development.

However, others have questioned the concept of place competi-tiveness. To Kitson *et al.* (2004: 992) it was 'an elusive concept', that is 'contentious and far from well understood'. Lovering (2001: 350) said that 'competitiveness' when applied to cities and regions loses coherence. There is certainly competition between firms, but do geographical areas really compete with each other? Krugman (1997), for example, has argued that a company and a region are fundamentally different. So in what senses do places compete with each other, and in what ways can an urban area or a region impart competitive advantage to firms located there?

What do the theorists say?

The writings of Porter (1990, 1995, 1996, 2000, 2003) have been fundamental in making the argument that there is a connection between the qualities of a city or region and the competitiveness of the firms located there. Porter (1990: 622) argued that: 'Interna-tionally successful industries and industrial clusters frequently con-centrate in a city or region, and the bases for advantage are often intensely local.' Furthermore, Porter saw policy interventions as key factors in shaping these local advantages. Lever and Turok (1999) summarized Porter's arguments. They said that economically suc-cessful places provide local access to concentrations of specialized knowledge, rival firms and related businesses, and supporting insti-tutions. Furthermore, many of these local assets exist as a result of cooperation between the public and private sectors, sometimes with civil society involvement.

Krugman (1995, 1996a, 1996b, 1997) contended that firms, not cities, compete. Cities are only the base for the enterprises. Firms make decisions about where to locate their business. To Krugman, the central question in understanding the location of firms is who takes what decisions that can increase returns within a market context? How would self-interested individual entrepreneurs act, and how would the sum of their individual decisions affect such decisions? Firms can indeed gain benefits from the kind of factors noted by Lever and Turok: however, to Krugman, discussion of competitiveness must be rooted in an explanation of the motives of firms seeking to maximize their returns. Thus Krugman's perspective focuses on things like labour markets. Firms in a large urban area can gain advantages over competitors elsewhere because the large urban labour market makes it easier for them to take on more staff quickly when demand rises. In this way they can manage the uncertainties created by fluctuations in supply and demand better than can firms in an isolated small town. However, the basic point remains: unlike firms, regions do not go out of business.

Crucially Krugman placed a lot of emphasis on productivity, but productivity is influenced by national and regional policies on matters like training, and on the regional labour market. Therefore, he appears to share common ground with those who have advanced the idea of place competitiveness. However, his different starting point does have some practical implications. Like most economists, Krugman believes that competition ensures specialization and optimal supply of goods at optimal prices. At the local level this would imply that places should specialize in what they are best at. In this way comparative advantage would 'naturally' benefit the firms there. If an economic development agency seeks to attract other types of enterprise or restructure the economy in some fashionable way, so that its portfolio of enterprises includes, for example, growth or high-technology sectors, then this implies a distortion of the outcomes that would be created by pure market competition. Exciting images and bullish terminology drawn from the corporate language of competitiveness are not substitutes for a careful analysis of the direct economic benefits that companies can expect from place-based policy interventions.

For a fuller analysis of the implications of Krugman's work, see Boddy (1999), who drew on Martin and Sunley (1996). Camagni (2002) added a further insight. He argued that some places may have an absolute competitive advantage over others. For example, they may have better infrastructure or special institutions that benefit the firms in that area. While international competitors might be able to compete by lower wages or favourable currency exchange rates, firms elsewhere within the same currency and legislative zone will not have those options. Hence the competitive advantage is absolute, not just comparative.

Thus it is argued that some combination of regional attributes and the strengths and weaknesses of the firms that are there can impart a spatial dimension to competitiveness. In addition there are situations when territories – political units – compete for events and activities that are not really reducible to the relative market advantage of companies within their territory. The obvious example is a bid to stage an event like the Olympic Games. Such competition may not be rational economically but it certainly happens, and is motivated by a range of political and social ambitions that in practice may not be easy to unravel from the purely economic considerations. This reminds us of the fundamental point. Cities and regions are not just about the 'bottom line' of profitability. Their politicians have ambitions and their administrations have to weigh economic advantage alongside social inclusion and environmental sustainability.

The question of scale

Kitson *et al.* (2004: 997) pointed to a further complication in debates about regional competitiveness: the question of scale. Researchers discussing competitiveness use a variety of terms to locate it: 'urban', 'regional', 'place' or 'territorial'. Yet effective economic development necessitates 'getting the scale right', mobilizing initiatives at the scale where they can be most effective. As Kitson *et al.* (2004: 997) observed: 'Some processes of regional competitive advantage may be highly localized, while others may operate at a more broad regional scale, and some may be national or global.' This is true, and so no single scale necessarily fits best, or in every part of the globe. In practice, the scale of a particular project is decided by the scale of government overseeing it, or by the scope of allotted budgets. Therefore in terms of policy design, it is important to ensure that policies at different scales are not working in contradiction to one another.

This leads to consideration of how scale should best be thought of, and where scale comes from. Such questions have become pronounced in academic geography for a number of related reasons. First, political and economic globalization has been fundamentally about the rescaling of politics and economics. With the end of colonialism, dissolution of the Soviet bloc, emergence of the semi-periphery, and decline of the first-world manufacturing hubs, many of the familiar groupings of political and economic space disappeared and, through technology as well as the workings of political economy, a new set of geographies emerged (Smith, 1984, 1998). A second driving force has been the influence of postmodernism in social theory. This theoretical turn has involved, most broadly, a questioning of the given and absolute categories of modernism, and the strictures of scale are prime examples of such assumed absolutes (Berman, 1982; Dear, 1986; Harvey, 1989).

Particularly important has been the argument that scale should not be assumed to be either stable or solely a matter of data aggregation. Rather, scale is produced through the workings of particular systems. For example, Smith and Dennis (1987) analysed data on manufacturing employment in the region known as the American Manufacturing Belt to show that deindustrialization fragmented the region into smaller entities that might be competing with each other for industry, rather than cooperating as a regional economy as they had in the past. Their work contributed to a larger body of work debating the appropriate scale at which to consider redevelopment (Cooke, 1987; Dear, 1987; Duncan and Savage, 1989; Harvey, 1987). This debate led to the idea of 'jumping scale' as a political tactic of grassroots organizing that sought to counter the fragmentation of the economy with locality spanning social organization (Adams, 1996; Smith, 2004).

Global processes – the emergence of a new international division of labour – are behind the fragmentation of the well-known economic regions of the core countries. The concomitant realignment of small-scale localities with global shifts was given the name 'glocalization' by Swyngedouw (1997).

Agglomeration and clusters

The idea that companies located close to each other can gain competitive advantages is fundamental to notions of regional competitiveness. It is not a new idea. Back in 1890 Alfred Marshall showed that firms would gain external economies by being located in a place that could provide ample supplies of common factors of production such as labour, capital, land and infrastructure systems. Hence industrial agglomerations would form. Marshall (1890) described 'industrial districts' which were concentrations of specialized industries in particular localities. In these districts small local firms would trade with each other and individuals moved from firm to firm. Thus the district is characterized both by shared industrial expertise and a common local industrial culture and identity. Within the district there is both competition and cooperation among the firms.

Porter (1990: 149) argued that 'the phenomenon of industry clustering is so pervasive that it appears to be a central feature of advanced national economies'. He stressed the importance of the local milieu to the competitiveness of enterprises. That local area is a key source of inputs to its firm, including a range of incentives and pressures. Porter (2001: 7) defined clusters as 'geographically close groups of interconnected companies and associated institutions in a particular field, linked by common technologies and skills'. He went on to say that clusters can take various forms but generally include 'end product or service companies; suppliers of specialized inputs, components, machinery and services; financial institutions; and firms in related industries'. Importantly, government and education and research bodies are also a common feature of a cluster, providing training and technical support. The essence of a cluster is the linkages and spillovers (e.g. in technologies and skills) that create economic opportunities and advantage to the companies involved. A famous example is the growth a cluster of computer and software companies along Highway 128 around Boston, Massachusetts. This is described in Box 3.1, though it also shows that triggers from outside the Boston region also shaped the development.

Edmonds (2000: 32–5) drew on the work of Finegold (1999) to set out what is required for a high-technology cluster to develop and succeed. The factors which he listed were:

- Catalysts – some sort of external trigger. For example in the case of Highway 128, defence contracts could be seen as an external catalyst.
- Nourishment – having universities nearby helps to sustain the cluster by pulling mobile talent into the area, training them and releasing them onto the labour market. Similarly, venture capital availability encourages risk taking.
- A supportive environment – this entails infrastructure, a supportive business and social ethos and a legal system that

supports commercial activity by making it easy to start up a business – and to go bankrupt if necessary!

- Interdependence – a shared focus on a particular sector or technology will fuel a learning process. In particular there are three types of linkages: horizontal ties among specialized firms, each with their distinctive core competence; vertical links between different points in the product cycle from product development through production and marketing; and last but not least, networks among individuals, who share and spread knowledge.

European enthusiasm for clusters came particularly from the practical example of what became known as the 'Third Italy' model of New Industrial Districts. Unlike the most commonly cited US clusters, it was not focused on high-technology industry and not tied to a major metropolis. In the 1970s, there were the old industrial regions of the north-west of Italy and the traditionally underdeveloped south; the 'Third' Italy was the fast growing economies of the north-east and central regions. In this Third Italy production seemed to be developed on a bottom-up model. To many people this seemed to be an attractive alternative to reliance on inward investment by multinational companies at a time of great uncertainty and change in international economic conditions. The components of the cluster were seen to be the physical proximity of small- and medium-sized firms with sectoral specialization, typically operating in a non-metropolitan, even rural environment. The example par excellence was Prato, where large traditional textile firms had fragmented into numerous small- and medium-sized specialized firms, who had developed strong horizontal networks (Camagni and Capello, 1990).

The idea that underpins the promotion of clusters as an economic development tool is that spatial concentration brings competitive advantages. This line of reasoning has similarities with the notion of cumulative causation, a concept invoked by Myrdal (1957) and Pred (1966) to explain regional growth and decline. Basically they argued that advantages translate into growth that begets more advantages, though conversely, when a period of regional economic decline begins it can also create a self-reinforcing downwards cycle. A region that is highly dependent on just one cluster is vulnerable if there is a serious downturn in that particular sector. Furthermore,

Box 3.1: A high-technology cluster, Route 128, Boston (USA)

In 1968–75 Greater Boston lost 252,000 manufacturing jobs, mainly from traditional engineering and textiles industries. In 1975–80 it gained 225,000 new manufacturing jobs, mostly in high-technology industries. Most of these firms located along Highway 128, the ring road around the city 15 miles from the centre. Further growth in the 1980s took new industries west and north-west around Highway 495, another arterial 40 miles from the centre of Boston.

In the 1940s and 1950s, US Defense Department contracts had led the Massachusetts Institute of Technology (MIT) to develop the cutting-edge knowledge and key personal contacts that triggered company start-ups in the 1970s and 1980s. Spin-off processes created new companies that clustered and began to enjoy agglomeration economies. Driving this growth was the computer industry. New companies were being created by engineers and scientists, often graduates or staff from MIT. Indeed there are 65 universities and colleges in the Greater Boston area providing skilled labour to high-technology industries.

However, we still have to explain the loss of jobs in the 1960s and early 1970s, and the growth that followed. Massachusetts actually lost

→

the World Bank (2009: 139) has reported that metropolitan areas that have a diverse industrial structure do better at being the locus for new products and processes than places characterized by clusters of similar firms. However, after innovation and start-up, the mass-production phase may then be located in a city marked by specialization. Ideally, therefore, the aim should be to have a number of clusters with connections between them that can spawn synergies without creating mutual dependence. Within a region a mix of specialized and diverse cities may be desired. Of course, it is easier to recommend this situation than it is to achieve it! The starting point must always be the assets that a region already has.

Most of the theorizing and examples of clusters come from North America and Europe. One of the few discussions from elsewhere can be found in World Bank (2009: 132) which summarized work leadership to California in electronics manufacturing when its older electronics companies failed to enter the emergent microelectronics field. Thus the reindustrialization of the late 1970s was independent of the area's old electronics base. It was started by new companies, most of which had been created after 1960, though Digital Equipment Corporation, founded in 1957, played a key role.

Although there were strong links with defence contracts, the real take-off came as the firms began to create computers for civilian use – computers doing the kind of word-processing and spreadsheet tasks we now take for granted. Then, as the world's computer industry experienced one of its downturns in the mid-1980s, the companies were able to switch back to military contracts, with the New England region receiving the highest level of defence spending per capita in the USA. The 'peace dividend' which saw military spending reduced after the end of the Cold War brought a new crisis phase in the early 1990s. Problems were exacerbated by global competitors in the civilian computers market, outdated corporate cultures and reliance on defence contracts that had eroded entrepreneurial skills in the firms. (Source: Castells and Hall (1994).)

in Indonesia. Four broad industrial groups were studied: chemicals, textiles, non-metallic minerals and machinery. The research found that the benefits of being located close to other firms in the same industry were strong for chemicals and textiles. However, these benefits were not in the exchange of new ideas but rather in more 'static' forms of interlinkage, such as access to a pool of labour with the required skills, or proximity to suppliers or opportunities for outsourcing. In comparison, the benefits of being able to pick up new ideas by being located in a large urban agglomeration were greater for the minerals and machinery sectors. Differences such as these have implications for policy-makers seeking to spread industrialization to under-industrialized regions. The findings imply that sectors such as textiles and chemicals are likely to be less dependent on an established urban location. However, such a strategy is not without problems. The spread of industrialization to Central Liaoning Province in China, which is summarized in Box 3.2, was

Box 3.2: Industrial agglomeration in Central Liaoning Province (China)

The industrialization of north-east China from the 1950s to the 1970s was done on a heroic scale. Large-scale, state-owned heavy industries underpinned the development of the city cluster in Central Liaoning Province. When China's reform programme began in the 1980s this was the most densely urbanized area of the country. Indeed the scale and density of urban industrialization in a region with coal, iron and oil resources was significant on a global scale, making it 'an urbanization miracle created by the planned economy' (Fan and Sheng, 2007: 49). There are three mega-cities (Shenyang, Anshan and Fushun) and two big cities (Benxi and Liaoyang) within a radius of 100 km. By 1978, manufacturing accounted for around between 68% and 81% of GDP in four of these five cities (in Liaoyang it was 55%) and heavy-industry output was between 62% and 93% of general industrial output (Fan and Sheng, 2007: 52). Anshan and Benxi are specialized in metallurgy, Liaoyang on chemical fibres and Fushun

→

achieved on a grand scale, but caused serious pollution, and the region has struggled to adapt to new economic needs.

Understanding of clusters and development of a clusters policy needs to be nuanced and specific to local situations. Kitson *et al.* (2004: 996) warned against assuming that the same economic drivers 'are equally important everywhere, and hence the same economic policy model is applicable'. Clusters do not guarantee success. Porter (2001: 17) stressed the need for distinctive strategies, warning that no single approach will work for all regions. Attempts to develop clusters need to be realistic. Small rural towns are not going to become powerhouses in global financial services. Large businesses have complex structures that may be geographically dispersed. Success in inventing a product does not necessarily guarantee success in producing or marketing it. For example, Edmonds (2000: 24) cited the example that the fax, video camera and recorder were invented by Americans and the CD player by on coal mining, petrochemicals and steel. In the planned economy key factors of production such as raw materials, energy and transportation, were provided at costs fixed by government (and sometimes the cost was zero).

Functional efficiency of the production process was a key aim, and an urban–industrial agglomeration a direct result of this process. However, there was a heavy environmental price to pay that was not included in the costs of the enterprises. Water pollution became a serious problem; pollution of the Liao River was the most severe among China's seven river systems. Also Fan and Sheng argued that the top-down system that created the cluster made it difficult for the region to adapt and renovate as China opened up to market forces. Local governments were unable to do much to diversify or upgrade the industrial base. Unemployment rose and local living standards have fallen below the national average. Fan and Sheng said that a 'core city' was needed to help to reconstruct the urban economy more towards service industries and create a base for knowledge and innovation in north-east China. The industries need to modernize technologies, create downstream products and value chains. Last, but not least, the deterioration of the environment that resulted from the dense metropolitan growth needs to be tackled. (Source: Fan and Sheng (2007).)

Europeans, but it was the Japanese who invested in actually making the goods and they became the world leaders for these products.

Notwithstanding these reservations, Cortright (2006) gave a strong endorsement of clusters as a practical economic development tool. He argued that clusters should be thought of as a general concept, rather than something that was precisely defined. Summarizing key lessons for economic development policy-makers and practitioners, Cortright (2006: v) stressed the need to diagnose a region's economic strengths and work with these rather than chasing industries at random. He called for ongoing dialogue with firms in existing clusters to inform policy. However, it is also possible that the mindset of local businesses may restrict the scope for new policies. For example, in the Liaoning example (Box 3.2), the influence of the culture of the local industries over local government was seen as a barrier to creating new urban initiatives.

Issues of scale (again)

Simmie (2001) questioned whether local and regional linkages are as important for innovation as the advocates of clusters and agglomerations suggest they are. Simmie's argument was that key new knowledge is likely to be sourced internationally rather than locally. Thus it is the big multinational companies located in the main urban cores that are likely to lead and reproduce the spatial forms of business innovation. He cited the work of Amin and Thrift (1992) who argued that major urban centres captured new ideas internationally and then provided the initial markets and the critical mass of local networks to provide rapid reactions. Their conclusion was that for many localities, aspiration to self-sustaining growth was an illusion in a world marked by increasing international control and integration.

The idea of 'glocalization' implies the weakening of the nation-state as a player in economic development. An extreme position is Ohmae's (1995) assertion that globalization means 'the end of the nation state'. More reasonably, Greene *et al.* (2007: 3) noted how the academic literature, in theorizing the importance of city–international linkages, instead of nation-to-nation linkages, had promoted the idea of city-regions. This implied 'an apparent re-scaling with respect to economic governance'.

It is therefore interesting to look at some research into the motors of growth in fast-growing cities in Africa, Asia and Latin America. While finding that agglomeration economies and good urban management were indeed present in many fast-growing cities, UN–Habitat (2008: 30) research highlighted the part played by national governments:

> In a number of rapidly growing cities, economic policies and investments grow primarily from national government decisions and allocations. The state, in its various institutional forms, exerts a critical influence on the growth of these cities. For instance, decisions to designate cities or regions as free trade areas or special economic zones are made at the central government level; likewise, the mobilization and allocation of huge public (and often private) investments for the construction of transport and communication infrastructure and the improvement of these services is often a central government responsibility.

This would appear to be consistent with more theoretical arguments about how states have had to adjust their roles relative to both smaller-scale and larger, supranational-scale actors (e.g. Agnew, 1997; Dicken, 2003; Leitner *et al.*, 2002).

Measuring competitiveness of places

Scale is also relevant to intra-regional equity. By definition any local-ized strategy will benefit some parts of a region more than others. Similarly, success in terms of regional-scale average measures may conceal a widening of differences within the region. So how do we know if a city or region is performing well in relation to its perceived competitors? Gross domestic product (GDP) might seem to be the obvious answer, as it is the most widely used measure of economic per-formance. However, used in isolation, GDP does not actually reveal much about the competitiveness of an economy: it largely reflects economic history. Annual rate of growth in GDP is a better measure, but it only really reflects outcomes; it does not probe the potential strengths and weaknesses of the economy. Gross value added (GVA) is a better measure of a region's income and the economic activ-ity within the area. GVA is the major component of GDP, the main difference being that GDP includes taxes (less subsidies). GVA is a calculation of the production of new goods and services per head, a measure of labour productivity, one of the key variables influenc-ing competitiveness of companies. When indexed against a national average and compared to an index of retail prices, GVA per head can be used to do comparisons of how regions are doing economically.

Other key indicators of regional competitiveness are invest-ment by companies and export of goods and services. However, researchers have tried to develop more sophisticated approaches that encompass indicators that are not purely economic in charac-ter, but stand for factors that will have an influence on economic outcomes.

Echoing Florida's (2002, 2005, 2008) ideas of a 'creative class', economy and cities, Begg *et al.* (2002: 102) defined successful cities as 'those that function well and compete effectively with other cities for private and public sector resources (the sources of jobs, income and quality of life). Unsuccessful cities tend to be characterized by a population loss and lack of employment or by an inability to surmount evident social and economic problems.' Lever and Turok (1999) argued that the rate of economic growth cannot stand as a single indicator for competitiveness. Rather, there will be a multiplicity of criteria for judging success, including distributional issues, economic development (not just growth), sustainability and quality of life. Quality of life might appear to be tangential to the real concerns of businesses. It is not easily translated into the bottom line. However, Rogerson (1999) quoted evidence that it really can be a factor in shaping location decisions. For example, surveys of industrialists and decision-makers by prominent property companies had found that around 10 per cent of the largest 500-plus companies in the EU include quality-of-life factors among the three most important attributes in their location decisions.

Yet 'quality of life' is very difficult to define. That is one reason why economic development agencies are unlikely to resist the temptation to define it in terms that put their own territory at the top of any rankings table! Rogerson (1999: 977) reviewed a range of quality-of-life studies and methodologies. He found that while there were variations, 'the focus is consistently on factors such as physical environment, climate, pollution, crime and social factors linked to education, health'. He noted that the way that quality of life was defined was typically socially skewed: it was quality of life as seen by business, not by poor residents, for example. He cited research by Macnaughten *et al.* (1995) which found that unemployed people actually resented the term 'quality of life' because of the gulf between it and their own material circumstances. One might also hypothesize that notions of quality of life would vary between different cultures and quite possibly between men and women also. It is a concept to be handled with caution.

The fact that knowledge and innovation are seen as so central to the dominant conceptions of regional competitiveness, yet are almost impossible to measure, raises obvious and fundamental questions. Greene *et al.* (2007) looked at 22 studies between 2000 and 2007 that attempted to measure the competitiveness of cities and city-regions. All of them were concerned with places in the USA, UK or Europe. Nine of the studies focused primarily on productivity as a key part of regional competitiveness. Innovation was also seen as very important, but it is difficult to measure directly, so proxy variables have to be used instead, such as employment of R&D workers. Most of the studies had also looked at educational attainment and economic activity rates, assuming that these were further indicators of regional competitiveness. Several also took migration flows as indicators of competitiveness. The characteristics of the firms (sectors, trends in their markets), along with measures of 'connectivity' and hard infrastructure (roads, airports, etc.) were also prominent. House prices, government financial support to business and even cultural factors also figured. In reflecting on these studies, Greene *et al.* (2007) argued that because the concept of spatial competitiveness was weakly developed as a theory, 'competitiveness' became no more than what the researchers had chosen to measure. A set of statistics about regional characteristics does not necessarily tell us much about how being in a particular place actually affects a firm's performance. Attempts to construct rankings of city or regional competitiveness were thus dismissed by Greene and his colleagues as no more than exercises in place promotion. Similarly, Boland (2007) was critical of the extent to which academics working as consultants and emphasizing regional competitiveness have set the policy agenda for the practice of local economic development.

A further problem in analysing competitiveness at local or regional level is that it is intertwined with the general level of the wider regional or national economy. Thus a town in a strong growth region may be seen to be performing better than another town in a declining region on indicators such as GDP per head or level of unemployment. However, that differential may be explained by the regional differences and not properly reflect local performance. To get a more accurate picture it would be necessary to see how well each town was performing in relation to similar towns in their own region. If this showed that the town in the growth region had lower GDP than the average for its region, and unemployment above the regional average, whereas the town in the declining region was performing better than average in its region, this would suggest a need to reconsider the comparison between the two towns. The same logic applies even more strongly for international comparisons, where the level of the national economy will account for much of the variations at local or regional level between places in different countries. Similarly, the inherited industrial structure – the type of economic activities within a territory – will influence its performance on measures of competitiveness. In other words, if measurements of place competitiveness are to mean anything, they need to compare like with like in terms of the territories, and to have a firm grasp of how place characteristics might really influence the performance of firms located there.

Regional resilience

One response to criticisms of the concept of regional competitiveness has been the development of a rather different way of looking at a region's performance through the notion of regional resilience. Again it is a rather vague term and is interpreted differently by different people. Fundamentally, it suggests that regions are vulnerable to 'shocks' that are triggered from outside the region. Examples might be a catastrophic weather event or other natural disaster or the kind of blows struck to regional economies by a major global financial crisis. How well can the region adapt to such changes and continue to prosper? What can policy-makers do to strengthen regional resilience?

Part of the answer to these questions is to understand the vulnerability of the region. Vulnerability is likely to be a combination of the risk of a shock occurring, the sensitivity of the region (compared to other regions) to that shock, and the damage that the shock will do to the region. For example, one risk from climate change is sea-level rise. Regions with a lot of low elevation coastal land will be more sensitive to such risks than mountain regions. Then a region where much of the economic activity is located on low-lying land will face the prospect of more serious disruption than a region where low land near the coast is not in high-value economic uses.

However, analyses of regional risk and resilience are not limited to environmental triggers. Christopherson *et al.* (2010: 5) noted how the open nature of the US and UK economies has left regions within them exposed to the risks inherent in global markets. In the wake of the sudden downturn in US housing markets in 2008 and the economic crisis that followed, they observed that:

> In the USA, a list of metropolitan regions least affected by the economic crisis contains a surprising (to some) number of old industrial cities. These cities' resilience is related to their diversified economies, including small advanced manufacturing industries as well as educational and health institutions. In addition, because they were poor candidates for

super-profits in housing, they avoided the speculation and mortgage fraud that resulted in deep financial losses in the consumption belt cities from California and Las Vegas to Georgia and Florida. (6)

When reviewing the emergent literature on how regions can best mitigate and adapt to shocks, Christopherson *et al.* (2010) recognized that each region will be different. Nevertheless, their listing of desirable assets reads very similar to those seen as key endogenous drivers by the theorists of regional competitiveness. The list included: a strong regional system of innovation; strength in factors that create a 'learning region'; a modern productive infrastructure (transport, broadband provision, etc.); a skilled, innovative and entrepreneurial workforce; a supportive financial system providing patient capital and a diversified economic base, not over-reliant on a single industry. They further suggested:

> successful universities with strong links between the universities and the regional economies; close collaborative relations between companies and with other organizations, locally and globally; high levels of trust among and between economic actors; companies adopting High Commitment Work Systems involving not just a skilled workforce but one that is consulted, involved, motivated and committed; a diverse economic basis in terms of ownership structures (with cooperatives, mutuals and co-owned companies as well as public limited companies) and with strong corporate governance arrangement that includes risk assessment and management; and a supportive regional government promoting the above factors, actively networked nationally and internationally, combining regional industrial policy and innovation policy into regional innovation strategies. (Christopherson *et al.*, 2010: 7)

The idea of regional resilience has been challenged by some authors. For example, Hassink (2010) argued that it misunderstands the processes that structure regional change. The underpinning notion of an equilibrium to which a region can seek to return was also challenged by Pike *et al.* (2010).

Territorial capital and territorial potential

The notion of regional resilience is more broad-based than the concept of regional competitiveness, though the underpinning notion of an equilibrium to which the system can return is itself suspect. It derives from a biological analogy and assumptions of some economists, but at this stage is not rooted in evidence or rigorous explanation. The definition and significance of a region as a significant scale for intervention is also subject to ongoing debate. Notwithstanding these reservations, what remains from the policy-led practice and theory of regional economic development is the idea that any territory has some unique combination of assets which carry some potential in furthering development. The Organization for Economic Co-operation and Development (OECD) developed the concept of 'territorial capital'. Territorial capital is the sum of the assets that are specific to the region. This encompasses natural resources, physical factors, financial, human and social assets. The proposition is that each region has its own distinctive combination of these assets that comprise its territorial capital. The combination will be shaped by history, landscape, the pattern of settlements and their connections, socio-economic structures and access to capital.

Waterhout (2008: 88) called the territorial capital concept a 'black box' and suggested that it would be difficult to operationalize. However, Pezzini (2003: 6) argued that the ability to properly exploit these territorial assets is very important. He said 'the difficulty is to transform stocks into flows: valorize natural and man-made assets, strengthen the economic environment, invest in human resources, improve the institutional capacity, etc.' While the 'etc.' begs questions, the thrust of his message is clear: there is scope to make a difference by understanding and using the territorial capital of a region. Underpinning this theory is a concept of market failure. In other words the market has failed to realize the region's potential. Examples of such failures would be a lack of information about, and imperfect understanding of, the nature and potential of the assets, lack of access and problems of converting public goods such as a splendid view into a revenue stream, restricted local opportunities for education and training. Public policy interventions are needed to overcome such failures. Such interventions can seek environmental and social ends, not just business efficiency.

The idea that regions have an endogenous potential that has not been fully realized and mobilized is particularly important in respect of rural areas and in thinking about the relation between a town and its rural hinterland. While the ideas of territorial capital and potential are also applicable in heavily urbanized regions, arguably the process of urbanization indicates that the potential of the place has at least been recognized at some point.

Drawing on the results of a number of OECD Territorial Reviews, Pezzini (2003) identified four main approaches to rural regional development. These were:

- Amenity-based development: many successful rural regions are able to offer high quality environments, beautiful landscapes and cultural heritage that can attract urban dwellers to visit or reside there. Perhaps the key is to avoid a situation where success in attracting people and investors begins to destroy these same assets.
- Diffuse industrialization in an 'urbanized countryside': some regions such as south-east Ireland or the Hiroshima-Kamo area of Japan have been able to attract industries despite not being able to offer agglomeration economies. Instead their draw is quality of life and skilled labour, which can pull in enterprises that do not need to be located close to their markets, e.g. accountancy or assembly of electronic components. In general though, regions succeeding with this type of approach tend to have some agglomeration of small firms already.
- Exploitation of natural resources: there are plenty of examples of regions based on the harvesting of their oil, timber, mineral or water resources. To be resilient they need to be able to manage two problems. One is the boom/bust syndrome, where decline can be triggered by exhaustion of the resource or by substitution as a result of technological change, or by fluctuation in world prices and exchange rates. The second problem is to avoid a situation where all value added is done outside the region – e.g. the processing plants and production and sales parts of the process.
- Major public expenditures: sparsely populated regions are often seen as good places to put the kind of land uses that few people want to live near, e.g. nuclear power plants, prisons, toxic waste dumps. They generate income and some measure

of economic activity, but they also create major obstacles to more diversified forms of development.

Pezzini (2003: 10) was of the view that the first two of these options – 'amenity-based development' and what he called 'industrial cluster-ing and networking' – are the ones likely to offer the best chance of sustainable growth. There is a need for case studies of these differ-ent kind of regions to explore what policies are applied in practice and how well they work. Of course, Pezzini's list represents simpli-fied categories of regions: any actual region may have elements of more than one of these ideal types.

The example of Falköping, discussed in Box 3.3, shows a bottom-up eco-modernization approach to rural economic development. Many of its assets were unrecognized for a long time. Traditional dairy farms and their products are intrinsic to this area, but if they were just seen as agriculture their full territorial potential was not fully recognized. Realizing that this kind of farming, and its unique local produce, can attract tourists and retain spending in the local economy unlocks some of the territorial potential of the area. The strategy plays to regional distinctiveness and targets local and national markets rather than chasing footloose international firms. Even then the entrepreneurs need to have confidence in the future of the area. In part this comes from investment by the Kommune in sustaining key services, such as village shops and com-munity halls managed by local volunteers. Active involvement of local stakeholders who take responsibility for the success of projects is vital.

Modernist farming had drained Falköping's natural wetlands. In the early 1990s the Swedish Environment Protection Agency responded to lobbying from ornithologists and ecologists and decided to restore a lake. Now, each spring thousands of migrating cranes arrive. These huge birds have the extra appeal that in Nordic mythology they are bringers of good luck. Bird watchers and tourists flock to the lake (150,000 visitors in April), go round the visitor centre, eat homemade food in the cafe, and hire cottages.

Summary

This chapter has shown that the concept of regional competitive-ness is contentious academically, but widely followed in practice.

Box 3.3: Amenity-based rural economic development: Falköping (Sweden)

In the nineteenth-century heyday of small dairy farming, even the poor soils on the Table Mountain above the Swedish town of Falköping were farmed. Now forests claim this marginal land. Farms are amalgamating as they struggle for viability. The area is losing its young people. Falköping Kommune, the local government unit, covers 2,400 square miles, and is home to 30,000 people, about half of them in villages and on farms. How can this kind of rural region, its level of settlement, lifestyle and landscape be sustained?

Niclas Fallstrom, the Kommune's rural development officer, explains 'When I was a boy here in the 1960s, growing up in the village where my parents and grandparents lived, many people in the village were able to make a good living from owning seven or eight cattle. Today, the median size of a farm is 30 cows. We still have 300 farms producing milk. Agriculture can still offer huge possibilities, but only if we use it properly.' About 700 are employed in agriculture and related jobs.

Fallstrom is convinced that 'clean agriculture' is vital to the future. 'There are two possible ways forward for agriculture. One is big businesses. You create bigger farms and produce a standard product in bulk, and sell it to the big butcher or the large dairy. People then travel to work in the towns, in factories like Arkivator in Falkoping who make mobile phones. A different way of rural living is possible, where people have small farms, think for themselves, keep animals free range, let cows stay with their calves, produce ecological foods and sell direct to their own customers.'

This philosophy infuses the Kommune's approach to rural economic development. Sorgarden, a dairy farm that supports one family, exemplifies the practice. Ten grass-fed cows supply milk for the cheese produced on the farm. Some cheese is sold to a nearby factory, but increasingly sales are made direct from the farm. Tourists visit to enjoy the rural landscape and sample homemade cheesecake. Crayfish, reared in a small pond at the back of the farmhouse, are a popular dish. Fallstrom says Sorgarden is an example for others: 'They had an idea and it is working. I would love to have about ten such "micro-dairies" because they would benefit each other by increasing the pull of visitors and customers.' (Source: C. Hague (2001).)

In terms of our typology from Chapter 1 it is an approach of the 'sharks', embracing pro-business competition to attract inward investment. As Bristow (2005: 293) has argued, one paradox is that the rhetoric of regional competitiveness emphasizes the importance of qualities and assets that are special to the region, yet results in standardized policies and practices. The notion of regional resilience offers a different perspective, rooted in rather different theory, and no doubt spurred by the increasing awareness of the vulnerability of regions to external shocks in the light of the onset of a financial crisis in 2008 and concerns about extreme weather events. Development strategies aiming to enhance regional resilience will fit on the right-hand side of our Chapter 1 typology: approaches that attach priority to environmental sustainability and social cohesion as well as to economic efficiency. The example in Box 3.3 from Falköping represents such an approach; it is environmentally led and backed by strategies of inclusion through sustaining public services.

The chapter has shown that local conditions are by no means the only influence on how a firm or indeed a region performs. International factors such as the fluctuating exchange rates of currencies are especially important to exporters. Similarly, in the rush to embrace regionalism it is important not to lose sight of the impacts of macroeconomic policy made by national governments. In particular there is some evidence that these can be very important in Asia, Africa and Latin America. Tax policies, and investment in education and training, make a difference. Similarly, there is evidence that multinational companies get new ideas internationally not locally. Nevertheless, the reason why regional development matters is because in the end economic activity does tend to concentrate in particular places – it is not spread out evenly over the land area of a territory. Furthermore it is clear that agglomeration can confer advantages in terms of shared services, markets for labour and goods, and access to ideas and know-how. These can be particularly important to some industries, though it is hard to measure just how important they are. There is great value in rigorous analysis of the region, its mix of firms, settlements and other assets, and its relations to other regions. Each case is unique and has its own challenges for equitable and sustainable development.

Topics for discussion

Imagine that you are working in a local economic development agency, and that you have been asked by your manager to produce a strategy for development based on clusters. How might you set about the task? What information would you need? Who would you talk to? What factors might influence your recommendations?

Can regions be made 'resilient'?

Related reading

M. E. Porter (2000) 'Location, competition and economic development: local clusters in the global economy', *Economic Development Quarterly*, 14, 15–31.

G. Bristow (2005) 'Everyone's a "winner": Problematising the discourse of regional competitiveness', *Journal of Economic Geography*, 5, 285–304.

Cambridge Journal of Regions, Economy and Society (2010), 3(2). (This issue contains several articles on the theme of regional resilience.)

4 Governance and Partnerships

Government, governance and economic development

Chapter 1 made reference to the 'New Institutional Economics'. It argued that many assumptions of neoclassical economics are idealizations that are not found in real-world situations. Thus, the political and legal framework is very important for the practice of economic development. The opening chapter also made the distinction between government and governance. The word 'governance' tries to capture the idea that governments work and negotiate with a range of other actors from the private sector and civil society, and the whole process spans different spatial scales. There were once clear distinctions between the different sectors, and governing was unambiguously the preserve of government; today the situation is more complicated.

Chapter 2 noted that regional policies were the classic form of state intervention to promote growth in local economies. These sought to steer firms to regions that were performing less well by using a mix of restrictions and centrally administered incentives. However, as Keating (2001: 372) noted: 'Since the 1980s, this model of planned and state-regulated spatial development has come into question as a consequence of the changing role of the state, economic and technological change, and a greater protagonism on the part of cities and regions themselves'.

This chapter focuses on how governments and the shift towards governance shape regional and local economic development. Among western academics there is a broad consensus that the governments have been 'hollowed out' during the current phase of globalization. This means they have lost powers and functions, for example through privatization. The state, instead of being a 'provider' has become an 'enabler' that works in partnership with the private sector and sometimes with citizens and NGOs. There is also strong advocacy of 'good governance' by international development agencies. For example, UN–Habitat (2006: 170) 'has been a major campaigner for inclusive, participatory decision-making in cities and devolution of power from central to local governments – two of the cornerstones of good urban governance'. However, when we look at how governments actually work in different countries, it is clear that there is not one approach, good or bad, but rather different cultures of governance. There is continuity but also change within these cultures. The pressures for change may have similar roots in different countries, not least concerns with place competitiveness. Furthermore, responses tend to be path dependent; that is to say they are shaped by the institutions, outlooks and practices inherited from the past. For example, the stamp of the public sector culture from the Soviet era remains in places and institutions in central and eastern Europe. Similarly, participatory approaches are difficult to nurture in societies without participatory cultures and traditions: yet also there are more ways of undertaking participation that western academics and practitioners imagine.

Some understanding of different governance styles and traditions is important. Without it the risk of inappropriate transplants of practices is high. Approaches which talk about 'best practice' without pondering the relation between the practice and the culture can be particularly problematic in this respect. In an effort to avoid such traps we propose developing the typology which was introduced in Chapter 1. Thus we approach the very real issues of governance in regional and local economic development not from preconceived theories, but in an exploratory way by using our typology that was derived from policy and practice.

Diagram 4.1 outlines the concept. The horizontal axis remains the same as in Diagram 1.2, and still defines the policy priorities. On the left is a policy approach prioritizing economic development alone, but as you move across the page to the right more weight is attached to environmental and/or social considerations. The top of the vertical dimension is still defined by faith in the market (as it was in Diagram 1.2), but now a broad governance consideration has been introduced. Thus the top of the axis also encapsulates the idea that the state has strong capacity to operate with and within markets. This combination of strong markets and strong states

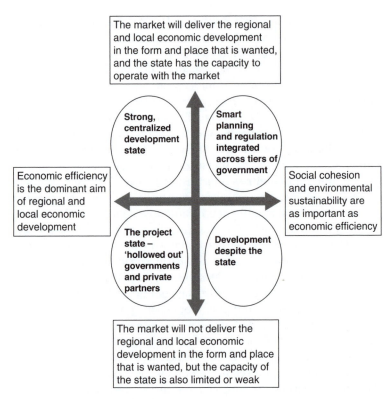

Diagram 4.1   **A typology of policy and practice related to governance**

dilutes as you proceed down the axis. At the bottom, the market itself is weak and/or not delivering what is wanted, but the state is also significantly constrained in its capacity to deliver change. In such situations governments work in partnership with the private sector or NGOs. In extreme cases states are themselves a barrier to development, and the development effort is led by others.

Our four metaphorical animals from Chapter 1 have now assumed the form of four types of governance in Diagram 4.1. The governance style of the 'sharks', whose policy and practice was pro-business competition to attract inward investment, is the Development State. Here government, not least central government, has a strong, forcing role. It can access land, provide infrastructure such as business parks, or work closely with the private sector to do so. It uses fiscal powers to create incentives through, for example, offering tax breaks to firms locating in special economic zones. The prize remains to capture foreign direct investment in the face of competition from other governments, regions or cities.

The idea of the Project State was introduced in Chapter 1. It is used here to characterize a governance approach to the pursuit of economic efficiency in situations where markets are not currently delivering the kind of development that policy-makers want, but the state is also limited in its own capacity to deliver the desired change. The pursuit of competitiveness still drives this approach. The difference from the Development State is that the government is weaker or 'hollowed out'. It needs partners to achieve its aims, particularly partners from the private sector. The government manipulates incentives and subsidies through an ever changing portfolio of time-limited, targeted projects that typically seek to tackle the problems of places where market failure is evident: e.g. there are assets (such as buildings or a good location) whose potential the market has failed to exploit.

In the top-right corner of Diagram 4.1 there is 'Smart Planning and Regulation'. This is a style of governance that has some similarities to the Project State. The main differences are that both the market performance and the perceived capacity of government are greater. Governments in places like Scandinavia, for example still retain some residual capacity and culture from the welfare states of the second half of the twentieth century (another example of 'path dependency'). In such situations, integration and better effectiveness of public policy are likely to be a key theme: public–public partnerships rather than only public–private partnerships. Similarly this style of governance can work in situations where the market-led growth is strong. In such situations businesses with strong green principles, for example, can deliver environmentally acceptable forms of economic development. Strong market pressure also potentially strengthens the hand of governments as regulators. Where markets are weak, regulation (e.g. strong environmental standards) may deter investment; but where markets are strong and market confidence is high, compliance with regulatory requirements is still 'a price worth paying' for businesses wanting carry-through development. So governments can operate through regulation (e.g. of new urban development) rather than having to rely on subsidies or other incentives, or opting to be direct developers themselves. In this governance style, governments are also conscious that they are accountable to a wide range of stakeholders, so need to balance claims for economic development against other priorities such as the environment. However, because of the basic faith in the benefits that market-led growth can bring, management styles are likely to mimic those of the private sector, for example through use of performance indicators and executive decision-making. There is also likely to be an enthusiasm for new structures of government, such as city-region authorities, as a means to create more effective channels for government intervention.

Finally, in the bottom right-hand corner of Diagram 4.1 we have 'Development despite the state'. There are many situations where the state is weak, and formal market processes are concentrating rather than disbursing wealth in a way that reinforces existing inequalities and marginalizes the poor and other groups likely to be disadvantaged such as women. Grassroots activists, NGOs and informal enterprises fill the gap, sometimes with support from multilateral donor agencies in the international development community. Decentralized actions such as community self-help and community involvement in partnerships are to the fore in this governance approach to economic development. This situation was exemplified in extreme form in Zimbabwe in the first decade of the twenty-first century. There was hyperinflation, rising poverty and unemployment. In May 2005 the government launched a mass slum clearance and eviction programme in which 700,000 people lost their homes and/or livelihoods. As a consequence of the eviction, it is estimated that 170,000 people were then accommodated by family and friends and a similar number by churches and voluntary organizations (UN–Habitat 2008: 96).

Transnational governance

The growth of transnational governance is one reason why the primacy of the nation-state is often seen to be reduced from what it was in the twentieth century. International trading blocks are both a consequence of, and a contributor to, globalization. Through them economic development has become an exercise in multilevel governance, rather than being led by national governments as in the era of traditional regional policy. The European Union (EU) is an example of an institution of transnational governance. By 2007 it had 27 member states. The Association of South East Asian Nations (ASEAN) formed in 1967. The five original members, Indonesia, Malaysia, the Philippines, Singapore and Thailand, have been joined by five more. ASEAN objectives are economic growth, social and cultural development and regional peace and security. The ASEAN Economic Community is working towards enhancing the region's economic competitiveness, through freeing trade and increasing the mobility of capital and labour within the region. Trans-Asian transport and energy networks are being created to increase economic integration.

In Africa, an Organization of African Unity (OAU) was set up during the decolonization period in the 1960s. In 2002 it was superseded by the African Union (AU) in an attempt to create a more dynamic body. The AU is loosely modelled on the EU. It inherited NEPAD – New Partnerships for African Development – that had been established in 2001 by the OAU. NEPAD's (2008) primary objectives are:

- to eradicate poverty;
- to place African countries, both individually and collectively, on a path of sustainable growth and development;
- to halt the marginalization of Africa in the globalization process and enhance its full and beneficial integration into the global economy; and
- to accelerate the empowerment of women.

Infrastructure improvement and human resource development are among NEPAD's (2008) priorities. In addition, regional free-trade areas are developing within the African continent. For example, the East African Community was formed in 2000. Its members are Kenya, Tanzania, Uganda, Burundi and Rwanda, and again it has economic development among its aims.

Similarly, there are regional trading blocs in the Americas. The North American Free Trade Agreement (NAFTA) was signed by Canada, Mexico and the USA and became effective in 1994. It is a looser form of cooperation than the EU. In Latin America there is Mercusor, the Southern Common Market. There are 10 members: Argentina, Brazil, Paraguay, Uruguay (the four original signatories to a treaty in 1991), Venezuela, Ecuador, Chile, Bolivia, Peru and Colombia. Thus it is clear that there has been a significant growth in intergovernmental cooperation to create geo-regional and transnational economic areas.

The development of regional policy in the European Union (EU) is summarized in Box 4.1. The EU grew and strengthened forms of

Box 4.1: EU regional policy

The European Economic Community (EEC), later the EU, was established in 1957. It initiated the European Social Fund (ESF) to provide money for job retraining. In the 1970s, as the EEC expanded, the European Regional Development Fund (ERDF) was established to reduce regional imbalances. The criteria that defined which regions were eligible for support were:

- regional per capita income below the EEC average;
- over 20% of the region's population dependent on agriculture or declining industry;
- unemployment persistently 20% above the national average; and
- a high rate of emigration from the region.

These problems were mainly found in regions that were peripheral to the intensely developed 'core' around the Benelux countries.

ERDF policy was closely aligned to national regional policies and redistributed money to compensate poorer regions for their disadvantages. Money was often invested in small infrastructure projects such as industrial estates, access roads or bridges (Williams, 1996: 71). From the early 1980s, when many member states were grappling with the impacts

economic integration after the early 1990s, and has a strong territorial component in its economic development policies. EU regional or, more recently, 'territorial cohesion', policy has contributed to implanting multilevel governance and development of the 'Project State'. Territorial cohesion stresses the need for regional development to deliver better integration between different sectors of policy-making, and to use concepts such as territorial capital (see Chapter 3) to reduce dependence on redistribution of funds from richer regions. It involves coordination and medium-term commitment from transnational, through national and on to regional and local levels, as well as cooperation in subsidized projects involving groups of regional or local authorities. Money from the EU supports local projects (which may well involve the cooperation of of industrial restructuring, rules for ERDF were changed to shift support away from 'one-off' projects to more sustained regional economic development strategies. ESF funds were also used to aid small- and medium-sized enterprises (SMEs) (Williams, 1996: 74).

These EEC efforts to improve the position of poorer regions succeeded. Between 1987 and 1997, per capita GDP in the poorest regions rose from 54.2% of the EEC average to 61.1%, and it was estimated that from 1989 to 1999 across all the assisted regions of the EU, 2.2m. jobs were maintained or created as a result of European funds (Drevet, 2007: 152).

After 2000, the 'competitiveness' agenda became prominent in the EU, which has failed to keep pace with growth rates in US and Asian economies. The Sapir (Sapir *et al.*, 2004) and Kok Reports (CEC, 2004a) argued this case, and 'Jobs and Growth' became the motto. However, the EU did not abandon the welfare state notion of regional equity. A new concept, 'territorial cohesion', emerged to support both competitiveness and poorer regions. 'The concept of territorial cohesion is a multidimensional one. Several aspects', explained Robert (2007: 28) 'are related to issues with a regional dimension, such as promoting territorial capital and regional identities, increasing the propensity of regions to anticipate asymmetric shocks and to face successfully the challenges of globalization, providing services of general interest and promoting intraregional integration'.

private companies) that are nested into a regional development strategy in line with national policies that link to the EU. This consistency creates confidence for investors. It contrasts with situations where local policy is subject to the whim of local politicians whose fate can change with an election. There is also an audit process to resist, though not entirely eradicate, corrupt practices.

Transnational state entrepreneurship

Development States can also operate at a transnational level. The government of Singapore is perhaps the outstanding example. It has established industrial parks in Indonesia, China, Vietnam and India (Yeoh *et al.*, 2007: 64), and examples from two of these countries are described in Box 4.2. The aim was to create 'Singapore-styled' facilities and business environments for utilization primarily by Singaporean companies. Pereira (2007: 297) described this practice as 'transnational state entrepreneurship.'

Singapore, a small, highly developed country, wanted its businesses to expand abroad. Overseas industrial parks gave Singaporean companies the opportunity to take advantage of cheaper costs for land, raw material and labour. In these industrial parks, the Singaporean government provided 'ready-built factories', telecommunications infrastructure, transportation facilities and other necessary aspects, to reduce the start-up costs of potential investors and encourage multinational companies to lease space in a business-ready environment (Pereira, 2004: 133). Host nations were happy to participate as they

---

Box 4.2: Singapore's overseas industrial parks

Singapore's first overseas industrial park was Batamindo, on Batam, Indonesia, an island 20km and a one-hour ferry journey from Singapore. It began operations in 1991. The 0.5 sq. km estate was designated by Indonesia as a 'duty-free export-processing zone' (Pereira, 2004: 134). Established as a joint venture between Singapore and Indonesian development corporations, the first users were companies who retained their headquarters in Singapore and relocated low-skilled jobs to Batamindo. In 1991, 15 companies located operations in Batamindo industrial park; by 1995, there were 77 tenants; and by 1997, 93% of the estate was occupied (Pereira, 2004). One immediate impact of the park was that it absorbed so much labour that it caused a shortage of workers elsewhere on the island. In response the Indonesian government initiated a short-term, internal migration programme to encourage people to relocate to Batam from elsewhere on the archipelago. In 1999, this movement of population led to riots as different ethnic groups came into conflict (Pereira, 2004).

Over the next six years, Singapore established six further parks (Pereira, 2007). The largest of them was at Suzhou in eastern China. This industrial park differed from Singapore's other efforts as

→

envisioned jobs and investment coming into their territories at little financial cost to them. Singaporean officials hoped that Singaporean companies and workers would attain 'local knowledge' about operating in different countries and economies and thus 'would be among the "first movers" within the region ... gaining significant competitive advantage over other agents' (Pereira, 2007: 291). These Singaporean 'enclaves' (Yeoh *et al.*, 2005) were intended to generate revenue 'that would eventually supplement Singapore's domestic economy' and were part of the country's Strategic Economic Plan, a regional economic development strategy pursued during the 1990s (Pereira, 2004: 132).

One of the weaknesses of the single-minded Development State approach is that economic development can rarely be the whole story, as the Liaoyang example in Chapter 3 showed. Also the nature of competition is that there are competitors! Initial competitive

rather than being 'developed and managed by Singaporean government-linked corporations', Suzhou 'was developed and managed by the Singapore government itself' through its establishment of the China Singapore Suzhou Development company and 65% shareholding in this institution, the other 35% being held by a Chinese consortium (Pereira, 2004; 2007: 287). This was a 'a hybrid state and for-profit corporation' (Pereira, 2007: 297). The Suzhou park was a direct effort at state-led entrepreneurship. Suzhou Industrial Park opened in 1994. It was planned to cover 70 sq. km by 2014, at a cost of US$30m. By 2007 the Suzhou Industrial Park employed 400,000 people, an estimated 2.5% of whom were not Chinese (Pereira, 2007). Unlike Singapore's other projects, Suzhou also contained residential buildings.

Between 1995 and 2005 Singapore's Suzhou Industrial Park attracted 'many multinational corporations seeking to locate in China in order to benefit from cheap labour and high-quality industrial infrastructure and administration' (Pereira, 2007: 294). In 1994, Suzhou Industrial Park opened with 14 tenants, reaching 82 tenants investing US$3bn by 1997 (Pereira, 2004). Despite this, the Singaporean government reduced its involvement in the project in 2001, becoming a minority shareholder and silent partner, and administration of the industrial park was passed to Suzhou local authorities.

advantage can undermine other similar businesses and also be undermined as new enterprises join the market. Transnational development is also likely to complicate issues of governance. For example, the success of Batamindo (see Box 4.2) saw other industrial estates in the area, which had been developed by local authorities, experience high vacancy rates. In addition, investors at Batamindo typically imported materials, processed them and exported the finished products. Technology transfers between the Batamindo industrial park and Batam island have been minimal. This weakness in local networks and partnerships could be seen as a risk in Development State strategies. Similarly, the Suzhou authorities (see Box 4.2) had initially proposed collaboration with the Singaporean project. Yet, Singapore's government proceeded to act independently and constructed the Suzhou Industrial Park on the eastern side of Suzhou city. The Chinese local authorities then built a competing industrial park on the western side of the city and this Suzhou New District, developed between 1990 and 1997 began to out-perform the Singaporean site as it offered foreign investors land at lower costs (Pereira, 2004; 2007).

Singapore's overseas industrial parks have achieved some economic success. Infrastructure, land and labour costs, basic factors in any firm's operation, were provided in the package which created locations that could be competitive. Singapore's recognition of the benefits available through access to local knowledge is also interesting. However, the problems reflected inadequate attention to issues of governance and equity. On any international venture like this, inter-governmental relations (including relations with local governments) are vitally important for success. There also has to be consideration of the impact of inserting a high-value production capacity in a poor, low-wage regional economy.

Tax breaks and Export Zones

Export Processing Zones (EPZs) emerged in the 1950s as a way to attract foreign direct investment to disadvantaged regions and stimulate economic development, and continue to be part of the approach of Development States seeking to capitalize on globalization. Early EPZs often occupied coastal sites for ease of shipping and offered advantageous taxation and tariff rates. EPZs gave investors a quick route through what might otherwise be formidable obstacles posed by local legislation and procedures.

China has been at the forefront of utilizing EPZs. Using other EPZs as models for the nation's economic development, such as those operating in Taiwan, after 1978 the Chinese government devised policies to establish a range of zones such as Economic and Technological Development Zones (ETDZs), High-Technology Development ment Zones (HIDZs), Free Trade Zones and EPZs (Wong and Tang, 2005). They were intended to reduce China's overreliance on heavy manufacturing industry (again think of the example of Liaoyang). At the forefront of these policies has been the Special Economic Zone (SEZ). There are numerous early overviews of China's SEZs initiative (Wong and Chu, 1985; Jao *et al.*, 1986; Wong, 1987).

In 1979 the Chinese authorities granted Guangdong and Fujian, two provinces on the country's southern coast 'special economic privileges' to develop 'non-conventional, market-oriented, and outward-looking measures in promoting economic development' (Ge, 1999: 1286; Crane, 1994). Four sites were chosen in these two provinces for the establishment of Special Export Zones, subsequently renamed Special Economic Zones. The first four SEZs – Shenzhen, Zhuhai, and Shantou in Guangdong Province and Xiamen – were chosen because they were near to major trading hubs outside of China, Hong Kong, Macao and Taiwan. In other respects though, these four areas were seen as 'backward' and in need of economic development and infrastructural investment (Ge, 1999).

Foreign enterprises that located in an SEZ received permission to repatriate profits and capital investments, duty-free imports on raw materials, tax-free exports and a limited licence to sell products in China's home market. The SEZs and ETDZs also allowed foreign companies to lease land and premises at below-market rates. In effect an SEZ is a masterplanned industrial park complete with the necessary physical infrastructure – roads, water, power, etc. They were generally developed on greenfield sites close to a large city and with good transport connections. One example, from Guangdong, is described in Box 4.3.

The governance context for this experiment was very specific to China at that time. Part of the 'Open Door' reforms following the death of Mao Zedong, SEZs allowed China to experiment with market economics while maintaining a centrally planned

---

Box 4.3: The Guangdong Development District (China)

In Guangdong Province one of the sites was an area east of the provincial capital Guangzhou. By 2005 the Guangzhou Development District (GDD) comprised four separate segments: an ETDZ, HIDZ, EPZ and Free Trade Zone. Together these Guangdong zones covered an area of 215.5 sq. km which housed over 120,000 residents. The zones utilized around US$50bn of foreign capital in 2001, and provided 2,490,600sqm of industrial building space in 2002 (Wong and Tang, 2005). Although dominated by manufacturing production, particularly in chemicals, electronics and food processing, service sector jobs were growing in this zone (Wong and Tang, 2005). Initially the zones were dominated by low-wage, labour-intensive manufacturing jobs, but as the Guangdong zones developed, more high-technology and high-value production began to emerge.

The Guangdong experiment spread far beyond what was initially proposed in the late 1970s and consequently, the Development District 'finds itself dealing with increasingly complex responsibilities that are not only concerned with the attraction of inward investment, but also community building, urban management and public welfare' (Wong and Tang, 2005: 314). Thus what began as a stand-alone industrial development became a major urban community. This has not come without a price and Guangdong Province suffers from some of China's highest levels of pollution, with acid rain being a particularly serious issue (Liu *et al.*, 2007).

---

economy. They aimed to bring foreign investment into China, albeit in a limited manner, increase international trade, and ease China's entry into the globalizing economy of the late-twentieth century. Ge (1999) maintained that in addition to providing industrial and economic stimulus, these SEZs were also the locations for testing new ideas and developments in education, tourist and entertainment practices, and research and development, though again the environmental costs demonstrate the primacy of economic aims.

The experiment was extremely successful economically. By 2008 there were five SEZs and 54 ETDZs; the city of Shenzhen had

330,000 residents in 1980 but 8.5 million by 2008 (ProLogis, 2008). Each national ETDZ is managed by its provincial or municipal government through a management company. The company's role is to ensure the delivery of public services, manage land and construction, look after the fiscal health of the park and – very importantly – manage the labour relations in the park. In addition, each ETDZ also has its own Development Company working to attract foreign companies into the park. This means competing with the other national ETDZs and with other municipal and provincial business parks (ProLogis, 2008: 8).

Zhu (1994: 1619) studied Shenzhen and found that the major beneficiaries of the land-lease policies in the SEZ were 'developers and investors'. Furthermore, whereas enterprises within the SEZ were monitored, regulated and held to mandatory pollution standards, those locating outside the SEZ boundaries were not held to the same standards. As a result, Liu *et al.* (2007) discovered that not only is land now cheaper to utilize immediately beyond the Shenzhen SEZ border, but with lax environmental controls, production is often cheaper as clean-up costs do not have to be met. Consequently, despite a great deal of increased pollution in the Shenzhen area since the establishment of the SEZ, it is locations like Guanlan River outside the SEZ, rather than the Shenzhen River within it, which have borne the brunt of pollutants.

Gender and the Development State

Despite such problems, China has been able to operate a development instrument – SEZs and ETDZs – that was competitive and strongly pro-business, with low wages and a large, disciplined labour force. This workforce is primarily female, a situation that is not uncommon in other EPZs (Table 4.1). In Shenzhen's SEZ, for example, 79 per cent of the workforce was female in 1992 (So *et al.*, 2001: 106). Many of the women employed in China's SEZs are young (18 to 23 years old) and from rural regions. While this can be seen as creating employment opportunities for a group often marginalized in formal labour markets, concerns for gender and other forms of equity are generally not to the fore in the Development State.

The data in Table 4.1 are from the late 1990s and shows that Mexico has one of the lowest percentages of women employed in EPZs. Mexico's EPZs are some of the world's oldest. They contain factories (called *maquiladoras*) and were established following the 1965 Border Industrialization Program. The United Nations Development Fund for Women report 'Progress of the World's Women' (Chen *et al.*, 2005) found that female employment in Mexico's *maquiladoras* had fallen from 63 per cent in 1998 to 54 per cent in 2004. The report stated as the jobs became better paying (partly due to labour organizing and higher competition for workers), male workers became a greater percentage of the workforce. Also, since 2000, 200,000 jobs have been lost in *maquiladoras*, with a greater proportion of women among those unemployed. The result is that while the rise of *maquiladoras* initially led to an increase in female employment, women were not better off in terms of living standards. In the *maquiladoras*, as in most EPZs elsewhere (see, for example, the description of the Kingston Free Zone in Box 4.4), women work the lowest-paying jobs and have the least chance of advancement. Further, when an EPZ loses employers women bear the brunt of the job losses.

Table 4.1   **Employment of Women in Export Processing Zones (source: Seager, 2003: 64)**

Country/industry	% of workforce that is female
Mexico	50
Malaysia	65
Philippines/electronics	76
Philippines/garments	81
Guatemala/garments	80
Costa Rica	65
Nicaragua	80
Sri Lanka	85
Panama	95
South Korea	70

Institutions and institutional thickness

As we saw in Chapter 3, there are now many arguments suggesting that businesses benefit from agglomeration economies through local knowledge spillovers and networks and links between firms and government, education and research bodies. This is a key reason why 'good governance' at the region or city-region has been seen as an integral aspect of economic development. When reviewing factors determining urban competitiveness, Kresl (1995: 51) included institutional flexibility, public–private sector co-operation and urban strategy, alongside more traditional concerns with infrastructure, amenities and location, etc. Amin and Thrift (1995: 100) summarized these 'soft' factors as:

> relationships of trust; a strong sense of common industrial purpose; social consensus; local institutional support for business; and agencies and traditions encouraging innovation, skill formation and the circulation of ideas. (Hirst and Zeitlin, 1991; Sabel, 1992; Salais and Storper, 1992)

Similarly Oatley (1998: 6) said:

> 'successful' localities display certain characteristics in terms of local institutional arrangements. At the centre of these arrangements is co-operation between a wide range of governmental and non-governmental agencies institutionalised within various forms of partnership. The aims of these partnerships are to establish consensus and a shared vision for the development of a locality; the mobilisation of skills, expertise and resources to enhance competitiveness; to engage in networking and lobbying in relevant markets and political arenas; to exercise clear and effective leadership while maintaining flexibility; and to deliver on plans. (Oatley and Lambert, 1997: 3)

The essence of the argument is that globalization has increased the importance of actions at the level of the city or agglomeration to pursue competitive advantage. Local government together with local civil society has the capacity, and the imperative, to foster and sustain innovation and business competitiveness. These ideas have been important in developing a Project State approach

Box 4.4: The rise and fall of Jamaica's Export Processing Zones

After the mid-1980s Jamaica pursued a deregulated, 'export-driven economy' (Rickard, 2003: 81–2). Previously Jamaica had aspired to self-sufficiency through government borrowing, subsidies, high tariffs and protectionist trade measures. Mullings (1998: 151–2) said the new strategy was 'neither stable nor sustainable', and seemed 'to entrench rather than eliminate existing inequalities'. Jamaica hoped to develop high-technology information-processing and telecommunications industries, but the reality was low-technology data-entry jobs and garment manufacturing (Mullings, 1998). The Kingston Free Zone (KFZ), established in 1976, was the first of Jamaica's five EPZs. It is examined in Stephanie Black's 2001 documentary film *Life and Debt*.

Technically and legally the KFZ was not part of Jamaica. Factories located within were not answerable to local taxation laws, control or regulation (Mullings, 1995). In the KFZ, textiles were imported from the USA, assembled and exported. The finished products were sold in the US as brand-name clothing for Hanes, Brooks Brothers and Hilfiger. In the mid-1980s around 4,000 people were employed, growing to a mid-1990s peak of 35,000 workers, before falling to a mere 6,000–7,000 employees ➡

and have also shaped the Smart Planning and Regulation style of governance.

Amin and Thrift (1995: 101) differentiated between three different types of contact network. The most basic type exists between members of different firms and between firms and major clients. Such networks may be enduring but they do not necessarily demand trust and commitment to shared values. The second type of network comprises specialists who form interest groups. These are often expressed through professional or social institutions that share knowledge, attitudes and values. Finally, there are 'epistemic communities' where knowledge, interests and attitudes are shared, and there is a commitment to act and to promote policy agendas.

Amin and Thrift (1995) connected these ideas together in the concept of 'institutional thickness', arguing that it is a key factor in shaping capacity for local action. There needs to be a substantial number of diverse organizations in an area, namely 'a strong institutional presence' (102), including firms; financial institutions;

in 2002 (Lezama *et al.*, 2004; Rose, 2008). At its peak in 1995, Jamaica's garment industry produced $566m. in exports with around 90% going to the USA (Rickard, 2003: 90; Lezama *et al.*, 2004: 95).

Jamaica's EPZs declined after NAFTA, established in 1994, made it more profitable for US companies to locate in Mexico. International companies departed; by 2002, only around 15 local garment companies remained. The last foreign-owned processor, Jockey International, closed after 24 years, in 2008 with a loss of 575 jobs (Rose, 2008).

In 1998, 95% percent of the employees in the KFZ were women (Ricketts, 2002: 128). Most were single parents between 30 and 37 years old and had migrated to Kingston from rural areas in their late teenage years in search of jobs (Ricketts, 2002). They were typically the primary wage earners in their families. On average, one to two weeks in a KFZ garment factory earned around J$800–1,200 (US$20–30) which was 'unlikely to raise women's incomes sufficiently to take them out of poverty' (Ricketts, 2002: 130). Many KFZ workers supplemented their incomes by selling goods at markets or doing domestic service jobs. In such conditions, and commutes to KFZ that were long and difficult, absenteeism was high and factories were unable to staff night and weekend shifts (Rickard, 2003).

chambers of commerce; training agencies; trade associations; local authorities; development agencies; unions; government agencies providing premises, land and infrastructure; marketing boards, etc.

However, it is not enough that such institutions simply exist. Institutional thickness requires that they interact with one another. Such contact and information exchange is seen as building individual interests into a collective representation. Costs, as well as control of 'rogue behaviour', are shared. Participants from different institutions become aware that they 'are involved in a common enterprise' (Amin and Thrift, 1995: 102) with a shared agenda, albeit one that may be loosely defined, shared habits and routines. Amin and Thrift (1995: 102–3, original emphasis) described this framework of mutual support:

> a local institutional thickness composed of interinstitutional interaction and synergy, collective representation by many bodies, a common

industrial purpose and shared cultural norms and values. It is a 'thickness' which both establishes legitimacy and nourishes relations of trust. It is a 'thickness' which continues to stimulate entrepreneurship and consolidate the local embeddedness of industry... what is of significance here is not only the presence of a network of institutions *per se*, but rather the *process* of institutionalisation.

Amin and Thrift (1995: 103) stated that 'institutional thickness can have a decisive effect on economic development'. However, all places are operating in a competitive framework. Institutional thickness does not guarantee success, because there is competition between places. Economic opportunity is mediated by market and governmental action at other spatial scales, not purely the local. Further, institutional thickness can also help to resist change and innovation. Businesses may have a limited involvement in partnerships (Curran *et al.*, 2000), and localities where a few traditional companies dominate, and where local politicians are used to looking outside the area for help and decisions (e.g. to company headquarters or to national government), may achieve inter-institutional cooperation, but are likely to struggle to develop and deliver innovative local economic development strategies.

The Stuttgart region (population 2.6 million) in Baden-Wurtemberg, south-west Germany provides an example of a region where there are strong links between research, education institutions and local industries, together with regional-scale public bodies that operate strategic economic development policies. A short summary is given in Box 4.5. There is a further example in Chapter 5 where the case of North Carolina's Research Triangle Park is described in Box 5.1.

Smart Planning and Regulation

The formation of the Verband Region Stuttgart described in Box 4.5 illustrates the appetite that exists for institutional reform in the Smart Planning and Regulation form of governance. Rationalization and rescaling of powers is seen to create more efficient and effective public sector bodies better able to operate at the city-region scale or beyond and to foster the kind of networks that seem to help businesses to prosper. However, a note of caution should be sounded in respect of this example. A survey in the Stuttgart region found that companies saw user–producer interaction as more important than networking with educational bodies in the region (Strambach with D'Lorio and Steinlein, 2001). Thus local institutional thickness, notwithstanding the efforts of the Verband Region Stuttgart, was secondary to the ability of firms to manage in an international knowledge economy. It is important not to isolate institutional thickness and imagine that it can automatically deliver economic development.

Public authorities may work in partnership to mobilize and target resources for regional development. Bailey with Barker and MacDonald (1995) identified a number of reasons for creating partnerships. These were:

- Synergy: two or more partners working together can achieve more than working separately.
- Transformation: each partner tries to influence the values and objectives of other partners.
- Budget enlargement.
- Unlocking land and development opportunities.
- Place-marketing and promotion.
- The coordination of infrastructure and development.
- Confidence building and risk minimization.

Box 4.6 provides an example of a public–public partnership in Roubaix, a town in northern France. This again involves a rescaling of governance and multilevel joint working between the local authorities and a city-region authority, the Lille Métropole Communauté Urbaine.

The project state: public–private (and community?) partnerships

Public–private partnerships are typical in situations where a development project would be too risky for a private company to invest, but the public body wants to see the development happen, but is reluctant or unable to undertake the whole project itself. In such situations a partnership can create a win-win situation: the company gets its required profit and the public body gets the development it wants without having to pay for it all from the public purse. Policies

Box 4.5: Institutional thickness in the Stuttgart region (Germany)

In the late twentieth century the Stuttgart region consistently achieved above-average rates of economic growth, and lower levels of unemployment, than other parts of Germany. It had the highest share of people employed in manufacturing within Germany (41.4% in 1994). Some 85% of industrial firms employed fewer than 200 people (around 28% of the area's jobs) while 5% of the firms employed over 50% of the region's workforce. Around 40% of production was exported.

Stuttgart's three technology clusters (mechanical engineering, road vehicle construction and electronics), employ 75% of the workforce and are vital to the regional economy. Daimler-Benz and Porsche, which originated in this region and operate headquarters there, dominate the auto industry. Mechanical engineering comprises primarily medium-sized firms. In electronics, Bosch and subsidiaries of multinationals have their German headquarters there. Proportions of scientists working in the Stuttgart region exceed national averages, as do the rate of patents per 100,000 population. These factors give the Stuttgart region its competitive advantage.

Public institutions have played a role in this industrial success story. There are over 20 universities and technological institutes in the region. These institutions specialize in sectors that are relevant to the regional

→

like Enterprise Zones (Chapter 8) and Tax Increment Financing (Chapter 11) are examples of policies encouraging public–private partnerships. A key concept in such partnerships is 'leverage', which means the ratio of public authority's initial investment to the total investment generated by the project. Such investment will include private investment, but also possibly funds from other public bodies, such as ERDF (Box 4.1). Box 4.7 gives an example of one successful public–private partnership, the Bird's custard factory in Birmingham, England. It tells a typical story of public money being used to get a project started, so that eventually more private investment came forward. The result was the conversion of a derelict factory into a multi-use facility.

industrial clusters and, consequently, the region's large firms buy research from their local universities and employ their students. There is a strong system of vocational training and overlapping qualifications, encompassing skilled workers, technicians and engineers. This helps to transfer knowledge into production.

With the aim of identifying the area's innovation deficit, *Wirtschaft 2000* ('Economy 2000') was set up in the 1990s and two new institutions were created: an Academy for Technological Assessment and an Innovation Council. Their task was to reduce inherited rigidities and promote coordination and linkages across policy areas.

The Verband Region Stuttgart (Stuttgart Region Association), a devolved parliament with legislative powers, was created to overcome the problems of coordinating five administrative districts and 179 independent municipalities. The Association focuses on strategic land use and transport planning, particularly the location of residential development, landscape conservation and economic development initiatives to promote clusters in fields such as microelectronics or new media. Stuttgart Region Economic Development Corporation (WRS) has established Regional Competence and Innovation Centres to provide assistance and advice on market entry; network regional expertise and innovation by organizing dialogues; and, stimulate collaborative projects. (Source: Strambach with D'Lorio and Steinlein (2001); Bohne *et al.,* (1999).)

Public–private partnerships are most likely to be satisfactory where there is an agreed development objective such as developing a difficult site. However, elected public authorities are always vulnerable to being reminded that economic development is not the only priority, and that private developers are not the only set of stakeholders. Area-based regeneration partnerships can therefore involve governments, the private sector and local residents. Through consultation, cooperation and coordination of services, these partnerships can help to establish long-term spending priorities, which reflect local conditions and needs, and improve delivery or development or services. An OECD (2001) report concluded that partnerships set up to stimulate economic development strengthen social cohesion, improve governance and enhance people's quality

---

Box 4.6: A public–public partnership, Roubaix and Metropolitan Lille (France)

Roubaix (population 100,000) is a town in the Lille conurbation in northern France. It became run-down in the 1980s when its main traditional industry, textiles, collapsed in the face of foreign competition. Unemployment reached 33% in the late 1980s, and 20 years later was still around 20%. However, the town is making significant progress. Roubaix's revival has been part of a coordinated effort by all the local authorities in the conurbation. They have worked together through a city-region authority, the Lille Métropole Communauté Urbaine (LMCU).

All 85 elected municipal councils in the conurbation are represented on the LMCU assembly that steers its work. The rationale behind the LMCU is to plan and coordinate investment in key public services at the metropolitan scale in a way that none of the municipal councils could do by themselves. The LMCU signed long-term agreements with central and regional tiers of government to provide integrated investment and funding in economic, physical and social regeneration.

Key projects in Roubaix involved revitalizing the town's economy, improving the town centre and the housing stock and creating safe and attractive public spaces. All new investments were linked to employment and training opportunities for local people. A partnership between LMCU and the Municipality of Roubaix carried through this work. (Source: Cadell *et al.* (2008: 69–90).)

---

of life. However, the same report noted that mixing public policy and partnership can raise difficulties:

- Civil servants taking part in partnerships can find it difficult to reconcile local and institutional loyalties.
- Partnerships challenge the power of local elected officials, who have a mandate from their electors, on issues that the partnership may want to debate.

Box 4.7: The Custard factory, a public–private venture, Birmingham (UK)

For many years Bird's custard was produced at a factory in Digbeth, a typical nineteenth-century industrial area on the edge of the city centre of Birmingham, UK. However, the factory closed and the buildings became derelict. Developers did not come forward to risk money on buying and modernizing the premises. Then in 1992 £800,000 of public money from a grant scheme was made available to begin refurbishing the empty buildings. This levered in £1.6m. of private investment. The result was 145 low-cost starter units that became occupied by small firms in creative industries such as design, music and dance. The first phase created something like 300 jobs and around half of the occupants had previously been unemployed. By 2007 there were 300 companies there, as well as bars, restaurants, nightclubs and shops employing around 700. In 2007 a further £6.4m. of public investment was announced for a £20m. scheme to refurbish two further buildings in the complex. (Sources: Noon *et al.* (2000: 68); PRZOOM (2007).)

- Trade union and employer organizations, which often defend the interests of their members, may see cooperation and the involvement of civil society as a threat.
- Sometimes, community-based groups and NGOs are not represented in partnerships. This can undermine the legitimacy of the partnership and limit institutional commitment to it.

The OECD (2001) made a number of recommendations. It stressed that the contribution of each partner should be explicit and transparent, with each having a defined role and accountability. Similarly, partners should identify the benefits they expect from the cooperation, and on this basis, they need to establish evaluation criteria.

In the end, the success of partnership will depend on the results achieved. Proliferation of partnerships that do not deliver tangible results from the point of view of the partners will soon generate 'partnership fatigue' and reluctance among partners to continue to participate. Similarly, a plethora of partnerships in an area covering a wide range of different and non-integrated topics is another pitfall to be avoided, since such a situation drains resources and creates confusion. Partnerships can offer benefits, but are not an instant or automatic solution to an area's problems.

Summary

Different countries have different structures and traditions in terms of governance, e.g. the degree of centralization or decentralization. While legacies of these traditions still stamp approaches to economic development, globalization has posed new challenges. There has been the growth of transnational development institutions and also a new emphasis on decentralization. For example, since the 1980s, there has been a clear trend towards decentralization (United Nations Centre for Human Settlements (HABITAT), 1996: 161). The emphasis on an active role for sub-national scales of governance derives in part from perceptions that knowledge spillovers and institutional thickness are important drivers of competitiveness at regional and city-regional scales.

Cox and Mair (1989) argued that local dependence was a necessary condition for the formation of business coalitions seeking to boost local economic development. However, such companies may not be the key economic players, and a formal partnership may not be the main driver of the regional economy. As networked relations become more important, whether vertically within forms internationally or among different tiers of government, or horizontally between different players within a region, the links and cross-over points are very important. They are the generators of the synergies that make networks and partnerships more than the sum of their parts.

The chapter has hypothesized that the typology of policies and practices developed in Chapter 1 can be linked to different approaches to governance. Four types have been set out and three of those have been related to examples in this chapter. As we work through the rest of the book, we invite readers to test the usefulness of these typologies against the array of examples of policy and practice that we will present.

Topics for discussion

Why might a government seek to establish a free-trade or export-processing zone? What could help to make such a zone a success? What problems should be anticipated?

Is the importance of local governance overstated?

Related reading

S.-W. Wong and B. Tang (2005) 'Challenges to the Sustainability of "Development Zones": A Case Study of Guangzhou Development District, China', *Cities*, 22(4), 303–16.

M. P. Fernández-Kelly (1997) 'Maquiladoras: The View from Inside', in N. Visvanathan, L. Duggan, L. Nisonoff and N. Wiegersma (eds.), *The Women, Gender and Development Reader* (London: Zed Books).

'Governing from the Bottom, Governing from the Top, Connecting the Two', in UN–Habitat 2006, 170–4.

5 Land and Premises for Business

Businesses need sites and premises to operate from, even if it is just a room in a house or a table at an internet café. This chapter is about land and commercial property as key requirements for most forms of business. Retailing is discussed later, in Chapter 10. There are some fundamental points to remember. First, land and buildings tend to be quite expensive items, and compete for investment with other areas of a business, e.g. with marketing or product development. Second, land and buildings are not easy to shift around or even alter as needs change. Thus a growing firm may well find that growth can only be achieved in new premises in a new location. Third, the environment around its premises may have impacts on the performance of the firm. If clients visit the premises, the look of the place, and the area around it, can influence their perception of the firm itself. How much this matters will depend on the type of firm it is: a canal-front site in a grim urban setting may add to the 'edgy' image of a graphic design company, but may not be the place for somebody making health-care products. In addition, some firms face absolute imperatives about the environment around them – for example they may depend on secure and high-quality supplies of water, or easy access to a highway. Last but not least, buildings will affect running costs through their energy efficiency. Concerns over carbon emissions make energy performance important.

Much of the practice of local economic development grew out of the provision, marketing and management of industrial premises. Development of business parks remains a key element in much local economic development work, even if the kind of firms may have changed with the growth of service sectors and high technology. In general, office provision is likely to be undertaken through the market. Users of office space are more likely to be able to adapt their activity to fit the physical layout of existing properties than is the case for a manufacturing firm, so the risks to the provider are less. Similarly, warehousing is relatively cheap to provide and adapt for new occupiers. Such factors, together with the historical perception that equated economic development with manufacturing, mean that industrial premises continue to be a prime focus.

Different premises for different businesses

Economic change has prompted an increasing diversity of types of enterprises with different property needs. As industry has become business, so the mass labour force arriving by bus has tended to give way to car-based journeys to work. This is especially true in edge-of-city sites which may not be easily served by public transport, and also where workers operate outside a routine 'nine-to-five' day. Similarly, industries have become cleaner, employ more office staff and in some cases sell products direct from the factory. Thus the divide between premises for manufacturing and for services has become more blurred.

Extending the categorization of the kind of properties used by manufacturing and by service-linked industries proposed by Ratcliffe *et al.* (2004), who drew on Worthington (1982), premises for different businesses can be summarized as follows:

- Hazardous industry: specially built plant on peripheral or remote site surrounded by security area and 'no development' zone.
- Flatted factory: multi-storey industrial buildings, with goods elevator and corridor access to some small independent tenancies. Likely to be provided in urban setting where land is expensive, and occupiers need to be close to suppliers or customers.
- Industrial estate: mixture of manufacturing and service uses. Industrial character where delivery areas predominate. Developed on edge-of-city sites for ease of access by road, though earlier sites are now surrounded by later urban development.
- Trading estate: warehouse areas with some offices. May attract retail warehousing and trade outlets. Access to and visibility from main highways is important.

- Industrial park: aimed at clean manufacturing organizations with a landscaped setting and leisure amenities for staff.
- Commercial/business park: a high-quality, low-density environment. Aimed at firms requiring prestige or a high-calibre workforce. Mixtures of manufacturing, office and sales functions. High-quality landscaping and attractive views are sought.
- Trade mart: a multiple-tenanted building with office showrooms and centrally provided exhibition, conference area, reception and support services. Normally developed around a theme, and located so as to be accessible by private and public transport.

As the importance of research and innovation has been increasingly recognized, so new types of development have appeared. These include:

- Innovation centre: an individual building, immediately adjacent to a university campus, providing small units 30–150sqm for starter firms growing out of research projects within the university and drawing upon its facilities and support services.
- Research park: sites or advanced units for young or established firms in the field of research or development. Often close to a university and associated with university research laboratories and amenities. Such schemes are often joint ventures.
- Science/technology park: with universities and research institutions within a 30-mile catchment area. Attractive lifestyle, low-density development aimed at scientific or technology-oriented companies.

In addition there are less conventional forms of provision for less conventional enterprises. These would include:

- Community workshop: small workshops aimed at encouraging embryo enterprises by developing skills and providing equipment and administrative support. Typically located close to residential areas in old buildings in regeneration areas.
- Working community: a group of independent small firms co-operating in sharing a building and joint services. The object

is to enjoy a scale of premises and facilities normally only available to larger companies. Usually selective of compatible or complementary firms.

- Home-based industry: typical in sectors like garment manufacture that include a high proportion of women in their workforce, working in conditions where there is little or no regulation of premises or working conditions. Home-based industry may also involve activities like car-repair and servicing, with the workshop on the ground floor and living premises above.

While some service activities are associated with manufacturing, as indicated above, there are also some distinctive types of service industry premises:

- Company headquarters: usually a prestigious, high-rise office block where high-paid employees work, often downtown in a major city, but accessible to airports and main stations.
- Back offices and call centres: extensive space in cheaper premises, often in a large or medium-sized city, but where land and property is cheaper, and a large labour force can easily be accessed.
- Teleworking: on the internet, which may be done from home.

To get a better understanding of the way the different approaches to regional and local economic development address issues of land and premises, it is useful to explore the demand and supply aspects.

Demand for sites and buildings

As indicated above, a business's location and accommodation requirements will depend on the nature of the activities to be undertaken. As firms change, their infrastructure requirements are also likely to change. Adapting premises or getting new ones takes time. Delays will undermine the company's efficiency. A study in 2002 estimated that UK businesses were losing £18bn a year through inefficiency in their use of property, and that elimination of this wastage could increase gross trading profits by up to 13 per cent (Capital Economics Ltd, 2002). There is no reason to believe that a similar situation would not be found in other countries.

Industrial premises are difficult to adjust. Fothergill *et al.* (1987: 56) observed that 'Of all inputs to production, buildings are the most indivisible. A new factory building is almost always a very large investment, and extensions tend also to require a major financial commitment'. Survey work by these authors in the UK in the 1980s led them to describe the relation between firms and their buildings as 'idiosyncratic'. However, there are signs that since then the demand for industrial properties has become increasingly segmented, with different categories of users having different requirements (Ratcliffe *et al.*, 2004).

In the UK, property costs are typically the second biggest cost for businesses after salaries. Paying for space and premises is a cost on turnover and/or ties up capital. Attitudes of firms to such costs vary, and the viewpoint of a particular firm is likely to be influenced by how well it is performing at any one time. Fothergill *et al.* (1987) reviewed a range of factors that affect a firm's decisions about property. In summary these are:

- Lease or purchase? Renting ties up less capital and gives more flexibility to relocate. This may be the preferred option for new or rapidly growing businesses. However, the disadvantage is that adaptations to the premises are likely to depend on the landlord. This is why firms with specialized needs may opt for a 'design and build' arrangement to ensure the property meets their requirements. Cadman and Topping (1995) and Wilkinson and Reed (2008) observed that this arrangement has become increasingly common with respect to warehouses. There is some evidence that those firms who are owner-occupiers are less aware of their property costs than are firms which rent premises. Owner-occupied office space is less densely occupied than leased space for all categories of offices (Capital Economics Ltd, 2002: 7). There are also variations in the extent to which firms choose to own or rent their buildings. Owner-occupation is almost the only approach in Greece, Spain, Italy, Switzerland and Luxembourg; 80 per cent of firms in France are owner-occupiers – though only 20 per cent of industrial property in the Paris region is owner-occupied; and 70 per cent in the Netherlands; but only 30 per cent in the USA (Capital Economics Ltd, 2002: 84).

- Scope for expansion on the site is a consideration, as is the size of the building and the type of space available. A firm will not want to be paying for unused or unusable space, but it will probably prefer to expand on site rather than face disruption by a relocation. Where space shortages are encountered, a common solution is the search for warehousing premises nearby. This can be one advantage of location on an industrial estate where there is likely to be a constant turnover of local premises.

- Design requirements include such matters as floor loadings and ceiling heights, layout of spaces and provision, whether the property has to be single storey, and the amount and nature of the land around the property. Again precise requirements will depend on the firm's activities: some can use a standard unit, others need buildings tailored to their particular needs. Specialized types of activity may be very demanding in respect of the environmental control systems within the buildings. Offices are likely to need cable connections and internal networks for computers.

- The trend has been for firms to require higher proportions of the floor area to be devoted to office uses. Similarly car parking is another requirement, especially when staff are mobile from a base, or for enterprises which receive regular visits from representatives of suppliers or clients.

- Some firms may require an architecturally distinctive building. This is most likely to be the case with firms who wish to project a prestigious or perhaps contemporary image. Most firms are likely to be less concerned about visual aspects of design than about the costs and functional efficiency of the building for their uses.

- Security is also likely to be an issue. Valuable raw materials or stocks of products need to be safe from theft. While employment of security guards is a means to increase security, the location and nature of the premises is also a factor. Fences, gates, barriers and secure entry systems, are all likely to be part of the package.

Overall, the users of commercial property are likely to want flexibility – to be able to get premises when they need them and to avoid paying costs on unused or underused space.

Supply of premises: developers' criteria

The dynamic and competitive nature of business activity makes provision and management of commercial property a risky business. It takes some time between conceiving and completing a development, and during this period investment is not delivering a return. Fluctuations of the economic cycle or structural economic change can mean that the market demand has changed before the premises are ready to be occupied.

When major economic or technological change occurs, such as deindustrialization or the advent of computer networks, it leaves an oversupply of buildings that are no longer fit for purpose. Often such buildings are difficult to adapt, with high maintenance costs and locations that no longer fit demand. Oversupply of such premises further reduces their market value, though this will also open up opportunities for start-up businesses seeking cheap space. However, the lack of demand can also feed what Weber (2002: 532) called a 'narrative of obsolescence' which reinforces the sentiment that it is impossible to adapt an old industrial building to current uses, frightening off potential investors. This is just one example of how market failure occurs in the supply of premises for business, a failure that shapes the approach to local and regional economic development, as outlined in our typology in Chapter 1.

In considering whether to undertake a new development for business uses, a developer will have to assess a number of factors. First and foremost is 'what is the market demand?'. In particular, what level of rental income might be expected and how likely is that level to be forthcoming? Generally developers know what the existing rentals are in the region for different types of property in different locations, but there may be occasions when an innovative type of development is envisaged and there is no local comparator. Such schemes are likely to carry more risk. Closely linked to the question of rental income are the type of premises to be provided and their likely users. As already noted, different users have different requirements.

Of course, a developer also has to find a suitable site. This is likely to be the first step. Sites need to be accessible to transportation and to a local labour force, available for purchase and developable. Meeting these criteria can be difficult, and a further cause of market failure. For example, an irregularly shaped site is unlikely to be attractive for large units, since the layout of buildings and access roads will be difficult and there is the risk of being left with some unusable areas. Similarly, natural features such as slopes, woodlands, drainage conditions and flood risk, will all have to be taken into account. Steep slopes, for example, cannot be easily built upon, but may provide an attractive landscaping feature. In respect of urban sites there may be concerns about security and trespass. Geological conditions and land contamination also need to be checked out. In greenfield sites there will be a need to calculate costs of equipping the land with essential infrastructure.

There may be uncertainty about whether the landowner(s) will make the site available, and if so, what it would cost to purchase the land and develop it. If there are multiple owners, it is likely to be more difficult and expensive to assemble the land for the site. Furthermore, as the developer will probably be borrowing money to purchase the land and fund the development, the preferences of those lending the money may well influence site selection and development decisions. Most banks and financial institutions will favour 'prime sites' and tried-and-trusted forms of development. Prime sites are those that are always going to be in demand, because of their location both regionally and locally. In times of economic boom, lenders may become more willing to take risks; however in bad times they are likely to become much more conservative about the kind of developments they will fund.

There is also the question of whether planning (or zoning) permission will be given for the development. A statutory land use plan for the area can act as a guide and give developers confidence by providing certainty. Smart regulation also protects developers against the risk of new uses on adjacent sites that could undermine the value of their asset, for example a noxious industry being located alongside an office building. Land development and planning systems differ from country to country, both in their scope and performance. Smart plans are up to date, and enforcement regimes are proportionate (covering only what needs to be regulated) but also consistent, predictable and effective. Within Europe, there is much more consistency between what the plan says and what happens on the ground in countries like Sweden and Germany than is the case in the south of Italy or Spain. In general, a land use plan will show what use is permitted, and also a plot ratio (also termed a floor-to-area ratio (FAR)). This is the ratio of the floor space to the size of the site, and indicates the permitted intensity of the development. This is a key measure for office development, where a developer will want to maximize the amount of floor space, and hence potential rental income, while the regulators will be concerned about trip generation, congestion and the impact of a tall building on views and the skyline.

The plan may well set out other requirements, e.g. about access to and from the site, landscaping, etc. While most planning authorities are likely to be supportive of employment-generating land uses, they may be reluctant to countenance development on what might otherwise appear to be prime sites, e.g. in attractive landscape on the edge of a settlement. Conditions or other obligations attached to a planning permission may significantly affect the costs of the development and eventual income flows from it.

The developer has to relate the anticipated costs of the project to the anticipated sale price or flows of rental income that it will generate. In essence the costs will be made up of:

- costs likely to be incurred in acquiring the land;
- the costs of designing and developing the site;
- interest payments for money borrowed to carry through the project before it begins to realize a return of the income through sale or lease; and
- various associated costs in marketing, professional fees, etc.

By calculating the net income expected from the properties as a proportion of the total costs, a developer will work out the likely return that the investment would produce. This figure will be compared with the norms that the company will generally aim for, and on that basis, a decision will be taken on whether to develop or not. This calculation also tells the developer what price can be offered for the land if the overall project is to be commercially viable. Developers will not supply premises on sites (such as polluted brownfields) or for types of buildings (starter units for new businesses with high risk of failure) where the return is seen to be inadequate and the risks unacceptable. In such situations, where the market does not deliver the kind of development that is perceived by policy-makers to be wanted, regional and local economic development agencies are likely to intervene. They may directly provide the premises, or 'gap-fund' the developer through grants or cheap land. This means that the gap between the developer's calculations and desired return is bridged, and the developer provides the desired premises.

Above all, those who own and manage commercial property want to have premises occupied by companies who can be relied upon to pay the rent. In this respect, a mix of tenants is less risky than a single major occupier, or than a grouping of companies in the same line of business. Similarly a well-established company with a long and successful trading record is preferable to a new business, given the extra risks of failure that attach to company start-ups. Branches of well-known national and international companies are likely to be seen as 'safe' in terms of the flow of rental income, whereas smaller, local businesses are more risky. Such conservatism is unlikely to assist local economic development policies seeking to foster innovation and new firms. This is one reason why public sector landlords often play a major role in accommodating such ventures.

Partnership and targeting sectors

The provision of conventional premises for conventional businesses is likely to be undertaken by the private sector or, as we saw in the examples from Central Liaoning Province (Box 3.2) and Singapore's overseas industrial parks (Box 4.2) by what we have styled 'development states' (see Chapter 4). However, where regional economies are less strong, and/or public agencies have less power to act directly as developers, public–private partnerships targeting key sectors such as research and development are more likely. North Carolina's Research Triangle Park (RTP) is a famous example of a partnership creating a leading research park. It has become a model of science industry-led economic development. Box 5.1 describes this case, which, as noted in Chapter 4, also illustrates the principles of 'institutional thickness'.

Research Triangle Park is a good example of a successful public–private partnership project in using development of commercial property as a means to promote innovation and kick-start regional adjustment to economic restructuring. It has certainly become a driver of the regional economy. However, as with any economic development project, there are debates about who gains and who loses, and about the impacts on local people and labour markets. In this example other municipalities in the area feel that they have not benefited from the jobs, development or economic investments that have resulted. Durham, NC, for example, has contested its supply of cut-rate water to RTP and in the 1970s and 1980s it threatened to annex the RTP in an effort to gain access to its tax base (Havlick and Kirsch, 2004). Other critics point to the growing

---

Box 5.1: Research Triangle Park, North Carolina (USA)

North Carolina's traditional economy, tobacco, textile and furniture production, began to decline after the Second World War. Faced with falling population, low per-capita income, and growing out-migration particularly of college graduates, public officials, banking industry leaders and private real estate developers came together to devise an economic development plan. One aim was to give graduates from local universities a location where they could live near to high-paying jobs and pursue long-term careers (Link and Scott, 2003). University administrators became involved and, after initial reluctance, so did North Carolina's governor.

After a positive feasibility study in 1955, Research Triangle Committee, Inc. lobbied potential occupants to persuade them to move into the proposed Research Triangle Park (RTP) (Link and Scott, 2003). Developers began to acquire contiguous plots and assemble parcels in preparation for the establishment of RTP, which was to be strategically located between three major academic institutions (Duke University in Durham, North Carolina State University in Raleigh and University of North Carolina in Chapel Hill). Initially, the Research Triangle Committee and state officials determined that RTP

$\longrightarrow$

---

divergence in incomes between those employed in high-technology jobs in RTP and others in the supporting service industries, such as cleaning and landscaping the RTP site. Furthermore, the *Wall Street Journal* noted in 1988 that 'the Research Triangle has spawned little work for people cast out of tobacco and textile jobs and fewer than anticipated research-related manufacturing plants. It may symbolize ... the widening gap between urban and rural [communities], white collar and blue collar [jobs]' (Helyar, 1988: 1ff.).

Such criticisms can in turn be countered. Local governments can be parochial in outlook. Turning around a regional economy takes time. Injection of higher-wage jobs may pull other wages in the region up over time. Perhaps more fundamental is a weakness identified by Porter (2001: 15) who found that the high levels of R&D (more than six to seven times the national average of R&D

would be privately financed but, after having trouble gaining adequate investment, these bodies developed a public–private partnership to acquire land. The result was a non-profit agency, the Research Triangle Foundation of North Carolina, to oversee land ownership and management.

Research Triangle Park opened in 1959, as did the Research Triangle Institute 'for the purpose of doing contract research for business, industry, and government' (Link and Scott, 2003: 169). By 1960, 200,000 ft^2 of space was available for businesses (Havlick and Kirsch, 2004). In 1965, the US Department of Health, Education and Welfare and the computer company IBM announced the first major commitments to facilities in RTP (Link and Scott, 2003).

The park covers 69,000 acres (*c.*28 sq. km), with 15,000,000 sq. ft of floor space for offices and laboratories. Around 50,000 people (42,000 of them full-time knowledge workers) are employed by over 170 companies, including global corporations such as IBM and GlaxoSmithKline. Havlick and Kirsch (2004: 263) said that this economic development strategy promulgated a 'local and regional transformation' and RTP is 'production utopia' where strict regulations prohibit noise, odour and air pollution, and control building size, design and landscaping. The result, Havlick and Kirsch (2004: 269) argued is 'quiet clean economic output in a setting that confers an aura of prosperity and modernity'.

investment per worker) in the Research Triangle were not matched by the levels of commercialization. In other words, more needs to be done to transfer knowledge from the research institutes to companies in the region.

The criticisms summarized above expose major debates in economic development about the relative merits of people-based and property-based approaches (for further discussion of this debate, see Chapter 9). Development of science or research parks is not necessarily addressing the needs of those in the local labour market who lack the skills to command high-technology jobs. At best, such approaches are seen as lifting the general level of the local and regional economy, in the hope that additional service jobs and other benefits will then 'trickle down' to help those people who are more marginal in the labour market. One remedy is to support property-led approaches with training schemes and other forms of outreach to help local unemployed people access the service jobs that will follow. Similarly, proximity does not by itself ensure commercialization of ideas: that has to be worked on by people and institutions. Last but not least, this example shows the need to use several different indicators to assess the performance of an economic development initiative, rather than relying on just one or two measures such as the number of firms or jobs.

Eminent domain

It is common for the patterns of land ownership to be very fragmented, with many different individuals, companies or institutions owning plots of land that are adjacent to each other. Land is a very inflexible resource – you cannot move it from one place to another. Similarly, it is very difficult to shuffle the ownership of sites around so that a site large enough for development can be brought into a single ownership. The nature of land means that it confers a sort of monopoly to a particular plot. In a competitive market, one owner can potentially hold adjacent property owners to ransom, if, for example, they need that plot to gain access to their own land. A single landowner could effectively veto a development that other land owners supported and which promised extensive benefits to the wider community.

It is not realistic or reasonable to expect unanimous consent for large-scale projects. This is why many societies have recognized that sometimes the public interest needs to take precedence over the private property rights of a landowner. This is typically achieved by giving a public body the legal right to force a purchase of a piece of land from a landowner. In such circumstances the purchase price is typically based on the existing use value of the land, plus some further compensation for the loss and inconvenience caused. However, the price paid is likely to be significantly below the monopoly price that could be achieved in an entirely free market. This approach is widely used by 'development states' and in area regeneration projects.

This process whereby a public body can enforce a land transaction has different names in different countries. Many call it 'expropriation', while in the UK it is known as 'compulsory purchase' and

in the USA it is 'eminent domain'. It can be controversial in societies at times when the political culture and legal system strongly
favours individual rights over collective rights, or where states are
distrusted and perceived to be corrupt. Furthermore, the ethical
issues and political controversy are heightened when the purpose
of the acquisition is to pass the land onto another private enterprise, rather than retaining it (along with any increase in value that
occurs from the forced transaction) in public ownership.

The Poletown case (see Box 5.2) illustrates some of the difficult
decisions that such area regeneration work poses. On the one hand,
GM was probably the most iconic business in Detroit, 'Motown'. It
is no surprise that the city authorities felt that they had to do all
they could to retain the company and its jobs. However, a public
body forcing the displacement of a low-income community because
a mega-company wants its land and properties, can be criticized as
undemocratic and inequitable. Despite offers of compensation and
cash incentives to relocate quickly, many residents refused to move.
In the end, around 1,500 homes, six churches, a school, a hospital
and numerous small businesses were razed (Nolan, 2000). After
the City of Detroit financed the clearing and clean-up of the site,
adding roads, sewers and other infrastructural improvements, the
entire 650-acre site combining the Hamtramck Dodge Plant and
Poletown neighbourhood, was sold to GM.

A further twist followed. GM's plans were never fully realized.
The opening of the plant was delayed for two years. Thereafter, due
to downturns in the automobile industry, the plant often operated
at less than full productive capacity. By 2006, the GM plant on the
site continued to employ around 3,000 people, but much of the
area that was cleared among such contestation in 1981 remained
unused (McKenna, 2006). Predicting future business needs is an
inexact science.

The use of eminent domain has remained a highly contested
practice in the USA. There was a landmark case in 2005, *Kelo* v.
New London in which the Supreme Court ruled, on a split 5:4 decision, that public authorities could indeed use eminent-domain laws
to seize privately owned property and sell it onto another private
developer to stimulate regional economic development. The case
had a lot of similarities to the one in Detroit a generation earlier.
New London, Connecticut, had suffered economically in the late
twentieth century as traditional maritime jobs declined. The city

Box 5.2: Using eminent domain to achieve economic development: General Motors and Poletown, Detroit (USA)

In 1980, Detroit, Michigan, was in dire straits. The impact of high oil prices on a city reliant on the car industry saw unemployment rise to 15%. Income from taxes plummeted, threatening the city with bankruptcy. Detroit lost 11,137 stores (and with them 59,706 jobs) between 1954 and 1977 (Wylie, 1989). General Motors (GM), threatened to move its operation and 6,000 jobs to another US location or Mexico, unless they could build a $500m. car assembly plant that could utilize 'just-in-time' manufacturing practices (Wylie, 1989).

GM requested a 'greenfield site' and targeted a recently closed automobile manufacturing facility at Hamtramck and an adjacent 465-acre community sandwiched between two major highways called Poletown (Wylie, 1989: 49). Around 4,000 people, many of them low-income and of eastern European descent, lived in Poletown. City officials hoped that by helping GM to invest within Detroit, other major employers would follow suit, and revitalize the region's economy.

In July 1980 GM told the City that unless the Poletown site was available by 1 May 1981, the new plant would be developed elsewhere

→

was declared a 'distressed municipality' in 1990 and a US naval base closed in 1996, further increasing unemployment (*Kelo et al.* v. *City of New London et al.*, 2005: 2). Municipal officials planned to stimulate economic development in an area known as Fort Trumbull, a 90-acre peninsula that had long been used for manufacturing and commercial purposes and as a consequence had degraded both environmentally and in its infrastructure (Carroll, 2006). Plans were drawn up for a mixed-use development, and the leasing of the acquired land to a private developer for 99 years, during which period the developer would gather rents from the tenants of the residential and commercial properties on the site. After this duration, the Fort Trumbull development site would revert to the ownership of New London.

The plan sought to stimulate economic development, bringing jobs into the community and increasing both the tax base and

(Wylie, 1989). Invoking a recently passed Michigan law that allowed city officials to 'tak[e] private property in order to encourage commercial development,' Detroit pursued the seizure of property in Poletown (Wylie, 1989: 54). Acquiring the land, however, 'under the auspices of the state's eminent domain law, would require the most massive and rapid relocation of citizens for a private development project in US history' (Wylie, 1989: 52). The city's actions were opposed by the Poletown Neighborhood Council, a community organization.

Michigan's Supreme Court ruled that Detroit could use eminent domain and 'condemn property for transfer to a private corporation to build a plant to promote industry and commerce, thereby adding jobs and taxes to the economic base of the municipality and state' (*Poletown Neighborhood Council* v. *City of Detroit*, 1981: n.p.). The Court stated that the public benefit of the GM development outweighed residents' concerns: 'The power of eminent domain is to be used in this instance primarily to accomplish the essential public purposes of alleviating unemployment and revitalizing the economic base of the community. The benefit to a private interest is merely incidental ... If the public benefit was not so clear and significant, we would hesitate to sanction approval of such a project' (*Poletown Neighborhood Council* v. *City of Detroit*, 1981: n.p.).

land values. To achieve this vision, however, New London had to assemble the lots on the site. Susette Kelo found her home, along with others, would be demolished. Kelo's case was that New London was not seizing the land for public use, but was acquiring it to pass onto a private developer for private use (Leef, 2005).

The court decided that New London was taking advantage of additional economic development opportunities that a major new industrial plant would generate. They ruled that eminent domain could be used to acquire Kelo's and the other holdout properties so that the economic development plan could be enacted. This decision met with strong opposition and provoked widespread debate. One of the Court's dissenters, Justice Sandra Day O'Connor, stated that 'Under the banner of economic development, all private property is now vulnerable to being taken and transferred to another private owner, so long as it might be upgraded – i.e. given to another owner who will use it in a way that the legislature deems more beneficial to the public – in the process' (Leef, 2005: 14). Again, however, the development proposals were never fully realized. The industrial users did not come and proposed condominiums, a hotel and shops were never built. By the end of 2009, most of the land where houses had once stood remained vacant (Nelson, 2009).

One possible way forward is to create a special purpose development corporation (SPDC), an idea advocated by Lehavi and Licht (2007). Such a body would be a subsidiary of a municipality's regular economic development corporation. The powers of eminent domain would be delegated to the SPDC. The landowners whose property is being taken over would be offered the option of either taking conventional compensation or taking shares in the SPDC to a value equivalent to their legal compensation. Lehavi and Licht (2007: 19) further proposed that the SPDC 'could either negotiate land rights with the private developer who initiated the project, or auction its land rights... Then the SPDC would distribute the net proceeds from the sale as dividends to its shareholders'. Its work completed, the SPDC would then dissolve.

We have dealt at some length with the issue of eminent domain because it is an important one that goes to the very core of regional and local economic development. Interventions by development agencies of various sorts are usually a response to market failure in some form, and seek to restore market operation. Put another way, public powers are used to create private benefits because there is perceived to be wider public benefit from the outcomes – such as jobs, environmental gains or tax revenues. Other private interests may be harmed in the process, and typically these will be individuals, firms or groups with less power and wealth than the ultimate private beneficiaries of a development. There is no easy calculus to weigh the merits on either side – and a fall back on democratic politics and accountability to make the decision may not protect minority rights. However, ethics, transparency and an active search for equitable institutional solutions can provide valuable guidelines.

Informal business

So far in this chapter we have concentrated on formal businesses and their property needs. However, in many poorer countries and in poorer neighbourhoods in rich countries, the informal sector plays a vital economic role, and is likely to be central to pro-poor approaches to economic development, and to demonstrate in practice what we described in Chapter 4 as 'development despite the state'.

The distinction between formal and informal economies was developed in the 1970s by the International Labor Office (ILO). The informal sector is widely recognized as being particularly important for new migrants from rural areas as they seek to get a toehold in a town or city. Some, e.g. Castells and Portes (1989) have characterized the informal economy in terms of its operating beyond the law. Used in this way, it becomes clear that informality is not confined to the poor. It is also important to stress that the borderline between formal and informal is now recognized to be not as clear-cut as the terms might suggest. For example, formal companies may trade goods and services with informal operations. People who work in the formal sector supplement their incomes by also doing work in the informal sector.

The informal economy poses obvious problems for any formal agency involved in economic development. It may well be a significant source of income, not least for poor people unable to find jobs in the formal sector. In particular the opportunities open to women in formal labour markets are often restricted, and so the informal sector can be important both for income and empowerment. On the other hand, its extra-legal nature means that the businesses are not paying tax, and there is little or no redress against exploitation and working conditions that fall well short of any statutory norms. Children may be kept away from schools so that they can work instead. Furthermore, one reason for the growth of the informal economy in many poor countries has been the loss of formal public sector jobs following closures or privatizations, resulting from the Structural Adjustment Programmes enforced by the international financial bodies as a condition for loans. For example, in Zambia, formal employment fell from 30 per cent of the labour force in 1980 to less than 10 per cent in 1990, while informal sector employment increased from 1.8 million in 1986 to 2.3 million in 1993 (Kazimbaya-Senkwe, 2004: 99–100).

Increasingly the trend has been for economic development bodies to give support to the informal economic activities, 'though not necessarily under that label' (Hansen and Vaa, 2004: 17). For example, provision of micro-credit is discussed in Chapter 8. In terms of business premises, the focus of this chapter, the main concept is the 'home-based enterprise' (HBE). The obvious advantage of an HBE is that it enables people to be economically active even if they cannot access a formal job or afford to hire business premises. It also allows all members of the household to help, whether or not they have also been able to find formal employment.

The precise way that HBEs operate will depend on local cultures and circumstances. Box 5.3 illustrates an example of HBEs based on a small study in Zambia's Copper Belt. The houses in Zambia typically sit within a parcel of land – in Kazimbaya-Senkwe's example even the people living in low-cost housing had 200sqm of free land on their plots. Thus many of these business activities took place outside the actual house, in workshops built attached to or separated from the main property. In contrast, Kellett and Tipple (1997) researched HBEs in India and found that as there was no space available outside the house, the enterprises operated within the house itself. Similarly, the advantages and disadvantages of HBEs will vary for different groups in different situations.

Generally land-use planning systems have sought to separate employment and housing, and thus planning controls may be used to prevent the development of HBEs. However, the reality is that HBEs are typically robust enough to reappear even if planners wish to do away with them. There is a message in this that planners need to heed. In some situations public authorities have indeed responded by tolerating special industrial estates for 'home industries', where typical activities are things like vehicle repairs, welding, small-scale manufacturing and trading, and business laws are not implemented. However, as Kamete (2004: 135) showed in respect of Harare, Zimbabwe, relations between the local authority and the home industries ranged from 'the very amicable to the confrontational'. Within Harare's local government structure the home industries were dealt with by social workers rather than by the council's economic development arm. However, as Kamete rightly noted, HBEs are business entities, even if they appear abnormal to officials used to operating only with formal businesses.

Finally, we should note that business premises can be an attraction for thieves. Hence security of premises is important. This in turn creates job opportunities in the security industry. Such jobs typically involve working antisocial hours and maybe some personal

---

Box 5.3: Home-based enterprises in Kitwe (Zambia)

Kitwe is a city of about 400,000. About half of its heads of households are in full-time informal employment. A sample of 11 residents drawn from six different types of neighbourhood (from low to very high income) found different types of HBE operating. These activities were: reed mat making; carpentry; shoe making and repair; battery acid manufacturing; tailoring/hairdressing; a nursery school; and trading. Most were long established (over 10 years) and have been the main lifeline for the household over that period. Educational qualifications were low and generally skills had been learned on the job. Unless they were very young, children were generally involved in the work. There were informal support networks from friends and business partners: e.g. the mat maker was part of a group of four women who collected reeds together and made and sold mats for one group member at a time. In general the interviewees felt that they were better off than if they sought work in the formal sector.

The fact that the property was perceived to be rent-free in respect of the business was a major reason for operating from home, though the location away from main traffic centres was seen as a drawback by some. In general those offering services saw their home as a logical place to operate from, while those manufacturing had aspirations eventually to move their business out of the home.

Lack of start-up capital and appropriate skills were identified as barriers to setting up HBEs. Also those in the poorer areas in particular suffered from lack of, or uncertain supply of, basic urban infrastructure – water, roads, sewers and electricity. This undermined their efficiency – for example the tailor had no electricity so in the evenings had to use candles and commented 'sometimes I have to work in the day only'. (Source: Kazimbaya-Senkwe (2004).)

---

risk for low pay, but require few skills. They can thus be part of a pro-poor strategy, a means of getting unqualified unemployed people into work. Depending on the situation, there may be scope for economic development initiatives to build in the creation of local job opportunities in the security side of property management.

Summary

Land and premises for business are an essential part of regional and local economic development. Indeed until the 1970s provision of factory units and zoning of land for industrial use in land use plans were almost the sum total of local approaches to supporting business. However, policies and actions have become more sophisticated as new forms of businesses have developed, and as the significance of the informal sector has increased in the economy of many countries. The root problem remains one of market failure, albeit in various forms. While in classical economic theory the market should provide the kind of premises for which there is a demand, the reality is that the risks involved and the problems of land assembly frequently mean that the theoretical optimal situation does not happen. Decisions necessarily have to be taken on the basis of imperfect knowledge – would the city of Detroit have backed the assembly of so large a site at Poletown if it had known that it would never be fully used? This does not mean that there is no point is trying to assess needs and impacts of interventions in land and property markets – quite the reverse. Those working in regional and local economic development need to be able to understand the property markets and the most likely consequences of their own interventions.

Topics for discussion

Discuss the proposition that the Research Triangle Park demonstrates the strengths and weaknesses of research parks as a tool for regional and local economic development.

Debate the case for and against the use of eminent domain as a tool of regional and local economic development.

Related reading

A. N. Link and J. T. Scott (2003) 'The Growth of Research Triangle Park', *Small Business Economics*, 20, 167–75.

6 Infrastructure and Communications

All businesses depend to some extent on infrastructure and communications. Transport is necessary to move raw materials, people and goods. Information technology is increasingly important in the age of teleworking, internet shopping and e-business. Although much of the infrastructure is literally out of sight, water and effective sanitation systems underpin urban economies. Thus infrastructure and communications provide an essential foundation for regional and local development. Infrastructure and communications are major sources of employment, both during construction and then in the operation of the systems. Although provision of gas, electricity and water was typically a municipal concern in the nineteenth century, in the decades that followed big business and state monopolies came increasingly to dominate such sectors. However, more recently we have seen the decentralization of infrastructure provision and infrastructure becoming an increasingly important aspect of local economic development (United Nations Centre for Human Settlements, 2001: 146).

This chapter therefore connects back to Chapter 5 insofar as infrastructure and communications, such as land and premises, can be seen as 'hard' or 'physical development' approaches, and also leads into Chapter 7, which examines the environment. Sources of power and energy – electricity and gas networks – drive the wheels of commerce, but energy systems are also part of the environment and greenhouse gas emissions from transport systems are a major environmental concern.

Infrastructure does not last forever. Systematic asset management is important: planned maintenance is likely to be more efficient and effective than unplanned maintenance responding to breakdowns and crises when they occur (Leung, 2004). Care for existing

113

infrastructure is at least as important to economic development as provision of new infrastructure, yet it is often overlooked. Similarly, funds are often easier to access for new capital projects – such as installing a new sewerage system – but the revenue costs needed to maintain the quality of the system, especially in the face of increasing demands upon it, may not be budgeted for effectively. This is especially likely to be the case with publicly provided services, where there is political kudos to be won in delivery of the project, but no votes in making consumers pay for the costs of using and maintaining it. This is one reason why international donors have encouraged privatizations of infrastructure or at least 'full cost recovery' pricing systems.

The delicate balance between regional development, infrastructure and the natural environment is well illustrated where there is rapid growth in an arid region. In such situations the governance of water becomes a critical issue. The south-west of the USA is a good

---

Box 6.1: Water conflicts in a rapidly growing arid region: San Diego County, California (USA)

Throughout the twentieth century, California relied on heavily irrigated agriculture, diverting water from rivers and draining underground aquifers (Reisner, 1986). This agricultural economy is in increasing competition with cities, especially since the 1990s when many Sun Belt cities such as Phoenix, Las Vegas, Denver and Houston experienced rapid growth. With a population of over 3 million, and sprawling over multiple municipalities, San Diego County's water problems became acute as the population grew and water conflicts intensified. In 1998, the county was importing up to 95% of its water, with a considerable portion coming from the Colorado River more than 240 miles away (Alexander, 1998).

Since 1946, San Diego has been a member of the Metropolitan Water District of Southern California (MWD), a body established to manage the importation of water from the Colorado River to Southern California. Golf courses, farms, factories, small towns and major metropolises such as Los Angeles and Tijuana all compete for the river's water. The MWD is dominated by Los Angeles interests. For this reason, and because of

→

illustration of these problems. As Box 6.1 shows, the administrators of San Diego County are competing with other administrations and water users to secure a sufficient supply of water to support the county's growth.

Networks, hubs and corridors

Firms and other organizations can now build networks that cut across sectors, and connect distant places. Indeed the network has arguably become the distinctive form of twenty-first century business, yet it is one that has been fundamental in transport and infrastructure for a long time. So what exactly is a network, and what features of infrastructure networks create economic opportunities? The essence of a network is that all points on the network (its nodes) are connected to each other. For example, on a road or

---

drought in the area in the late 1980s and early 1990s, San Diego sought to lessen its dependence on the MWD by purchasing water from the Imperial Irrigation District (IID) (Alexander, 1998). The MWD, IID and other municipal and agricultural water management boards are governed by the 'Law of the River', 'a collection of legislative instruments, judicial decisions, and other legal documents that have been realized since the middle of the 19th century, to regulate the use of the Colorado River's waters' Maganda (2005: 494). The legal structure of the Law gives priority to 'those who arrived first', meaning that today's burgeoning cities are fighting not only with earlier and older cities, but also against the major farming districts that dominated the Southern California landscape before it became predominately urban (Robbins, 2003).

Growing demand from the states that share use of the river with California meant that smaller states, especially Nevada, the USA's fastest growing state in the 1990s, put pressure on the federal government to restrict California's overuse of the Colorado River. The result for San Diego has been a need to diversify water sources, and so the county has put a new emphasis on reclaiming and recycling water, as well as expanding research and development of desalinization plants (Archibold, 2008; Renstrom, 2004; Robbins, 2003).

rail network it is possible to reach any place on the network from any other place on the network. However, the way to get there may not necessarily be the shortest straight-line distance. This is because networks have structures and are typically made up of sub-networks that are components of bigger networks. When on a railway for example, you often have to change trains to reach your final destination. Similarly long-distance air travel often involves a change and more than one leg to the flight.

The point of entry to the network – the 'gateway' or 'portal' – is vitally important – it makes the difference between being connected and not connected, between being able to access the benefits of the network and being unable to do so. Similarly the points of interchange – the hubs – are very significant, as they are the points where different networks cross over and connect. This has advantages and disadvantages. The volume of traffic (and hence potential customers) moving through them will be high, but with that comes the risk of 'bottlenecks', especially at peak times. Thus the design of these hubs matters for the efficiency of the system as a whole, as well as for capturing the local economic opportunities that they create. Tolley and Turton (1995: 217) noted key features that all good transport interchanges have in common: 'they are simple, safe, comfortable and uncrowded, providing the passenger with short walking distances and waiting times, clear information display and an attractive environment'. Transport interchanges are increasingly seen as catalysts for urban regeneration. However, any planned interchange needs to be realistic in transport terms: train operators, for example are unlikely to be willing to slow or divert existing services unless the catchment opened up by the interchange makes it commercially justifiable to do so.

What about the places in between? Are they corridors or tunnels? In a corridor you have several points of access to the network. While this may reduce the efficiency of movement on the network as a whole, it does make it possible for more users to access the network. Highway junctions are the obvious example. In contrast in a tunnel there is no access. Thus, for example, a high-speed train may pass through a region, but not stop at any stations there. This is a tunnel effect.

These different network configurations will greatly influence the economic development opportunities. Other things being equal, hubs will have competitive advantages over other points on a network. Similarly corridors will have potential that is not there in a tunnel situation – but corridors are also much more vulnerable to congestion. Crucially, in regional development terms, access to a network is likely to be more important than the quality of the network itself. Strategies to improve the connections between a regional centre and the national capital, for example, are likely to widen the development gap within the region between the regional centre (which is on the international network) and those other places in the region not connected to that international network. For road networks, regional access depends on the density of the interchanges and on the quality of the local networks connecting to those interchanges.

One of the outstanding examples of using infrastructure connections to achieve regional economic development is the visionary construction of the Øresund (Danish) or Öresund (Swedish) Bridge. Copenhagen and Malmö are only 30km apart but are separated by the Øresund water and a national boundary. An 8km bridge, 4km tunnel and 4km artificial island opened in 2000. It includes both road and rail links, and connects to the airports of both cities. A step towards European integration and a powerful regional economic development intervention, the bridge cut travel times across the Øresund from one hour to 10 minutes. What were once two separate housing and labour markets merged. Malmö offered cheaper housing and lower living costs; Copenhagen more jobs, a more diverse labour market and better wages (Øresundbro Konsortiet, 2008). Existing cooperation between the region's 12 universities developed into the Øresund University partnership with 150,000 students and 14,000 researchers and teachers. Other similar partnerships, such as the Øresund Science Region, also developed.

The Øresund bridge demonstrates smart, strategic planning. It illustrates how filling in a 'missing' infrastructure link can have significant advantages, by increasing the critical mass of a region and extending labour and housing markets. In a survey in 2006 it was found that 70 per cent of the Swedish companies that had established themselves in Denmark and 60 per cent of the Danish companies that had gone in the opposite direction had improved their results following their move across Øresund (Øresundbro Konsortiet, 2008: 48). While the major benefits in the example were to the region itself, there were wider gains that rippled through the rest of Scandinavia and the Baltic – other places connected to the network.

The Øresund example emphasizes the economic development potential of a corridor and the importance of being connected to networks. Regent, North Dakota in the USA is a world away from this transnational European link. It only has a population of 211, and is remote from urban centres. Against all the odds, one man there has his own vision to create local economic development by using a network connection. His endeavour to transform a rural road into an 'Enchanted Highway' is described in Box 6.2. This case study shows the economic development potential of a road: those passing along are potential customers. It also shows once again how public funding (in this case only $500) can be a lubricant that makes it possible to mobilize support from elsewhere. Last but not least, the Enchanted Highway is a reminder that many projects need a long time to come to fruition, and that success needs to be measured relatively rather than in absolute terms.

Box 6.2: The Enchanted Highway, North Dakota (USA)

Regent, North Dakota is hundreds of miles from any sizeable city. Between 1995 and 2005, Regent lost around 25% of its residents; most of those remaining were over 50. Could anything be done?

The Enchanted Highway is the idea of local resident Gary Greff. In 1990 Greff set about creating a series of gigantic metal sculptures. By 2008, seven sculptures had been erected along a 32-mile stretch of rural road. Many were constructed from old farm equipment, welded together to form gigantic fish, pheasants, deer, grasshoppers and people (see Real ND, 2009).

The Enchanted Highway connects Regent to North Dakotas' major east–west highway. Greff aimed to use that connection to attract car drivers to visit Regent. His vision is to make Regent the world's 'metal art capital', with a motel, theatre, café, metal-art theme park and camping facilities.

Residents and local government officials were sceptical. However, with few other options to stimulate the economy, the Regent City Council provided a $500 start-up donation. Local organizations, businesses and residents followed, raising $8,000 for the first sculpture.

→

Attracting new economic growth through improving transport and infrastructure

Provision of new or improved transport and communications infrastructure is a common approach to regional economic development through competition to attract footloose industry and foreign direct investment. Business interests often lobby governments for infrastructure improvements. Graham and Marvin (2001: 390) stressed how 'Premium network spaces must continue to maintain connectivity with wider, public infrastructure networks and systems of technological mobility'. This idea finds practical expression in Malaysia's Multimedia Super Corridor project (see Box 6.3).

The MSC project shows how a state strongly committed to leading development and attracting foreign investment has integrated information and computer technologies (ICT) into national development policy. A range of e-government initiatives have been

By the late 1990s, local government had invested $25,000 in the project; but the predicted tourist boom had not happened. Donations and funding slowed; volunteers aged or disappeared. Greff kept his faith. He planned a sculpture of flying geese to be located beside the interstate highway junction with the Enchanted Highway and raised over $150,000, more than four times the annual budget of Regent City Council, from the National Endowment for the Arts, North Dakota Arts Council, local city and county government bodies. Completed in 2001, and at 110-ft high and weighing 80 tons, it got listed in the *Guinness Book of Records* as the world's largest scrap metal sculpture (Figure 6.1).

By 2005, the summer tourist season saw around 100 people per day travelling to Regent and visiting the metal-art store and Enchanted Highway giftshop. However, revenues remain small and mainly generated from purchases such as snacks.

With the internet and national radio broadcasts bringing attention to Greff's work, 11 sculptures are planned. 'I have an image of ... taking people from Regent', said Greff in a 2005 radio interview, 'having them stay at the theme park in Regent, at a motel, [then] taking a limousine and stopping at each site'. (Sources: Greff (2008); *Talking History* (2005); *Roadside America* (2009); Real ND (2009).)

Box 6.3: Regional development through a cyber corridor: Malaysia's Multimedia Super Corridor

---

The Multimedia Super Corridor (MSC) was launched in 1996 with a plan to cover an area of roughly 50km by 15km between the capital city Kuala Lumpur and the Sepang International airport (Bunnel, 2002; Lepawsky, 2005). Promising multinational companies and high-technology businesses that the MSC would come provisioned with 'intelligent buildings', 'fiber-optic networks, research facilities, tax breaks' and new 'cyberlaws', this huge regional development project, has an estimated cost of US$20bn (Einhorn and Prasso, 1999: 83–4).

The MSC project includes high-technology clusters such as an 'intelligent city' or 'brainport' called Cyberjaya, a new federal government complex at Putrajaya, and a Multimedia University (Ramasamy, *et al.*, 2004; Sood and Pattinson, 2006). By March 2008, according to the MSC website, 63,000 jobs had been created, over 2,000 companies were active in the MSC, and 1,815 patents had been filed by MSC researchers. Research and Development expenditure had surpassed RM814m. (US$251m.), generating RM13bn (US$4bn) in revenues and RM5bn (US$1.5bn) in annual exports.

The Malaysian government played a critical role in establishing the MSC. The central vision for the MSC was codified by the Malaysian

→

---

packaged into the spatial form of a 750-sq. km corridor as a means of propelling Malaysia towards its aim of being a knowledge society and a developed country by 2020, using twenty-first century communications technology to get there.

Thus Phase One (1996–2003) saw the creation of a corridor through development of five cybercities as well as the decanting of civil servants to Putrajaya, together with supporting investment in transport infrastructure such as the new international airport, the expressway road linking it to Kuala Lumpur and the development of a light-rail fast link which puts Cyberjaya only 20 minutes' travel time from Kuala Lumpur's Central Station. This spatially targeted approach enabled some rationalization of the very high costs of infrastructure provision at the outset. The aim of Phase Two (2004–10) was to grow MSC into a global ICT hub. This involved extending cybercity status to centres beyond the corridor – Penang

Federal Department of Town and Country Planning in 2000 in a document entitled *Physical Design Guidelines for the Multimedia Super Corridor* (Lepawsky, 2005). Federal legislation sets out financial and other incentives to encourage businesses to locate in the Corridor. These include government research and development grants, multi-year exemptions from Malaysian income taxes, duty-free allowances for importing of equipment, ability to recruit foreign workers without restriction, intellectual property rights and unfettered internet access (Ramasamy *et al.*, 2004).

The Malaysian state has also funded infrastructural and educational developments to spur operations in the MSC. Part of the rationale for the MSC, contends Bunnel (2002), is an effort to reverse the 'brain drain' which has seen Malaysian high-technology workers move overseas; instead the MSC aims to produce a 'brain gain' where skilled Malaysians stay at home or return from overseas, to be joined, it is hoped, by world-class researchers and engineers from elsewhere. Consequently, the MSC has attracted investment from major global high-technology corporations, such as Microsoft, Oracle, Nippon Telegraph and Telephone (NPP) although arguably at levels below those desired by Malaysian authorities (Einhorn and Prasso, 1999; Ramasamy *et al.*, 2004). Major areas of established business include software development, web design, telecommunications and manufacturing.

and Kulim Hi-Tech Park – and designating five 'cybercentres'. In this way the aim is to spread the benefits geographically while increasing the critical mass of the whole MSC, by creating a web of corridors. The growth process is backed by attempts to increase Malaysia's ICT services and products. Then Phase Three seeks to bridge the nation's digital divide by spreading the knowledge society across Malaysia as a whole (MSC Malaysia, 2009).

The agenda behind the MSC may be even more challenging. Bunnel (2002) saw the project as an attempt to revision Malaysia as a multicultural nation, balancing the nation's Malay-centred history with greater visibility of Chinese Malaysians and other ethnic minority groups. The MSC is the flagship for an economy based on education and merit, rather than ethnicity and lineage. However, Bunnel also commented that whereas Indian nationals are being recruited into high-technology positions, many Malaysians

Figure 6.1   Geese in Flight **sculpture, Interstate-94, North Dakota**

of Indian descent who worked on the farms and plantations in the area that became the MSC are employed as low-wage security guards and cleaners for the new corporate and government facilities that have replaced the agricultural land.

As ever, the MSC project shows that there is more to regional and local economic development than just economic development – both in terms of the steps needed to promote development, and the wider aims and impacts of policy. Similarly, the power of the state in Malaysia has been crucial to developing and delivering this very integrated and planned model for economic development using a top-down approach. It would be wrong to assume that the model can be transplanted to situations where the preconditions are very different. It is interesting therefore to compare the MSC project with another ambitious attempt at modernist planning to tackle the diseconomies of congestion, that of Abuja, Nigeria, which is summarized in Box 6.4.

Just as Malaysia decanted government ministries to the new city of Putrajaya, so Nigeria sought to relocate its civil servants to the planned new city of Abuja. The 'new city' solution is perhaps the most drastic of all ways to try to solve problems where poor infrastructure and congested communications networks are

Box 6.4: The challenge of congestion and infrastructure: Abuja (Nigeria)

By the 1970s the growth of Nigeria's capital and largest city, Lagos, was becoming a problem. Nigeria's military government decided that Lagos had become so congested and insecure that it would create a new capital city, Abuja. The site chosen was much closer to the geographical centre of the country and on land that did not have a major tribal ownership, unlike Lagos which was mainly identified with just one of Nigeria's many ethnic groups. The new capital was also seen as having a regional development function, and was to be a symbol for Nigeria's greatness.

The Master Plan for Abuja was completed in 1978 by International Planning Associates. It was a classic piece of functionalist modernist planning, with a clear hierarchy of roads and wide boulevards – but no railways or subway system (indeed there are no railways in Nigeria at all). The centre of the city was given over to federal buildings and judicial and legislative functions along with a business district. The plan was for a city of 3 million people. Abuja became the capital in 1991.

However, infrastructure problems have emerged in Abuja. Provision of affordable housing proved inadequate. The prospect of getting employment in Abuja has attracted thousands of families who have constructed informal settlements which typically lack basic infrastructure, though the settlements do have boreholes and electricity connections and single- or double-lane dirt roads connect them to formal, paved roads. The Master Plan was not followed and commercial buildings have gone up where they were not intended to be, while new housing has been built on sites planned for open space or schools. One consequence is that electricity distribution networks quickly became overstretched and power cuts are a chronic problem of day-to-day life.

The Centre on Housing Rights and Evictions/Social and Economic Rights Action Centre (2008: 39–54) estimated that as many as 800,000 people were evicted from informal settlements by the authorities in Abuja between 2003 and 2007, though the officials contest this figure. Land is not allocated for low-cost housing because of the high costs of infrastructure provision. Prices of plots for housing are even out of the reach of the middle classes.

hindering economic growth. As the Abuja example shows, delivery requires effective planning and regulation. It can be argued that in economic terms Abuja is a victim of its own success. Over 200,000 government staff were relocated from Lagos, along with embassies and other international agencies. It is no surprise that this influx created jobs in services, for example, and thus attracted further in-migrants as well as opening economic opportunities for people who were already resident in the area of the new capital. However, what is more significant is the way that officials have resorted to forced evic-tions to try to ensure 'orderly development' in tune with a plan that was almost 30 years old. The scale of the disruption to livelihoods and economic activity as a consequence of the evictions is incalcu-lable, yet appears to have been little addressed. Economic devel-opment gains from improving infrastructure and communications must always be weighed against their potential destructive impacts, particularly in relation to poor people and their livelihoods.

A similar point was made by Kalabamu (1987) in respect of attempts in Dhaka, Bangladesh, to ban rickshaws. The conventional wisdom of Dhaka's engineers, police, professional planners and local media, was that rickshaw operation created congestion and should be prohibited. However, Kalabamu argued that such measures would impact adversely on the low-income groups who earn their living from, or use, the rick-shaws. 'There is absolutely no need to ban rickshaws simply because the elite wants to modernise the transport system', he commented, while also arguing that road widening and new road construction were 'nei-ther economically feasible nor socially desirable' (1987: 129). Instead he advocated a variety of less intrusive traffic management measures to address the problems of congestion and accidents. Like the Abuja example, this illustrates how economic development approaches that prioritize economic efficiency risk adversely affecting poor and mar-ginalized groups.

There is some evidence that transport infrastructure benefits businesses (Leitham *et al.*, 2000). For example, better transport sys-tems can reduce the cost of buying and supplying goods. Similarly, lower-travel costs for staff and customers (such as tourists, for example), will be beneficial to business. It is also the case that for many firms 'time is money'. Businesses producing a product that quickly perishes and loses its value – e.g. fresh fruit or newspapers – really do rely on the quality of their transport systems to distribute their products to their markets. Indeed this principle of 'just in time' has become quite pervasive in many areas or business since the 1980s, enabling firms to reduce capital tied up in storage where it is not earning a return. Transport access also matters at a more local level: for example, a new road connection can open up a previously inaccessible piece of land, making it available for development and better designed streets can encourage pedestrian traffic and generate greater access to retailers and businesses (Vojnovic *et al.*, 2006). Since the mid-1990s, for example, city planners in Hamilton, Canada, have designed streets that 'ensure freedom of movement for those who are infirm or permanently or temporarily physically challenged, and senior citizens' (Tomic, 2003: 41) by, among other things, texturing and grooving pavements to indicate direction, major and minor roads, building entrances, pedestrian crossings, bus stops, etc.

Of course, different types of companies have different transport needs. This ought to inform policy decisions taken to promote local economic development. For example, Leitham *et al.*'s (2000) research in the UK found that location choice is based on different hierarchies of location factors, depending on the origin of the firm: local relocations, foreign inward investors or branch plants sourced from national bases. Foreign inward investors rated considerations of workforce and premises considerably more highly than road links, which were considered to be a relatively unimportant factor. In contrast, branch plants sourced from national bases rated motorway links the highest of any of the groups of firms. Local relocations fell into two distinct groups in the importance attached to road links, between relative importance and non-importance. Good public transport was a significant factor for larger intra-regional locating firms.

Reservations about the relative importance for economic development of transport infrastructure were also expressed following research that examined the impact of the EU's policy for Trans-European Networks (Institut für Regionalforschung *et al.*, 2005). The study found that enhanced regional accessibility through transport improvements translated into relatively small increases in regional economic activity. However, this was much more the case in regions where both accessibility and economic development were already high. In regions that had poor transport infrastructure and low economic development, the impact of better connections was more noticeable. This research largely echoed previous findings in the UK. The Standing Advisory Committee on Trunk Road Appraisal (1999: 3) found that 'the effects of transport on the economy are subject to strong dependence on specific local circumstances and conditions' and that in mature economies with well-developed transport systems, the impacts were likely to be modest.

Even the poorest-quality roads – or other transport links such as regional airports – open up a region, facilitating regional imports as well as exports, and exposing local firms to outside competition. It is also important to recognize that access to any kind of network does not just depend on the physical infrastructure itself, but is also shaped by pricing, which in turn depends on market conditions and public policies. There are arguments that congestion arises because there is no charge for the use of road space. Thus forms of road pricing or 'congestion charges' have been introduced in cities such as Stockholm, Oslo and London. Such moves can be interpreted as 'smart regulation' in practice, aiming to ensure that companies and individuals cannot push onto others the costs of the congestion they create. Such strategies are politically contentious, and opponents argue that they create a competitive disadvantage for the places where they are implemented. In fact, much depends on the nature of the competition: large cities able to offer unique advantages are less vulnerable than smaller centres whose competitors do not go down the pricing route. Different firms will also be affected in different ways depending on the extent to which their business demands road trips.

Public transport and economic development

There is some evidence that investing in public transport can bring benefits to the local and regional economy. Smith *et al.* (1998) cited examples including Portland, Oregon, where a new light-rail system acted as a catalyst for the rejuvenation of the city centre, which grew economically and in particular increased its share of retail expenditures. In addition Smith *et al.* (1998) highlighted the need to look at the amount of jobs created by the construction of different types of transport infrastructure. They argued that investment in public transport systems brings more jobs than for roads and drew attention to how money spent on transport is recirculated within the local economy, with higher levels of 're-spending' within the local area generated by public transport than for roads.

Fundamentally, access to transport systems is likely to increase demand for land around the interchanges. This basic recognition provides an opportunity to stimulate local economic development. Retailers and other businesses (especially hotels or those involved in distribution) are always likely to find a highway interchange to be an attractive location. However, developments in such locations are typically out of town or on the edge of town, and while they may boost the regional economy they can undermine the economy of a local town because of the competition they provide to in-town businesses. So is it possible to use in-town public transport such as metro systems – 'transit' as it is called in the USA – to capitalize on the value created around stations? The answer seems to be 'yes, but it requires some clear thinking'.

The example of Arlington, Virginia, described in Box 6.5, shows how transit stations can be used to boost economic development around them, and how a strategic planning approach can help to deliver regeneration along a corridor. A key point in the success was the effort and investment put into the plans for each station and the area around each station. However, these plans were rooted in understanding of the real estate market. Developers were allowed to build to higher densities provided they followed the plans, but were also expected to negotiate a package of community benefits (Nguyen, 2008). In this way it has been possible to fund design improvements to the public areas around the station, thus consolidating the attraction of the corridor.

Consistency and clarity in planning policy have been critical to making the transit-led regeneration work at Arlington. The private sector got strong signals that the public bodies were going to back the regeneration of the Rosslyn–Ballston Corridor for the long term, and this built confidence and discouraged attempts to force development in locations that were ruled out by the planners. However, despite this success story, it is important to recognize that transit-oriented development may not work everywhere. Building confidence and partnerships is not something that happens overnight – it has to be worked at and is a slow process. In addition, in some cities transit may have a negative image, being associated primarily with use by the poor: this can deter potential investors. Finally, it may not draw as much retail development as policy-makers imagine (Dunham, 2007).

Box 6.5: Transit-oriented development for economic growth: Arlington, Virginia (USA)

Arlington, Virginia, is on the western edge of Washington, DC. In the 1970s it was in decline as developers sought greenfield sites for new development, pushing out the edge of the conurbation, but leaving run-down older settlements behind. Arlington's main commercial area, a 2-mile stretch along Wilson Boulevard between Rosslyn and Ballston, showed classic signs of decay. This corridor, and the areas around it, were haemorrhaging people, shops and jobs.

There was a plan for a new section of interstate highway (I-66) around the edge of Arlington with a subway line in the middle of it that would connect the expanding suburbs to downtown Washington. This infrastructure proposal was the cheapest option to build, but it would have exacerbated the economic problems in the older part of Arlington. Instead the local administration of Arlington lobbied the Washington Metropolitan Area Transit Agency and advocated a different solution: put the subway underneath Wilson Boulevard. This would cost more, but would mean that the rail line could be used as a driver to regenerate the Rosslyn-Ballston corridor.

→

Water and sanitation

As the example of San Diego (see Box 6.1) showed, water is fundamental to economic development, and as a regional or local economy grows the demands it makes on water supplies increase. Similarly, sanitation is basic to health and so to the productivity of workers. However, water and sanitation are provided through networks, and competitive advantage accrues from being linked into the leading networks, and from being able to connect across the limits of networks or to innovate new networks. Similarly barriers are erected or premiums are charged to control entry to networks. The 'one size fits all' infrastructural service delivered free of charge at the point of use, by a state body operating in the public interest has been widely replaced – and of course in some parts of the world and in rural regions in particular, it never existed. Graham and Marvin (2001) talked of 'Splintering Urbanism'. Their

Five subway stations were developed along this short strip. This meant that nowhere in the corridor was more than a 10–15-minute walk from a station. A strong planning strategy was developed through a process of public consultation. The area immediately adjacent to each station would be a focus for intensive and mixed use of land, with densities and building heights then tapering away.

The strategy also gave a distinct function to each of these nodes of development. High-density headquarters offices were planned for the area around the station nearest to Washington. The next station was to be an area for government buildings; then the third station, which was in the heart of the old declining downtown of Arlington, was the focus for an area of commercial retail businesses. Virginia Square, the next stop, is the educational node (including training space for insurance businesses, and George Mason University). Finally, the fifth station is the centre for a mixed use area, with both public and private buildings, including back office uses (e.g. processing of accounts).

The project has attracted something like 40 million sq. ft. of development so far. From 2002 to 2006, land values in the Rosslyn–Ballston Corridor grew 84%, from \$2.18bn to \$4bn (Dunham, 2007). (Sources: Dunham (2007); Nguyen (2008).)

argument was that the new technologies and privatized systems of provision are fragmenting places, and challenging traditional ways in which academics and policy professionals, such as those engaged in local economic development, have conceptualized the city.

As we saw in the example of Abuja (described in Box 6.4) it is very difficult to fund infrastructure in situations of rapid urban growth. Where local government is responsible for water and sanitation but there is no adequate tax base, there is the risk of overloading, inadequate maintenance and the collapse of systems. It is essential to adopt a lifecycle-costing approach to essential infrastructure. This means taking into account not only the initial capital costs of the project, but also the operation and maintenance costs and the costs of paying off any debts on loans for the project. Ways to fund such ongoing costs need to be addressed.

In these circumstances, public–private partnerships have emerged as a way to attract investment from the private sector while also

enabling local resources to be mobilized. Typically in these arrangements the role of the public bodies is to reduce the risk to the private investors, who bring money and expertise not immediately
available to their public partners.

Box 6.6 gives an example of China's first venture into water
supply through a public–private partnership system known as
'build–operate–transfer' (BOT). The Chengdu project has elements of a 'Smart planning and regulation' approach. As well as
the direct economic benefits, the project is also expected to deliver
gains in terms of knowledge transfer from the foreign firms to the
Chinese. Use of major infrastructure projects to build local skills
and capacity is a dimension that is important for long-term local
and regional economic development, and is one of the attractions of international public–private partnerships of this kind.
It is also worth noting that the city's administration has started

---

Box 6.6: Financing water supply in Chengdu (China)

Chengdu (population 10 million) is the main urban centre in south-
west China. It is a centre for scientific and industrial clusters such as
electronics, mechanical engineering, metallurgy, chemicals, textiles,
aeronautics, and space and nuclear industries. Its rapid industrial
growth in the 1990s, together with rising standards of living, created
serious water problems. Traditional water sources became polluted.
Water quality deteriorated and there were severe water shortages. The
spread of squatter settlements along the banks of the local rivers made
the situation worse.

From 1993 onwards the city began to clean up the rivers. Firms whose
waste was polluting the rivers were more tightly regulated. Affordable
housing was provided to resettle 30,000 squatter households, and public
parks were developed along the riverbanks. In the first phase of the
work, the city council committed a substantial proportion of its annual
budget to the project. The second phase involved the construction of
a water-treatment plant and 27km of pipe to connect the plant to the
city's main networks and cost US$107.6m. The Asian Development
Bank provided loans of US$26.5m. and helped to get further loans
from commercial lenders for US$21.5m.

→

work on watershed rehabilitation – deforestation had contributed to the mounting water supply problems in the 1990s. This response to environmental need demonstrates integration and awareness of the long term as well as procuring necessary short-term investment.

While water and sanitation systems typically are huge engineering projects, as was the case at Chengdu, small projects that help the rural poor can also be very significant in local economic development and a vital element in pro-poor approaches. One such example is described in Box 6.7. The building of wells and toilets in the poor rural region of Khurda, India, not only brought investment into a local economy, but also built skills and confidence, and contributed to health improvements which allow people to be more productive. Initiatives such as that described in Box 6.7 encourage people to work together for the development of the

---

Although water supply projects had traditionally been funded by China's provincial or national governments, to obtain the capital needed for the Chengdu project, a public–private partnership joint venture company was formed with a French water company (Compagnie Générale des Eaux-Sahide) and Japan's Manubeni Corporation. This resulted in a build–operate–transfer (BOT) scheme. The French and Japanese companies together invested US$31.9m and a further US$26.5m. direct loan came from the European Investment Bank. After 18 years of operation, the ownership of the plant will be returned to the municipal government (World Water Council, 2009).

The municipal government guaranteed to purchase bulk quantities of treated water. This significantly reduced risks for the private investors. Chengdu's ongoing plans to maintain its infrastructure and renew its airport also built investor confidence. According to the Asian Development Bank (2005) the project delivered access to treated water for local industries and 3 million people. The World Water Council (2009, n.p.) reported that the Asian Development Bank found that the project enhanced 'the economic potential and productivity of the region as a result of the increased accessibility to safe, affordable water provided to households and industries' and improved public health. (Sources: World Water Council (2009); United Nations Centre for Human Settlements (2001: 153).)

place they share: without such cooperation it is hard to achieve change in poor communities for two reasons. First, no individual is likely to have the means or inclination to work independently for village development. Second, top-down approaches are unlikely to be sensitive to local values and customs and so will prove unsustainable.

Another noteworthy aspect is that WaterAid India was able to bring together a range of local NGOs to form the Water Sanitation Hygiene Promotion Network (WSHP Net). The Network had the capacity and critical mass to act strategically and provide the training necessary to enable local communities to take on responsibilities for water and sanitation. Networks like this one enable ideas, success stories and lessons to be disseminated and shared. They also make the outreach process to reach new members easier: WSHP Net has been able to help 86,000 people in 150 villages (WaterAid, 2008: 7). As this example demonstrates, the replication of local initiatives can have a substantial impact, even if each initiative is quite small scale. This again is an important principle.

Summary

This chapter has shown that approaches to regional and local economic development that prioritize competition for inward investment are likely to focus on provision or upgrading of networks, particularly, but not exclusively those of roads and telecommunications. However, there is evidence that the impacts of transport developments on a regional economy may be less than is conventionally assumed. In addition, different types of enterprise have different transport priorities. Nevertheless, mega-scale public works projects will inevitably impact on regional economies at least during the construction phase, and are likely to remain attractive to states and institutions with a strong development ethos.

Smart planning and regulation is typified by integrated approaches like this, which take a long-term view, looking to link economic benefits to good environmental standards, whether through new provision or better regulation. Use of road pricing to tackle congestion is another example. Such approaches need effective agencies and enforcement if they are to succeed. Development will generally follow infrastructure, and we have seen examples of attempts to capitalize on the opportunities along corridors and at hubs in

---

Box 6.7: Building wells and toilets in a poor rural region: Khurda district (India)

Durgaprasad and Deuli are twin villages in the Indian state of Orissa, a state with a very low level of economic development and very poor communities. Their combined population is about 2,500. The main economic activity is agriculture, which is rain fed. However, drinking water comes from groundwater accessed by wells. Villagers lacked basic sanitation and so defecated outside. Diarrhoea and dysentery were common.

The agents for change were a local NGO called Gram Bharati, which worked with the Village Water and Sanitation Committee, which reached out to all the villagers. People who had been reluctant to build toilets have now done so and new wells have helped in the management of water supplies. Involvement of women was a key part of the programme. Gram Bharati provided them with interest-free loans to build toilets for their families. Through this work, self-help groups in the villages gained confidence and began to take on more responsibilities for village development. Gram Bharati promoted the work of these village women, who were then able to win a contract to provide a midday meal for a local primary school. Loans were taken out to spread the toilet campaign around neighbouring villages. Eventually, the women in the Nayapalli-Haripur village, a village with only four or five toilets, were convinced of the case for toilets. A bank loan was raised to allow 30 families to build their own toilets. (Source: WaterAid (2008).)

---

networks, such as transit stations. Overall a theme running through the chapter has been the close interrelation between infrastructure and the focus of our next chapter, environment. Smart-planning approaches would seek to make regions resilient environmentally.

Infrastructure is expensive and provision usually requires large-scale construction followed by effective maintenance. In weak states there are likely to be significant infrastructure gaps. We have therefore pointed to examples of self-help practices led by NGOs. Through working together important improvements can be made to livelihoods to the direct benefit of very poor people. As in the example of the sanitation project in the Indian villages (Box 6.7) there is often a strong gender dimension to such projects, in contrast to more conventional approaches to infrastructure such as those discussed elsewhere in this chapter, which are typically male led and gender blind.

Last, but not least, the imagination and ambition of Gary Greff, his scrap-metal sculptures and his vision to make Regent, North Dakota, the 'metal-art capital' of the world should be recognized. It embodies a spirit of enterprise as the Enchanted Highway endeavours to attract visitors and their spending to a town that is small, remote and in demographic decline. He uses virtual and physical networks (the internet, national radio and the highways) to connect to his markets. The scale is much closer to the self-help approach to sanitation improvements in India than to the Malaysia's Multimedia Corridor, confounding some assumptions in our typologies from Chapters 1 and 4. It provides a useful reminder that typologies in seeking to simplify and codify can never encompass the unique features of what practitioners actually do.

Topics for discussion

How do road improvements and street design help businesses?

What problems and opportunities arise from the decentralization of responsibility for urban infrastructure?

Related reading

S. Leitham, R. W. McQuaid and J. D. Nelson (2000) 'The Influence of Transport on Industrial Location Choice: A Stated Preference Experiment', *Transportation Research A*, 34, 515–35.

S. Handy (1996) 'Understanding the Link between Urban Form and Non-Work Travel Behavior', *Journal of Planning Education and Research*, 15(3), 183–98.

UN–Habitat (2001) Cities in a Globalizing World: Global Report on Human Settlements 2001 (London and Sterling, VA: Earthscan), 146–58.

---

7 Economic Development and the Environment

'The bottom line of green is black.' This snappy observation is the title of a book (Saunders and McGovern, 1993). It means that looking after the environment makes good business sense. Large companies are increasingly aware that a bad environmental record is likely to be reflected in consumer resistance to their products. But small businesses can also grow by using green business practices, and there are many opportunities for niche markets based on products that have authenticity and natural qualities. These insights contradict the traditional dichotomy between economy and environment. They underpin a key approach to economic development that was outlined in Chapter 1, eco-modernization. This chapter will explore that concept more fully and more critically, demonstrate its practice, and also point to the way that environmental concerns and opportunities have influenced other approaches to regional and local economic development.

The definition of sustainable development from the Brundtland or World Commission on Environment and Development (1987: 43) is often quoted: 'development that meets the needs of the present without compromising the ability of future generations to meet their own needs'. Since 1987 the idea of sustainable development has been widely adopted internationally, though not without considerable debate over what exactly the term means and what practices it entails (Redclift, 1987). The underlying idea then is that it is not development itself that is bad, but forms of development that have detrimental effects on the environment and deplete non-renewable natural resources. However, it is also important to point out that the 1987 report went on to recognize that sustainable development should be interpreted in relation to needs (and in particular the needs of the world's poor, which should have priority). Thus in this chapter as in the others, one of our concerns is to highlight the ways in which poor people have taken economic actions.

Eco-modernization

The idea of eco-modernization developed in the 1980s, notably with writings by Huber (1982, 1985) and Jänicke (1985). It implied not only that firms would adopt new, clean technologies, but also that there would be broader shifts at a macroeconomic level towards production of different, ecologically sound products and services while waste would be drastically reduced. Thus the appeal to business, and the belief in the capacity of businesses to become 'green' was that less waste and pollution means more efficiency, and new market opportunities for new products and services. Thus eco-modernization contains a paradox; the proposition that a transformation was needed that would secure the processes of modernization. A skilful balancing of economic and environmental aims was sought, not the supremacy of environmental concerns. Technological innovation and market forces, rather than state intervention and planning were seen as the motors for this change.

Early formulations of eco-modernization pointed to such developments. A typical example is NaturVärme, which sells heat pumps to houses across Scandinavia. The pumps use geothermal heat and so reduce home energy consumption. The business is based in the small Swedish village of Junosuando, and employs 12 local people, a significant figure in a village of 450 persons. The company also runs an education centre to train local youth, prospective assembly workers and salespeople (James and Lahti, 2004: 90). Eco-modernization grew in Europe, and in particular in Scandinavia and Germany, places which combined strong manufacturing and innovation capacity with high levels of environmental concern.

However, development of the concept since the 1990s has placed less emphasis on technological innovations and more on the roles of governments and other institutions (involvement of NGOs for example), and also on issues of consumption, such as food (see Chapter 10). Mol and Spaargaren (1993) for example argued that the kind of transformation sought would require action by government. Issues of governance have therefore become wound up with the propositions and assumptions of ecological modernization. As well as embracing environmental concerns and respecting the dynamism of the market, there is an emphasis of the capacity of institutions to learn and adapt their practices. The prescription is for governments that are decentralized, participatory and consensus builders (see, for example, Fudge and Rowe, 2001). Thus Kitchen and Marsden (2009: 276) spoke of ecological modernization in very general terms, saying it was 'a broad-based amalgam of policy concerns that suggests more normative approaches for the practice of sustainable development through reform and transformation of social structures, governments, businesses and markets'. This is the sense in which in earlier chapters we have linked eco-modernization to a governance approach that we styled 'smart planning and regulation'. Thus in looking towards a rural eco-economy in Europe Kitchen and Marsden (2009: 290) said that 'The development of new regional and facilitative institutional frameworks and new forms of governance of markets for rural goods and services become critical … as do the abilities of regional governments and agencies to work in partnership with the growing array of ecological enterprise'.

Industrial ecology and eco-industrial parks

Eco-industrial parks were an early and influential step to putting ideas of eco-modernization into practice. In industrial ecology, networks connect firms so that there is recycling and reuse, leading to efficiency gains and reduced costs as waste becomes a marketable commodity. Ideally, the results are 'zero discharges', along with competitive enterprises and an attractive 'green' region.

As Gibbs (2003) explained, the focus goes beyond the individual firm and onto the wider industrial ecosystem. Industrial ecology looks at industry as a closed ecological system. This means it should be possible for one industry to feed off the waste of another, reuse it and create other products. There are some similarities here with the notion of agglomeration economies which was discussed in Chapter 3. One reason why firms cluster is that they can benefit from 'spillover effects' generated by other firms in the same agglomeration. Such benefits were seen to include skilled labour and access to know-how as well as easy links to suppliers and customers. However, it is worth remembering that reuse of waste products can also be part of such synergy. For example, Chicago's famous stockyards, where cattle were slaughtered on an industrial scale, generated waste that was used in numerous ways by other firms; manufacture of glue from the hooves and bones, and fertilizer from dried blood are familiar examples.

Given the similarities to the notion of clusters, it is perhaps no surprise that the early and most influential example of an eco-industrial park at Kalundborg in Denmark, was a spontaneous development rather than a planned park. In this city of 20,000 people, gas from a refinery, previously flared as waste, goes to a nearby local power plant whose waste steam is returned to the refinery and to a fish farm, the city and a pharmaceuticals plant. Fish-farm sludge and pharmaceutical waste become fertilizers for local farms, and so on. The approach has been replicated through public planning and design of such parks. This fits the notion of smart planning and regulation, though Desrochers (2000) argued against public planning such as this and that market processes are sufficient to promote recovery of resources. Despite Desrochers' fundamentalist stance that fails to address the urgency of some resource constraints, eco-industrial parks have developed widely since the 1990s. South Korea, for example, adopted a 15-year plan in 2003 to convert 18 existing industrial parks into eco-industrial parks (Korea National Cleaner Production Center, 2010). Other countries, such as Thailand have also created eco-industrial parks (see Box 7.1).

Despite a seeming proliferation of eco-industrialization initiatives such as these, Gibbs (2003: 262) expressed concern that eco-modernization entailed 'rather isolated responses that may allow policy-makers to "tick the environmental box" while getting on with the main business of economic development which may continue to be environmentally destructive'. He pointed to the fundamental conceptual weakness of eco-modernization as being the lack of a theory of power relations. Therefore, in further discussing the relation between environment and economic development we need to look at power and governance.

Cleaning up the mess

Industry has been and in many parts of the world industry remains a major polluter of air, water and land. This constitutes a form of

Box 7.1: Industrial ecology: a closed-loop water system in Thailand

The Eastern Seaboard Industrial Estate south-east of Bangkok has created a closed-loop water system. The essence of the system is that waste water is processed and reused. The Estate's companies use a lot of water each day, with supplies coming from reservoirs in the region, fed by rainfall. Nearly all factories in the estate are required to maintain their own pre-treatment plant, after which their waste water flows to primary and secondary aerated lagoons. The Estate maintains an emergency pre-treatment plant in case of breakdown of the factories' plants and an inorganic waste-water treatment plant.

A constructed wetland provides tertiary treatment and a holding pond ($600,000m^3$) which cleans the water to higher than the Industrial Estate Authority standard. Plants in this wetland are selected to remove residual heavy metals remaining after earlier treatment.

A holding pond is the last piece in the system. From here the water goes through a dedicated retreatment plant process and returns to a supplementary system of pipes that the Estate uses for landscaping and to supply several factories needing it for cooling. Management is researching the feasibility of using the recycled water for growing rice on adjoining farmland. Storm water will be integrated with the recycled water system.

The holding pond is home to 300,000 fish and diving ducks. The fish cannot be marketed for human consumption: though they test for heavy metals at a level below legal limits they would not have a good 'image'. Management is exploring the possibility of supplying them to an alligator farm. During the winter, migratory water fowl use the pond as a resting place.

A new treatment method will use gravel-filled ponds with floating islands to grow tropical flowers for market. The flowers, other plants, and fixing bacteria will aerate waste water, possibly replacing the mechanical aeration ponds and cutting the cost of their energy usage. Proceeds from export sale of the flowers will fund local education programmes. (Source: Lowe (2001).)

unfair competition, since part of a polluting company's production costs are in effect being shifted off to the environment. Place competitiveness bought at the price of environmental pollution is ultimately unsustainable. Contamination has a negative effect on place competitiveness; it deters investment and can even harm residents and other businesses. Indeed property developers are extremely apprehensive about many brownfield former industrial sites because of the risks of the land being found to be contaminated. Thus the possibility of contamination has a blighting effect beyond sites that are actually contaminated.

Industrial and commercial uses that create contamination typically include chemical works, mines and quarries, dockyards, oil refineries, power plants, yards, asbestos works, iron and steel works, paper and printing works, timber treatment works, leather tanning factories and sewage plants, though this list is indicative not definitive. Since groundwater moves, the effects of the contamination may be experienced beyond the actual site of origin. Economic development bodies ideally need to keep – or have access to – records of sites that have been polluted. Furthermore steps should be taken to try to get the polluter to repair the damage, though this is very likely to be a problem, since the original polluter may no longer be in business. Without such safeguards, new users of land are at risk and will be reluctant to invest.

Issues of power and governance are central to tackling such problems. Market forces are less responsive to problems of waste and environmental damage than authors such as Desrochers and free-market advocacy groups such as the Property and Environment Research Center might wish.

Isles, the NGO highlighted in Box 7.2, brings together environmental work with outreach to low-income communities. Its local community and economic development work is rooted in environmental improvement. Isles 'finds creative, low-cost ways to transform toxic spaces into beautiful, clean places by educating people to take control of their own physical environments and personal health' (Isles, 2009: n.p.). As well as its work on brownfield sites and training residents for jobs in cleaning up environmental hazards, it is involved with planting community and school gardens; building and renovating parks; educating adults and children about the environment and nutrition; testing and cleaning up unhealthy homes and schools; and creating opportunities for enjoyable exercise. This holistic, bottom-up and environmental-centred approach is a method well suited to marginalized communities in political cultures that have a strong participatory tradition.

Box 7.2: Community involvement in land reclamation for development: Trenton, New Jersey (USA)

New Jersey lies just across the Hudson River from New York. It has 8,400 sites that are known to be contaminated with toxic chemicals. Most are former industrial sites that are underutilized or vacant and lie in urban areas. Many of the sites are in Trenton (population 90,000), the State capital. Trenton's industrial base declined after the Second World War and left behind heavy metals, contaminants from fuels and other chemicals. The costs of cleaning up such sites make them unattractive propositions for development in competition with greenfield suburban sites. As is often the case, these vacant lots are mainly in neighbourhoods where low income and ethnic minority households live.

Isles, an NGO in Trenton, works with low-income communities to educate them about their environmental rights, collect scientific data on contaminated sites and use it to develop ideas for reuse with public authorities.

An example of their work is the 3-hectare 'Magic Marker' site, so-called because it had been used by the firm making felt-tip pens, before it closed the factory there. The legacy of contamination on the site came from an earlier use, the manufacture of batteries from the 1930s to the 1980s. From 1994 Isles began work on the site involving local organizations, clergy and heads of small businesses. A core group of about 40 people helped research the site, its owners and the health hazards that it posed. A training programme for these local residents was run through higher education institutions in the area. The group of activists formed the North West Community Improvement Association, which partnered city officials and other organizations in re-planning the site for the development of retail units, housing and open space. (Source: Antoniou (2001).)

There are perhaps two keys to the Isles approach. First, it is about partnership; and secondly, environmental improvement is approached as an economic and social opportunity, not purely an environmental problem. Similar concepts underpin one of Europe's largest projects to reclaim derelict land and turn around a regional economy that was in steep decline. However, the example of the Emscher Park, which is described in Box 7.3, illustrates how public sector investment was used to drive the transformation based on environmental business and good design, which draws in private sector investment.

The Emscher Park project was coordinated over a decade by the publicly established IBA Planning Company, with an initial funding allocation of approximately US$20m. from the state government. Actual project implementation, however, was dependent on investment from developers, which in most cases were partnerships involving local governments and private companies, though funding was also sought from central government and the European Union.

Box 7.3: Regional reclamation through an International Building Exhibition: the Emscher Park, North-Rhine Westphalia (Germany)

Germany's Ruhr valley with its steel mills, coke smelters, coal mines and chemical plants, dominated German industry during the nineteenth and early twentieth centuries. By the late 1900s, following the restructuring of the steel and mining industries, the area became blighted with economic decline and high unemployment, and scarred by pollution and dereliction.

In the late 1980s the State Government of North Rhine-Westphalia adopted the International Building Exhibition (IBA) approach already used in Germany for smaller-scale projects. This time the approach was to be applied to the achievement of 'integrated regional development', the theme of the exhibition, over an area of 800 sq. km, covering 17 cities and towns, with a population of 2 million inhabitants (MacDonald, 1995).

The strategy had a strong environmental focus, including:

- reuse of land to prevent further loss of greenfield sites;
- extending the life of existing buildings through maintenance, modernization and reuse strategies;
- incorporating ecologically sound construction practices for both new buildings and adaptive reuse; and
- transforming the region's production structure towards environmentally-friendly production methods.

→

Although it was a large-scale regional project, the implementation was quite bottom-up. There was extensive consultation with, and participation, of professional associations, environmental groups and the general public. The use of the concept of a 'building exhibition' meant that architecture, building and site design led the project. However, the ecological principles were also crucial and embedded throughout, as detailed in Box 7.4.

Challenging the 'narrative of obsolescence' (Weber, 2002: 532) and reusing buildings and infrastructure uses fewer resources than new construction. Similarly, reuse of derelict land avoids conversion of greenfields and farm land into urban uses. However, a key

---

Five projects sum up the kind of intervention used:

- **The Emscher Landscape Park**: this park stretches throughout a valley and unifies the whole Emscher IBA. It is based on the reclamation of coalfields and existing open spaces, integrated into a system of seven regional green corridors, often following former industrial roads and railway lines.
- **Industrial Museums and Historical Preservation**: existing industrial and mining facilities have been preserved, and converted to new uses. The former Zollverein colliery, a masterpiece of industrial architecture, was made into a centre for art and culture, with theatre groups, design studios and a museum. The Oberhausen gasometer was converted into an exhibition hall and contemporary theatre.
- **Housing on Brownfield Sites**: Emscher IBA includes 3,000 new houses, many of them on previously contaminated land, and the refurbishment of a further 3,000 houses. These were provided with facilities and infrastructure, and located in garden city residential villages.
- **Duisburg Harbour**: the docklands area in Duisburg was transformed into a waterfront development, including offices, a hotel, social housing, studios, galleries and cafés.
- **Redevelopment of the Emscher Waterways**: the entire Emscher drainage system, based on concrete channels, was ecologically re-engineered and new water treatment methods are reducing pollution. (Source: Environmental Protection Agency (2009).)

lesson from this project is that reclamation and redevelopment of contaminated land will normally require a significant input of public money. The financial models used by private funders such as banks are not likely to be able to accommodate the clean-up costs. As a general rule, smaller sites (which are likely to make up the majority of contaminated sites) are particularly difficult for the private sector to tackle alone. This is because they do not yield the economies of scale of a large site, and there is likely to be a strict regulatory regime to be negotiated, since the process of cleansing the site is itself potentially a polluting process. In general, the clean-up standards required for a site that will subsequently be used for industry are lower than when the new use is for housing.

The governance structures in the Emscher Park example are typical of those recommended in the eco-modernization literature. There are a lot of actors involved: different levels of government,

---

Box 7.4: Governance approaches to tackling environmental problems in Hong Kong

Air pollution, mainly from vehicle emissions, is a problem in Hong Kong. In the 1990s, the government's Environmental Protection Department aimed to tackle the problem by forcing taxis, buses and light-goods vehicles to switch from diesel engines to petrol engines. However, such measures were blocked by the country's Finance Bureau because they were seen as inflationary. Serious air pollution events in 1998 and 1999 forced reconsideration. Tighter fuel and vehicle emission standards were introduced. However, between 2000 and 2003 the government offered subsidies in the form of one-off grants to diesel taxis to convert to use of a cleaner fuel, LPG. There were other incentives. No excise duty was charged on LPG making it cheaper, thereby reducing taxis' operating costs. To ensure adequate provision of LPG supplies across Hong Kong, operators of dedicated LPG filling stations were granted sites at favourable rates. From 2002, incentives were also given to replace buses using diesel with LPG or electric vehicles. These initiatives proved successful, though air pollution remains problematic due to other sources.

→

private companies, special development agencies and professional bodies, and they all work within set rules, learn from each
other and adjust their outlooks and behaviour through being part
of the project. However, Sonnenfeld and Mol (2006) criticized
eco-modernization for being rooted in a set of values and assumptions that are strong in northern Europe, but by no means universal. Thus Gouldson *et al.* (2008) looked at the situation in
Hong Kong, where the governance culture is also strong but
different from what is seen as the northern European norm. The
tradition in Hong Kong was one of top-down regulation by government, rather than use of incentives and agreements with a plu-
rality of partners. As the summary in Box 7.4 shows, Hong Kong
addressed its challenges of air pollution and water management
through a combination of top-down regulation and more open,
inclusive policies.

Pollution of marine waters, especially in prominent Victoria Harbour,
also causes concern. Industrial change has reduced but not eliminated
discharges into the waters, which are also used for disposal of sewage
and effluents. The approach adopted in the 1990s was top-down and
engineering led, with construction of a new collection and treatment
plant and a longer outfall beyond the harbour. However, the project got
behind schedule and public concern grew. This led to renewed efforts
to address the problems after 2000, but these were much more open and
consultative, with use of websites and briefings for district councils.

Gouldson *et al.* commented that both examples showed 'a significant
departure from well-established modes of decision making in Hong
Kong' (2008: 327). Furthermore they reported that 'similar engagement
processes are now being pursued in connection with Hong Kong's
attempts to develop a sustainable development strategy', and so these
'more open, inclusive approaches have catalyzed broader changes in
the policy process' (2008: 327). However, they also argued that the
highly technical nature of the issues relating to the Harbour Area
Treatment Scheme mean that the public consultation 'should probably
be seen more as an attempt to legitimize decisions on expenditure
than to incorporate public concerns into the decision making process'
(2008: 327). (Source: Gouldson *et al.* (2008).)

The examples in Boxes 7.2, 7.3 and 7.4 highlight some issues of waste as a factor in economic development and a challenge for governance. In Trenton and in the Ruhr, recovery from deindustrialization was impeded by the blight caused from the polluting legacy of past economic activity. There are thus issues of intergenerational equity and, as Trenton showed, social equity in that wealth creation was achieved through leaving poorer people in a despoiled living environment. In Hong Kong, the problems of air and marine water pollution are more caused by actions during the current generation and are more generalized in their impacts. In 2001 the government of Hong Kong directly linked the water-quality issue to 'Hong Kong's status as Asia's World City' (Gouldson *et al.* 2008: 327), thus connecting environmental quality, and the process of consensus building around it, into global positioning and city marketing. However, part of the water and air problems in Hong Kong result from cross-boundary pollution emanating from the Pearl River and elsewhere in the region. How to handle such inter-regional and international flows, their origins and consequences remains a major problem of governance.

Although all three examples can be read as eco-modernization, and while they have some strong similarities in their governance approaches, each one also points to a different part of our typologies from Chapters 1 and 4. Trenton is about mobilization of poor and marginalized people to act together to improve their situation. The leading role was played by an NGO. The Emscher Park was about area regeneration through a 'mega-project' composed of numerous smaller projects, state led but with lots of partners. Hong Kong saw a strong development state linking the fight against pollution to global city status and so implicitly the attempt to hold and attract foreign direct investment.

Finally in this section, we need to make the obvious but often overlooked point, that in developing countries around the world solid-waste recycling is a key source of livelihoods. In the Philippines (see Box 7.5) as in other locations, solid waste creates both an economic opportunity and a health hazard for the poor.

Richer countries have disposed of their waste as 'landfill'. However, this 'solution' is itself problematic. In very urbanized regions the supply of sites to bury waste is finite and diminishing. Furthermore, burying rubbish means that the potential for reclaiming and reusing at least some of it is lost. Incineration is another alternative, so that waste can be used to create new energy and heating. However the environmental effects of such systems need to be considered carefully.

Waste strategies – at national or local level – can make a difference and there is scope for local economic development to be integrated with such strategies so as to capitalize on the opportunities they can create. Key environmental principles for such strategies should be proximity and self-sufficiency. In other words, plan to dispose of the waste locally, rather than using energy to transport it and then dump it somewhere else. These principles are also ethical – those who create the waste should clear it. However, they

---

Box 7.5: Waste collection and recycling in the Philippines

Solid waste is a common problem in informal settlements. It contributes to pollution of the water supply and creates hazards for health. Yet solid waste is also an economic resource and an environmental challenge, with disposal sites in short supply given the pace of urban development. All these elements are present in Metro Manila, Philippines, an urban area of some 12 million people that is growing fast. The lowest level of local government there is the *barangay*, which for the people in the informal settlements is the main link between government and civil society.

Many *barangays* organize local waste collection, as recycling of this waste can be a valuable source of employment. One example is Barangay Mameltac that borders a sanitary landfill site. The *barangay* organized the 'garbage pickers' so that they are employees of a firm that sells on recyclable materials to dealers. The work and hours are demanding – the picking starts at 4 a.m. when there is enough light to begin sorting the midnight dumping of waste. However, the involvement of the community through the *barangay* means that income levels are safeguarded, there is no use of child labour and the workers get free medical care.

Funds from the Ayala Foundation support the Barangay Integrated Development Programme. This Programme trains *barangay* leaders in community waste management strategies and business planning. Among the spin-off businesses have been one turning waste cloth from a jeans factory into high-quality paper. (Source: Carley and Bautista (2001: 111–12).)

also make economic sense in that there can be jobs in collecting, sorting and recycling waste. Pellow (2002) provides a historical case study of the issues of environmental justice and economic development around waste disposal in Chicago, highlighting the complexities of geography and technology that frame the issues. Of course, as with everything else, much depends on market demand and the relations between fluctuating market prices and the costs of recycling. Nevertheless, the need to dispose of waste will persist even if the market rate makes recycling it economic. In an ideal world the costs of other forms of disposal should be factored into the equations to assess the economic value of recycling. This can be done through taxation – for example by imposing taxes on landfill so that the real costs of disposal cannot be so easily externalized.

Regional energy risks and options

Energy systems are vital to the environment but also to economic development. If regional resilience is an aim, then resilience in the face of rising energy prices has to be part of regional development. In an analysis of the vulnerability of regions across Europe to rising energy prices Innobasque (2009) identified regions which have specializations in industrial sectors that make a high level of energy purchases. Typical energy-intensive industries are steel, aluminium, pulp and paper, glass and cement, though food processing is also an industry with large energy requirements. However, the Innobasque researchers also found that, within the same industrial sectors, there are significant differences between countries in the efficiency with which energy is used. While energy costs may not be the main production cost, nevertheless a regional economy in which key firms are using energy less efficiently than their competitors is going to be vulnerable when energy costs rise. Hence raising awareness of the economic benefits of becoming more energy efficient can be a wise component of regional economic development.

The Innobasque researchers also argued that regions with a high level of commuting are more at risk than regions with more self-contained labour markets in the event of energy price increases. The logic therefore is to begin to create regional land use and transport structures that make it easier to work locally and to use energy-efficient forms of transport. This implies a switch from cars towards public transit. This links back to themes in Chapter 6.

If the costs of conventional energy sources increase, then production of renewable energy will become a more viable proposition. In 2009, for example, China was developing a plan to massively increase solar energy generation. The country was earmarking something like US$600bn from its economic stimulus fund (set up to counter the economic downturn that swept the world in 2008) to provide incentives for solar farms and roof top panels. The plan was to boost China's domestic solar power market and so help the overall economy. China has already invested in wind and hydro electricity generation, and is the world's leading manufacturer of photovoltaic panels that turn sunlight into electricity, though in 2009 95 per cent of the panels produced were exported (Watts, 2009). Investments such as this will create significant economic opportunities for regions which are the base of enterprises involved in panel manufacture.

In Europe, Innobasque (2009) found that areas with high potential for generation of renewable energy were often peripheral regions with rather depressed economies. In the UK, for example, there is great potential for wave and tide power around the islands off the north and west costs of Scotland, an area which also has strong winds. However, there can be difficult environmental trade-offs that block the way to realizing the energy potential as the example from the Isle of Lewis in Box 7.6 shows.

The Isle of Lewis's proposed wind farm highlights issues of governance. Several tiers of government are involved in issues like this one, as well as NGOs and pressure groups. However, it also illustrates how policies from different arms of government (in this case EU Directorates) can have contradictory impacts at regional level. In Europe there are requirements to undertake Environmental Impact Assessments on major development projects and Strategic Environmental Assessments on plans and programmes. While the actual processes vary somewhat from country to country, the overall impact has been to give more weight to environmental impacts than to social and economic benefits when regulators consider possible development.

Sustainable construction

Like renewable energy, the construction industry is important to climate change mitigation and economic development. Energy

---

Box 7.6: Green energy and jobs versus birds, fish and peat on the Isle of Lewis (Scotland)

The Western Isles are located off the north-west coast of Scotland. They face all the problems of a remote region where residents have traditionally relied on farming and fishing, together with a short seasonal tourist trade, to make a living enabling them to buy goods that are brought in from the mainland. Unemployment is high, and much of it is long term. Young people have tended to move out to access education and well-paying jobs. The islands are swept by strong winds from the Atlantic and the Arctic, so have great potential for wind farm development. Furthermore, national planning policy made by the Scottish government requires local planning authorities to make positive provision for renewable energy developments. In 2004 a developer sought planning permission to build a 243 turbine, 702 MW wind farm on the Isle of Lewis.

However, the planners also have to work within the EU's Habitats Directive. This basically requires that protection is given to habitats of important wildlife species. The Western Isles also has extensive designations for Special Protection Areas linked to environment. The proposed wind farm encompassed three Special Protection Areas and encroached on important habitat areas for birds. Reduced CO_2 emissions, local jobs and benefits to the Scottish economy were on offer, but peatlands, birds and fisheries were under threat. As well as the various semi-state environmental conservation bodies and pressure groups opposing the scheme, there were almost 11,000 objections from the general public, most from outside the island.

The planning application was refused by the Scottish government in 2008 on the grounds that the development would adversely affect the integrity of a protected European site. (Source: Hague (2009).)

---

efficient buildings and other 'green' construction, helps reduce CO_2 emissions and operating costs. Saving energy in existing building stock is just as important as in new buildings. Awareness of the need to reduce CO_2 emissions can create the new business and economic development opportunities in sustainable building that champions of eco-modernization advocate. Construction is a major employment sector. Many of the jobs are relatively low skilled and thus can be accessed by people who cannot break into other labour markets. Also construction by its nature is very place based, and so can have quite immediate impacts on a local or regional economy. In general people in the locality are the first to access jobs in construction, though later they may be overtaken by people migrating to the area to get the jobs.

However, construction has significant environmental impacts. The construction, use, repair, maintenance and demolition of the built environment consume resources and energy and generate waste. Many billions of tonnes of minerals are extracted for use in roads, other infrastructure and buildings. Poorly managed construction processes can be a major source of pollution, generating waste materials, noise, vehicle emissions and contaminants released into the atmosphere, ground and water.

Energy, much of which comes from non-renewable sources, is consumed in the production of construction materials such as cement, bricks and metals, and in their distribution. Waste from construction and demolition materials generally exceeds waste produced by households. Its disposal typically extends the ecological footprint of a settlement.

The construction industry can play a key part in achieving sustainable development through:

- design which minimizes waste;
- minimizing energy in construction and use;
- not polluting;
- preserving and enhancing biodiversity;
- conserving water resources;
- respecting people and local environments; and
- training construction workers in sustainable development principles.

The nature of construction or adaptation for energy-efficient buildings will vary across the world, depending on local climates and raw materials. In New Delhi, for example, locally available mud provided a key building material for a new office building. The design and construction of the DA headquarters building, described in Box 7.7 illustrates some further approaches to sustainable construction – such as passive cooling, reuse of materials and avoidance of materials such as aluminium that come with high environmental costs in terms of CO_2 emissions. While construction needs the professional skills of architects and engineers rather than economic development specialists, it is still useful to be aware of such parameters.

Design and construction progressed incrementally, through multiple short experiments and cross-cutting collaboration between the architects and TARA Nirman Kendra, which is the construction and engineering arm of DA (Schalcher, 2008: 58). This is very much in line with our understandings of how innovation is triggered. Nonaka and Takeuchi (1995), for example, saw the process of converting knowledge into innovation as resembling a spiral involving collective learning, which as we have seen is an important mechanism to deliver the kind of transformation sought in eco-modernization.

Box 7.7: Sustainable building design and construction: the Development Alternatives office in New Delhi (India)

Development Alternatives (DA) is an NGO based in New Delhi that promotes commercially viable and environmentally friendly technology. In 1985 it acquired a site for a headquarters, but had few resources. To keep costs down, therefore, the design used the cheapest available building material: mud. Combining traditional methods with modern engineering, an office was constructed using compressed earth blocks. Highly innovative at the time, today compressed earth technology is a proven building method.

By 2006 there were 150–200 people working in the building that had been designed for 50. Something had to be done. There were three options: keep using the building but also find new space elsewhere; try to expand the building vertically or horizontally; or demolish and build anew. In the end the decision was to demolish, largely for economic reasons. DA had space on the site, but could not buy a suitable replacement site elsewhere, and a new building would give better energy efficiency.

→

Exchanges of ideas between those doing the research and those involved in production itself, are fundamentally important, involving people who have a lot of practical experience and draw ideas from that experience. Similarly, the most critical aspects of the innovation process 'are dependent *not* upon frontier research, doctoral graduates, gross expenditures and so on, but on spillovers, linkages, networks, inter-dependencies, synergies etc.' (De la Mothe and Pacquet, 1998: 31). ECOTEC Research and Consulting Ltd (2005: 8) say that the challenge faced by firms is how to strike the balance between *routines* (which help to steer the organization and keep it performing) and *creativity*, 'which is the lifeblood of innovation'. The need to respond to threats of climate change through more sustainable construction will generate innovation. Scarce resources can even be an advantage, favouring developing and transitional

---

Sustainability was central to the design of the replacement building. After extensive consultation between the designers and DA staff, it was agreed to substantially downgrade air-conditioning provision, thereby considerably reducing electricity consumption, but at the cost of significantly higher temperatures and humidity levels. In effect, staff were prepared to change lifestyles to move to more environmentally sustainable arrangements. Throughout construction, careful attention was paid to the energy consumed by materials and building methods. The earth removed from the original building was recycled as building blocks (literally) for the new one; fly-ash from a local power plant became a building material; and, decks and vaulted pre-cast domes that cost much the same as conventional reinforced concrete but required about 20% less embodied energy, were installed.

Another key feature of the design is how it brings nature into the building. Internal spaces connect to a courtyard. The building is shaded against the sun in the summer and catches the monsoon breezes. The design of each facade is different, especially the windows, taking account of the direction of the sun and the views. The building's environmental control systems allow users to vary the spaces internally and to control the internal climate of each wing. Similarly, all wastewater is treated on the site and recycled for flushing toilets and watering plants. (Source: Schalcher (2008).)

economies over rich countries, by making experiment and a revisiting of tradition the most realistic economic options.

Finally, we should note that 'many small contractors, local tradesmen, and poor itinerant workers were hired to work on the construction site. The idea here was to distribute wealth equitably through the project. The itinerant workers lived on the site during construction, and were provided adequate shelter' (Schalcher, 2008: 58). It shows how sustainable construction can contribute to job creation and social inclusion, key aspects of pro-poor economic development.

Summary

The interactions between environment and local economic development are multiple and complex. This chapter has necessarily been selective. For example, it has not sought to address whether an attractive environment makes a place more competitive, or arguments that environmental regulation is costly and reduces competitiveness. Decisions in regional and local economic development are rarely easy and clear cut. Examples in this chapter have shown that there can be 'win-win' outcomes delivering economic, social and environmental gains, but also there can be regional situations such as the Scottish wind farm example (Box 7.6) where there are irresolvable conflicts. Concerns for sustainable development have highlighted issues of intergenerational equity, and the chapter has illustrated some of these. But there are also issues of social equity and territorial equity, as when pollution generated in one region adversely affects an adjacent region. As always, we have to consider who benefits and who loses. This remains a weakness in the advocacy of eco-modernization. The early presumption that market forces will generate a new industrial ecology has some substance, in so far as businesses respond to new opportunities, but it is also flawed in its disregard of two things: businesses seek to offload production costs to increase competitiveness; and, it is not in the interest of a business to clear up a polluted site if there are cheaper equally well-located options elsewhere. Thus smart planning and regulation certainly have a part to play, but the way they operate will be shaped by governance cultures and the distribution of power.

Last, but far from least, is the issue of how climate change will reshape regional and local economic development. There is not space to examine this fully here, but we concur with Sanderson and Islam (2007) who propose that the greater frequency and intensity of extreme weather events will be unevenly distributed around the world. In different locations, therefore, as seasonal patterns change, agriculture could be devastated, existing property and communications networks damaged as sea levels rise, and growing numbers of international migrants and environmental refugees may result from water shortages, flooding or economic hardships.

Topics for discussion

Evaluate the concepts and assumptions that underpin eco-modernization.

What are eco-industrial parks, and how can they be made to work for the environment and for business?

Related reading

D. Gibbs (2003) 'Ecological Modernisation and Local Economic Development: The Growth of Eco-Industrial Development Initiatives', *International Journal of Environment and Sustainable Development*, 2(3), 250–66.

A. Gouldson, P. Hills and R. Welford (2008) 'Ecological Modernisation and Policy Learning in Hong Kong', *Geoform*, 39, 319–30.

E. A. Lowe (2001) *Eco-industrial Park Handbook for Asian Developing Countries*, Report to the Asian Development Bank, Environment Department (Oakland, CA: Indigo Development).

8 Support for Entrepreneurship and Business Development

Entrepreneurialism

In most regional and local economies today businesses are the main contributors to economic growth. Furthermore, it is small, young and independent businesses that tend to grow at the fastest rates. However, such businesses are also the most vulnerable and likely to fail. People who start businesses and drive them forward are entrepreneurs. Therefore fostering and sustaining entrepreneurship is a key part of regional and local economic development.

So what makes an entrepreneur and what can development agencies do to support entrepreneurship? While definitions of entrepreneurs vary, a common theme is that they are innovators who see a gap in the market and have the confidence and determination to fill that gap. While such actions necessarily incur a degree of risk, there is a danger in simply equating entrepreneurialism with risk taking, and with celebrating the risk-taking aspects of being an entrepreneur. Few benefits will arise if risk taking is on a scale that is likely to lead to failure. Most businesses, like most of the rest of us, are actually risk averse, and rightly so. There are enough unexpected factors that can tip a firm into making a loss and eventual bankruptcy without rushing headlong to take on more risks. Indeed one of the ways that economic development work can help entrepreneurs is by trying to reduce the risks they face.

The Global Enterprise Monitor tracks levels of entrepreneurship across more than 40 countries. The data for 2006 showed a relationship between a country's per capita GDP and the level and type of entrepreneurial activity. There were many very small

156

enterprises in countries that have a low GDP per capita. As incomes rise, larger and better-established forms of business appear to be able to serve more of the markets and become more significant in the economy. This coincides with a fall in the number of new enterprises. Then as GDP rises further, there is something of a revival of entrepreneurship. However, GDP does not tell the whole story: other less tangible factors are also operating. For example, in Sweden's affluent neighbour Norway, 9.1 per cent of the adult population are involved in early-stage entrepreneurial activity; this is well over twice Sweden's rate. Similarly the USA's 10 per cent contrasted with the UK's 5.8 per cent or even lower figures for other affluent EU economies (Bosma and Harding, 2007).

Thus the cultural, legal and political context, what the Global Enterprise Monitor report called the 'institutional environments', are significant influences on entrepreneurial formation and survival. Norway's performance, for example may reflect initiatives to develop entrepreneurialism through schools. *Entreprenorskap pa Timeplanen* ('Entrepreneurship on the Timetable') was a three-year pilot project initiated by the Ministry of Research and Education which was completed in 2002. It was carried out in three counties. *SimuNor*, at Bergland upper secondary school in Rogaland County, lets pupils set up simulated companies. Around 90 such companies in Norway trade (imaginary) goods and money with each other in a network (Aakre, 2006). Such initiatives are likely to develop a culture of entrepreneurialism.

What kind of people are likely to become entrepreneurs? The profile of entrepreneurs rather mirrors that of migrants (there are similarities and almost certainly direct overlaps). Again the research by Bosma and Harding (2007: 20) provides valuable insights. Early-stage entrepreneurial activity peaks in the 25–34 age group and is lowest among 55–64-year-olds. Men are more likely to start a business than women are, and the gender gap exists both for new entrepreneurs and among established businesses. People in work are more likely to start a business than people who are unemployed.

Setting up a business

What do you need to set up a successful business? The answer will depend on what kind of business it is, and in what conditions it aims to operate. Nevertheless some general factors will apply to many different kinds of ventures. There has to be an idea for the product or service that will be the focus for the business activity. However, the idea needs to be converted into a commodity for which there is a market. There are many steps along this road.

The process of making a business plan is both a key step in business development and also a good check on the factors needed to make the business a success. A key issue to be addressed is how to assess the likely market for the output of the enterprise. While a budding entrepreneur may have an intuitive feeling that there is a gap in the market just waiting to be filled, banks lending money to get the business going are likely to demand a more rigorous and quantitative assessment of the market prospects. This will involve reviewing the market trends and competition within the particular market being targeted. Is the market growing, static or declining? Is it cyclical or seasonal in nature? Construction, for example, is a notoriously cyclical sector, and business plans need to anticipate how a venture can survive through the downswing of the cycle.

A business is likely to need some capital to get started. However, banks are more reluctant to lend to new firms than to established and larger companies which will generally pose fewer risks. Also banks charge for borrowing money: the terms on which capital can be raised – the interest charged and the schedule for repayments – can influence the way that a nascent company manages its cash flow and ultimately its survival. Money is needed because even the smallest business has some start up costs. For example, a poverty-stricken migrant to one of the burgeoning slums in a poor country who decides that survival depends on becoming a self-employed street hawker will need some capital to buy in basic goods to trade. Micro-lending (see Box 8.5) is one way to fund such entrepreneurship. For more formal companies, start-up costs are likely to be needed for a wider range of provisions, such as equipment and marketing. In addition, any planned expansion should also be anticipated to require a further injection of capital.

While the internet has allowed some small businesses to be run from home, one issue likely to pose problems for a would-be entrepreneur is the need to get premises. As explained in Chapter 5, those renting premises to businesses are likely to prefer an established going concern over an unproven enterprise. This is simply because anyone leasing business premises wants to keep them occupied, and to avoid the risk of becoming a creditor owed money by a tenant that has gone bankrupt. From the point of view of the would-be entrepreneur, money will be tight and the priority is likely to be to produce, market and sell the goods or services. Having property from which to run the business is a means to an end, not an end in itself. Money invested in fixed assets such as property or machinery is not available for other purposes such as marketing. Thus new businesses are likely to need property that is affordable and can be quickly accessed – but also quickly and cheaply left if the business fails or expands.

Running a business also involves keeping an inventory of stock and assets, and proper bookkeeping. For any formal business this will be needed by the tax authorities, and may also be a legal requirement. If the product is genuinely new there will be a need to get it patented so that it cannot be directly copied by competitors. Again there is no guarantee that the innovator who has a bright idea for a new business will also have the aptitude to record cash flows and transactions, or understand the intricacies of company legislation.

Management is another requirement. Even a one-person enterprise will need to manage at least his/her own time and cash flow. Hiring and managing other people gets complex. What skills and qualifications are needed? How much should you pay for them? What are the obligations on an employer? How much responsibility should staff be given and with what structures of accountability? Will everybody be able to get along amicably together? How do you know how well staff are performing?

While this list is indicative rather than exhaustive, it will already be clear that business development is not for the faint-hearted or those who want an easy and secure living. Underestimating the challenges is one of the quickest routes to business failure. Hard work – and a little bit of luck – are likely to be prerequisites for success.

How can economic development help?

Looking again through the list of needs and pitfalls in the previous section, it will be clear that most people who are aspiring to set up a business could benefit from a helping hand. New businesses and innovators are crucial to the vitality of a regional economy, but they are vulnerable. That is one reason why there has been such a growth in economic development work through the public sector or through private sector forms of business support. This section reviews examples of how businesses can be supported, with a particular emphasis on new and small enterprises. In the literature (e.g. Storey, 2003) a distinction is sometimes made between policies that promote entrepreneurialism (and so focus on individuals who are about to start a business or have only recently started one) and policies targeted at small and medium sized enterprises which are already in existence (though to further confuse matters, definitions of what is 'small and medium' vary between countries).

It is important to recognize that very often it is the actions of national governments, rather than regional or local governments, which shape the prospects for business. Business tax rates, education and training, legislation on many matters concerning company practices and employment of labour are just some examples. Nevertheless, more local forms of business support can be more responsive to particular needs and can create local synergies that reinforce networks and share experiences. For example, national education policies will have important influence on the proportions of the labour force with degree level qualifications, but are not likely to address the specific skill needs of a small business in a small town, or even the demand for a particular set of skills within a region.

Thus regional and local initiatives matter. However, in delivering any form of business support, a public body has to consider whether it is at risk of creating unfair competition. For example, other things being equal, a company that gets a subsidized loan or below-cost premises from a public body might be able to undercut the production costs of rivals not enjoying such benefits. Thus if the aim is to create jobs by supporting a new local company, but the success of that company puts a local rival out of business, the public money will have been wasted, with no net gain in jobs – or maybe even a reduction in jobs if new, more efficient machinery has been employed. There are no easy ways round such dilemmas. Transparency, analytical in-depth understanding of the local economy and judgement are essential guides to action. Spatially targeted subsidies to firms, an approach often used in area regeneration to make marginal sites more attractive to developers and business, are particularly likely to have unintended results. For example, in the UK in the 1980s government created 32 'Enterprise Zones'. Companies locating there were able to benefit from tax breaks. Research found that most of the new development that Enterprise Zones attracted would have occurred anyway, though not necessarily in a Zone (PA Cambridge Economic Consultants, 1987). Thus the Zones tended to move firms and jobs around, rather than create new businesses. Famously, Rupert Murdoch moved newspaper production from central London's Fleet Street, to a nearby site in an Enterprise Zone. A major shopping centre was developed in the Enterprise Zone at Gateshead near Newcastle-upon-Tyne. While these were important sources of employment and area regeneration, they were not the kind of small manufacturing start-ups that had been expected.

The Employment and Economic Development (T&E)Centres which are described in Box 8.1 were set up on a regional basis by the government of Finland. They give an idea of a 'smart planning and regulation' approach to business support. Business support is given, but linked to social and environmental aims, and tailored to the regional situation.

The approach of the T&E Centres is rather typical of the situation in northern Europe, but is not without controversy. Storey (2003) challenged the notion of free provision of advice and services to small firms, within a context of orthodox economic analysis. From one standpoint, the provision of free support at the taxpayers' expense may be premised on the notion that small-firm growth will create not only private benefits to the firm, but wider gains for society as a whole. Such hopes are embedded in the aims of the T&E Centres, which encompass notions of employment and regional balance. Advice and assistance to small firms will, in the language of the economists, create 'positive externalities', by which they mean spin-off benefits to others that cannot really be made into a commodity and sold. 'A vital countryside' – one of the T&E Centre aims – is an example.

However, as Storey (2003) argued, it is also possible to view the problems faced by new small firms as an example of market failure. From this perspective, the problem is that the small businesses underestimate the real market value to them of buying good advice, while banks, in turn, do not have the necessary amount of information to make judgements about lending money to small firms. The result is that markets for business advice and loans do not work as perfectly as theories assume that they should. Thus public intervention becomes necessary to redress the market failure. However, as Storey argued, a 'market failure' approach does not point to the kind of rather generous and open-ended support system that

---

Box 8.1: Finland's T&E Centres

Employment and Economic Development Centres (Työvoima- ja Elinkeinokeskus or 'T&E Centres') are run by partnership between the Ministries responsible for Employment and Economy, Agriculture and Forestry and the Interior. They also draw on the expertise of the Finnish Funding Agency for Technology and Innovation. They operate on a regional basis across Finland. Their aims are:

- to strengthen expertise, enterprise and growth;
- to improve the level of employment;
- a balanced regional structure; and
- a vital countryside.

The Centres provide training, advice and consultancy to people wanting to start a company. They help analyse business ideas, and do the legal work necessary for company registration. Financing can be provided to help new start-ups, and services to new firms are confidential and mostly free of charge. Centres provide business-development funding for SMEs, channelling funds from national government and the EU, and help local firms develop export markets. There are also schemes to equip local job seekers with the skills needed in the local economy.

$\longrightarrow$

---

follows from an 'externalities' explanation of the need for business support. Rather the challenge becomes to bridge the information gaps. Thus business owners can be given subsidized short 'taster' courses of advice, so that they realize its value and then become willing to pay the market rate to avail themselves of the services of appropriate business consultants. In turn the consultants then have to deliver what the market wants, whereas in a model like that of the T&E Centres, there is a perception that the centres are delivering what government thinks the market wants, and the private consultants are 'crowded out' of the market.

Social enterprises and social entrepreneurs

As market economies have become more all-pervasive through globalization, so practices have developed that attempt to connect

Funds are also available to support job creation through initiatives from unemployed people or from local governments.

T&E Centres give specially tailored help to foreigners who want to start a self-employing business in Finland, but are faced with the need to secure residency permits and are unfamiliar with Finnish rules and regulations.

Finland is a very rural country, with extensive areas that are forested and/or sparsely populated. The needs of such regions are directly addressed through the T&E Centres. Direct support is available for farms and other rural enterprises. One aim is to support development projects that will strengthen the competitiveness of farms. The kind of activities covered includes not just conventional farming but fur farming and forest management. Funding can help a range of investments such as land purchase, conservation and enhancement of heritage sites or important buildings, or simply business planning. Through their regional base, the T&E centres manage the EU's rural development programmes, which support the diversification of rural economies and seek to sustain rural communities. Practical measures include developing tourism services and opportunities, e.g. by creating tourist routes through and between rural regions. The Centres also have roles in relation to fishing in a country where fishing is a very popular recreational activity, and can generate local income from fees and sales of fishing tackle. (Source: T&E Centres (2009).)

new economic value with social value. This involves finding ways in which businesses can serve poor and marginalized groups better, while also building enterprises around core values of social inclusion. Social enterprises are businesses that measure success in terms of profit but also in terms of the benefits they produce for their community. They may raise capital by offering philanthropic investors social returns rather than financial rewards. For example, VisionSpring was established in New York in 2008. It set out to raise US$5m. to enable it to deliver 650,000 pairs of glasses to poor people in Asia, Latin America and Africa, and to train 5,000 village-based entrepreneurs on how to sell the glasses (Ransom, 2008).

Typically such firms are run by social entrepreneurs, but such entrepreneurs may also be found working for not-for-profit organizations or in the public sector. They are characterized by bringing the qualities of a business entrepreneur to social projects. Social entrepreneurs thus are good at spotting opportunities and untapped potential – such as in sites, materials or people – and mobilizing that potential for public benefit. One such example is the work of Hernane Prates in setting up a music school for deprived children in a poor part of Brazil. Projeto Oxentin got volunteer teachers and sought to provide access to music education for young people too poor to afford conventional education and thus at risk of being drawn into a life of crime and drugs (Prates, 2007). Another South American example from Chile is summarized in Box 8.2. It shows how a community enterprise helped empower small-scale fruit harvesters.

Might social enterprises benefit from being clustered together in an industrial park specifically designed with them in mind? In 2009, a social enterprise in Spain's Basque region, Business Innovation Brokers (BIB), was planning just such a venture. They claim that it will be the world's first industrial park for social enterprises and cooperatives, 'a social Silicon Valley'. Similar parks were being considered in Australia, New Zealand, Portugal and Russia. The Basque region has a long tradition of cooperatives. They receive tax allowances in return for investing 10 per cent of their annual surpluses in the local community, supporting for example education or cultural activities. BIB's plan was that their industrial estate would provide a base for the growth of grassroots cooperatives run by unemployed people. It would include a business employment centre, a school for social enterprise managers, a social innovation centre and an international wing. The target was to have 1000 people employed there by 2012 (Benjamin, 2009).

Social enterprises are growing in numbers, with more and more countries making legal provision for their existence. However, there is sharp academic debate about them, and a tendency for governments and activists to approach them with differing priorities. Amin (2009: 31) commented:

> For many governments and other public policy actors the social economy should reintegrate the socially marginalised back into the mainstream economy. It should unlock the capabilities of people bypassed or damaged by markets and states, helping them to become future workers and social actors. In this view, the social economy acts as adjunct and safety net. Many actors within the third sector, however, see the social economy as a distinctive value system privileging meeting needs and building social power above all else. Some see it as a parallel system to states and markets, while others see it as an alternative system, an emblem of post-capitalist solidarity and human sustainability.

Box 8.2: A community enterprise in Chile

Región del Bío-Bío is near Santiago, but also had one of Chile's highest rates of unemployment: 9.7% for men and 17.4% for women. It had large forest-based enterprises, fishing and agricultural businesses, but the mechanization meant there were few jobs. Only the better qualified found work in these industries. The rest had to find low-paying jobs as farm labourers, with women and children doing harvesting. A community development not-for-profit organization, Taller de Acción Social (TAC) managed to organize wild-fruit harvesters to develop their own business initiative. That way, they were able to bypass the middlemen and deal directly with the produce marketers. A lot of the early work involved raising self-esteem and a sense of shared identity amongst a group who often were single women living with their children in remote rural locations. A collaborative network was built, and TV publicity helped to boost confidence and pride. Training in business skills was done.

A social enterprise was built up. With technical help from the Food Technology department at the Universidad de Concepción they were able to dry and package their products, and sell them to national agro-businesses, as well as foreign markets. 'By dehydrating the fresh produce, they could obtain five times the value. Additionally, their work could be extended from a seasonal activity to a year-round endeavor if they expanded their range of produce to incorporate a variety of vegetables and herbs' (Koljatic and Silva, 2006: 22).

They created the Coordinadora Regional de Recolectoras y Recolectores del Bio-Bio to do management and marketing and allow for participatory-governance processes. 'Each community elected two leaders of a board that met monthly to oversee the chain of production and marketing. Leaders shared information with community members, issuing a public statement of costs and revenues in order to foster transparency and accountability' (Koljatic and Silva, 2006: 22). In 2006, 57 women and 13 men were members. (Source: Koljatic and Silva (2006).)

As Amin (2009) observed there is also a division over whether social enterprises are a way of providing market competition (and discipline) as part of a wider programme of welfare reform, or an alternative to the state and the market, where business principles are mediated by environmental principles and commitment to social solidarity. These differences in interpretation make it difficult to assign social enterprises unambiguously to one box of our typologies. The view that links them to the marketization of welfare reform could be seen as a form of smart planning and regulation, sharing with eco-modernization the idea that the market can deliver social and economic benefits. On the other hand, the activists' perspective puts the emphasis on the pro-poor approach.

Furthermore, while in Brazil and Argentina there appears to be a confidence that 'worker cooperatives, microcredit schemes, reciprocal trading networks, community-led initiatives and social enterprises ... confirm the viability of local economies and community organisation in a corporatized global economy', the picture is different in developing countries. There 'the social economy languishes in obscurity, unsupported by the state, blending into the informal economy, frequently dependent on motivated individuals and third sector organisations, barely able to survive; neither partner nor alternative to the mainstream. If the term is used, it is to illuminate signs of life in desperate circumstances, the glimmer of possibility from grass-root organisation (Appadurai, 2000; Chaterjee, 2004), rather than a staging-post of post-capitalist hope' (Amin, 2009: 33). This provides a reminder of how difficult it can be to do 'development despite the state', as sketched out in Diagram 4.1.

Business Angels

The problem of getting capital to assist the start-up and growth of a young company has been addressed by what are known as 'Angel Investors'. These are often retired entrepreneurs or executives who are prepared to make loans or other investments to help new firms in situations where more conventional sources of credit are difficult to access. They may also provide advice and other forms of assistance.

Networks of such 'angels' have developed in some countries such as Canada, the USA and the UK, and there is also a European Business Angel Network that was set up in 1999. Chapter 12 includes an example from Savannah, Georgia. In some cases, such as in Alytus in Lithuania (see Box 8.3), the work of a business angel has become localized and supported through a local government, as well as through local businesses, so that it becomes a vehicle for local economic development.

It is important to emphasize that the Alytus Business Angel is not typical. As noted above, the typical angel is an individual investor maybe linked into a network. The Alytus model was inspired by a Swedish example, 'Jobs and Society' which in turn was influenced by the development of enterprise trusts in the UK. However, a key message from Alytus is that the form of business support that they set up was the one that they believed suited their local needs. In a small town in a rural part of a transition country, there simply were no seriously wealthy individuals around willing to risk their capital in assisting new firms. The base for the Alytus Business Angel was therefore the local governments and donations from existing local companies with good will to the area and to the idea of helping businesses to form. The economic and political weaknesses in Lithuania at the start of the twenty-first century mean that in terms of our typology in Chapter 4, this is an example of 'development despite the state'. The strong involvement with local youths may have been pragmatic, even accidental, but it is highly relevant in a transition economy, especially given the problems that small towns in rural areas have in retaining their brightest and best young people, for whom existing firms may not be able to compete with job offers from companies in Europe's capital cities.

There has been no rigorous evaluation of the success of the Alytus Business Angel. This situation is not uncommon in much local economic development work and is a weakness. However, it is also difficult to measure the success of this initiative in the short term. This is because the returns from investment in the entrepreneurship education of the young people – like all education – may not be evident for some time. There are times when the long view is more important than short-term results.

Better information to get a better service from business

Although conventional economic theorists often assume that all actors in a market have perfect information and use this to make rational decisions, the reality is very different. Businesses are no more free of prejudice and assumption than the rest of us, and miss out on opportunities because of it. Furthermore, even in rich countries, the informal sector tends to be important in poor neighbourhoods. Since the very nature of the informal sector makes it hard to record and quantify, the scale of local economic activity is

---

Box 8.3: The Business Angel in Alytus (Lithuania)

Alytus (population 70,000) is a town in southern Lithuania, a country that was part of the USSR. Following the break-up of the Soviet bloc, Lithuania's economy changed dramatically, as old industries closed and new private firms developed. The country joined the EU in 2004. Alytus had already begun to cooperate with local governments in Scandinavian countries through participation in EU programmes before 2004. Having seen approaches to local economic development in Scandinavia, the Alytus Municipal Council, with support from local companies, set up a Business Angel as a non-profit public institution. It is run by a board comprising people from local government, media and businesses. Vaclovas Gostautus became the Director of the Alytus Business Angel in 2002. A life-long resident of Alytus, Gostautus had practical business experience and wanted to help in the town's regeneration.

The Business Angel has done a number of things. It provides information and advice about running a business, while stressing the need to ensure that ideas and aspirations can indeed be transformed into viable businesses. One feature in Alytus was the work of the Business Angel with young people. Encouraged and supported through

→

---

often underestimated. The result tends to be that poor areas and their residents get a worse deal than they would if business followed a truly rational course in investment and marketing. In the USA, Social Compact, a non-profit coalition of businesses leaders has led the way in providing easily accessible data about low income communities and challenging the stereotypes and assumptions that have held back investment.

Social Compact has done work in many low-income US neighbourhoods. It does market analysis by using a methodology called Neighborhood Market DrillDown (see Box 8.4 for an example). This involves using data from over 30 different sources to build up a business-oriented profile for the area. Some of the data is already available in the public realm from sources like the census. However, such data is often out of date, especially in neighbourhoods where there has been regeneration or redevelopment. Thus Social Compact also collects up-to-date economic and demographic information two EU-funded projects, 'Planning, Innovation, Participation and Entrepreneurship' (2002–4) and 'Innovation Circle' (2005–7), about 100 youths were involved, a core group of around 50 being termed the 'little angels'.

The youths met weekly, taking leadership roles and discussing ideas and problems with the Business Angel. They visited local companies, met with politicians and participated in local events. Encouraged to experiment with their own business ideas, one successful venture was the production of a Business Map of Alytus showing the location of all local enterprises. Preparing the map brought the youngsters into contact with the local business community and helped build essential information about the town's business base that had not previously been brought together, providing new channels for local firms to publicize their services. It led to continuing involvement and monitoring of businesses by the 'little angels'.

The Business Angel helps people with tax forms, receiving donations in return. From 2004, young people were trained as assistants in this process. By 2006 the Angel was aiding in over 2200 tax declarations and earning over 25% of its budget from that process. Other groups within the Business Angel work on quality assurance, publicity and information technology. (Source: Verslo Angelas (2009).)

from people and businesses in the area. This includes data on building permits, and information from tax assessments and commercial credit companies. Connections to utility companies – for water, gas and electricity are used to calculate vacancy rates for property. The intuitive knowledge of local market leaders is also tapped to provide a fuller picture.

Social Compact has found it valuable to work in partnership with local economic development agencies at the early stage of a project. This usually helps in the engagement with other providers of data. Depending on the particular study, the public sector may provide much of the raw data. Where technical capacity is limited, Social Compact may partner with universities or other research organizations, to use expertise in Geographic Information Systems, for example. In short, the Social Compact model seeks to build buy-in and support from a range of local stakeholders across the public, private and non-profit sectors (C. Hague *et al.*, 2006: 22).

Box 8.4: Social Compact's (2007) DrillDown analysis in Detroit (USA)

Detroit, the home of the US auto industry, has been portrayed as a place in steep decline since the industry began restructuring in the 1970s. Its inner city is almost the archetype of a run-down area of poverty and crime, the kind of place where existing businesses shrink and new firms dare not venture. However, when Social Compact did its DrillDown analysis in 54 inner-city neighbourhoods in 2007 it came up with some different pictures.

One of the most basic findings was that the population was considerably higher than had been thought. This meant that the size of the local market was also greater than imagined. The inner-city population was put at 933,043, which was 62,000 more than the 2006 Census estimates. In some neighbourhoods the population was more than 20% in excess of the 2000 Census figure. Densities were also higher than in the suburbs, meaning that buying power was more concentrated, and though incomes were lower than in the suburbs, the density narrowed the spatial differences in overall purchasing capacity.

Average household income was put at 17% higher than the 2000 Census estimate, and the median household income at 12% higher. Nearly one-third of the neighbourhoods showed a significant increase in median incomes from the 2000 Census. The informal economy was significant. Its value to for the City of Detroit was put at $US803m. In several neighbourhoods the informal economy made up more than 10% of the economy.

The retail spending of Detroit was put at $US4.6bn but $1.7bn of this went outside of the city. The analysis confirmed that banking and other financial institutions along with grocery stores were underrepresented in the poor neighbourhoods, as is often the case. Not only are these examples of unmet market demand, but the consequences are higher costs for such services to local residents – or even total exclusion.

Another important part of the analysis looked at market stability and risk. This was mainly done by looking at crime, property values and owner-occupation levels, including situations where owners lived in part of a building and rented out other parts. (Source: Social Compact (2007).)

The aim is to identify untapped market opportunities that tend to get overlooked by more conventional market analysis models. The new data is then shared with corporate, government and community leaders, so as to spur new investment that will have benefits not just for the companies but also for local residents. The results consistently show that the communities, though poor, actually have greater buying power and are safer than firms had assumed them to be.

Markets work in ways that are partly specific to particular areas. Deprived and stigmatized areas are in a sense niche markets and a place where there are micro-markets that have been overlooked but have potential for investment, once investors can access accurate information. The result of the traditional neglect is that residents of such areas are denied the facilities others take for granted and often have to pay more than they should need to for goods and services.

While the Social Compact approach has a strong underlying logic, some critical questions still need to be asked. In particular, how far does its general narrative of hidden opportunities actually depend on the local housing market? US housing markets were strong for the years either side of the year 2000, but then plunged in 2007, with many home owners facing negative equity – that is owing more on loans taken out to buy their house than its current market value. Furthermore, the housing-led message, which comes through quite strongly in the Detroit study in Box 8.4, for example, can be interpreted as a model looking to gentrification to regenerate a neighbourhood.

Micro-credit

The problems of getting capital for a new business are especially acute in situations where the would-be entrepreneur is poor, even though the scale of the finance required may be quite limited. Indeed, this can be a problem in itself, since the time and effort involved for a bank in handling a loan application is pretty much constant regardless of the amount of money being loaned, and of course it is much easier for a bank to recoup these costs from interest payments on a big loan than on a small one. Thus conventional banks are particularly unlikely to support new micro-business start-ups by poor people.

The idea of micro-credit as a way to help poor people develop and sustain small enterprises developed in the 1980s, mainly in rural parts of poor countries. It was partly a reaction against the failures of rural development banks to really aid small farmers, for example. The movement developed through private not-for-profit agencies and NGOs, though by the start of the new millennium orthodox banks had increasingly become involved. One of the leading examples in the field of micro-credit is the Grameen Bank in Bangladesh, which was honoured by the award of a Nobel Peace Prize in 2006 for its work. The Grameen Bank also helps by offering retail outlets for clients' products. A key feature has been the lending to women who are home based (United Nations, 1998). It is argued that through such lending women have been able to enhance their livelihoods and become empowered. However, there are critics who suggest that the picture is more complex, with gains for women (and some of the loans) being translated into higher dowries and continued repression (Rozario, 2007).

Micro-credit is not a universal solution. Much depends on the circumstances of the potential clients. Those most likely to benefit are people like small farmers or self-employed urban workers, who may be working from home. Their numbers will include street vendors, shopkeepers, petty traders and artisans. The key point is that while they are poor, they have a reasonably steady source of income. The risk is that when micro-credit is extended to the poorest of the poor, they may be taking on loans that they cannot repay and thus their problems accumulate rather than are alleviated. Similarly, there are households where income may fluctuate, whereas micro-credit works best for those who can expect to be able to make regular and sustained repayments, and in situations where the economy as a whole is growing rather than declining. Furthermore the chances of success will be greater if micro-credit operates in association with other forms of business support, such as training and access to land, the latter being especially important in rural development.

The relation to traditional sources of loans, like the money lenders and pawnshops in Alexandria that are described in Box 8.5, also needs to be carefully managed. While moneylenders as a group may have few champions, they are an important resource for many

---

Box 8.5: Micro-credit in Alexandria (Egypt)

Small and micro-sized enterprises are a significant sector of Egypt's economy and an important route into employment for many poor people. However, they have limited access to credit. In 1989 the Alexandria Business Association, a non-profit NGO linked to the local Chamber of Commerce, set up a micro-credit scheme in what is Egypt's second largest city. USAID, America's international development body, provided a collateral fund of US$8m. and a further US$2m. towards running costs until the project could become self-sufficient. The scheme then offered small loans with few collateral conditions, flexible repayments over a few months and other advice. Interest rates were set high enough to cover running costs but below the local norms set by moneylenders and pawnshops, the traditional lending sources for the poor.

A key part of the scheme was the 'extension officers' as a link between the clients and the branch manager. They were people paid a basic salary, supplemented by performance in respect of loans and their repayments. The extension officers helped to decide on the size of the loan, organize the paperwork and monitor and collect repayments. A high repayment rate of 99.2% was achieved. Another indicator of success was that 72% of loans went to smaller, generally lower-income micro-enterprises. ABA covered its operating costs by 1992. By 2000 the project had served over 60,000 clients with 170,000 loans for almost US$125m.

Buoyed by this success the ABA founded the Alexandria Small Business Centre to provide assistance on other small business needs such as marketing, quality control, accounting, etc. In 2000 they set up another programme called 'Towards Self-Employment' focused on poor women and unemployed youth. This was an explicitly anti-poverty programme, again backed by USAID with funds for seed capital. (Source: Wakely and You (2001: 151).)

---

very poor people with few other options in times of trouble. As a tool for poverty alleviation, micro-credit schemes need to be part of a wider array of micro-finance mechanisms that incorporate savings schemes and forms of basic insurance.

A further issue for economic development workers within local or regional governments to ponder is whether they should seek to establish micro-credit facilities. In general, there are likely to be risks if the operation of micro-credit systems falls under political control. Politicians want votes and so will be vulnerable to the temptation to be over-generous in giving loans and too reluctant to chase defaulters. Information and facilitation is probably the better way for public sector development agencies to assist the development of micro-credit schemes in situations where there is a risk that the governance arrangements are not sufficiently robust to ensure transparency and protect against political manipulation.

Ethnic Minority Business (EMB)

This chapter began by making the point that levels of entrepreneurship vary between countries. There is also evidence that levels differ between different ethnic groups within a country. Some ethnic groups in some societies have a high level of self-employment. This feature of Asians in the UK attracted much comment in the 1970s and 1980s (for example, Ward and Jenkins, 1984). In the USA the employment patterns of minorities was also the focus for research (e.g. Light, 1972; Bonacich and Modell, 1980). The conventional explanation of such high levels of entrepreneurship is that migrant communities tend to help each other, and so are able to access distinctive resources and assets from within their networks in ethnic 'villages' within cities. In particular patriarchal relationships within tight-knit families were seen to create – or even enforce – the conditions for flexible working for long hours in sectors like small-scale retailing.

However, as ever, beware the stereotypes. Many migrants also provided, and continue to provide replacement labour for large employers in sectors where the indigenous workers were difficult to attract, such as textiles, hospitals and public transport. Even in English towns with large recent Asian immigrant communities and a high number of Asian small businesses, such as Bradford, Bolton and Rochdale in the 1970s and early 1980s, self-employment still accounted for a minority (Ward, 1985).

Furthermore, the pattern was not consistent across all recent immigrant communities. In the UK, for example, the Afro-Caribbean pattern of employment appeared to be much less entrepreneur- ial. This concern peaked after the riots in Brixton in 1981. The official report (Scarman, 1986) recommended that promotion of enterprise could address some of the social and economic problems. In the decades since then there have been a multitude of projects and initiatives funded by central or local governments in the UK seeking to support ethnic minority business develop- ment. Ram and Jones (2007: 8) drew a contrast between 'the neo-liberal deregulated Anglo-Saxon countries of Britain and North America, with their rapidly multiplying swarms of firms and the highly regulated regimes of mainland western Europe, where EMB development is comparatively stunted, apparently stifled by restrictive immigration, labour and other legislation'.

Despite these efforts there is still evidence that ethnic minority businesses tend to make less use of public sector business support than is the norm for small businesses. Ram and Jones (2007: 15) suggested this is because of 'a lack of awareness of business sup- port initiatives; a perceived lack of relevance of business support products; language barriers; an absence of trust between ethnic minority businesses and providers and cultural differences'. How- ever, the same authors noted a project called REFLEX (Regener- ating Enterprise through Local Economic Exchange) run by the London Borough of Islington. This project enabled ethnic com- munity organizations to employ business advisors and so develop their own business support capacity. More than 1000 ethnic minor- ity business owners were helped in this way in the period 2001–5.

In summary, it is important to recognize the diversity within and between ethnic minorities, and to engage with those communi- ties rather than to assume that a standard economic development approach will suit all, or that some ethnic groups are 'culturally predisposed' either towards or away from particular forms of entre- preneurial behaviour and patterns of business development. One area of recent emphasis has been on improving links between eth- nic businesses and the procurement practices of public or private bodies. In the USA, for example, the National Minority Supplier Diversity Council, which was set up in 1972, builds such contacts with corporate businesses for minority owned firms of all sizes so as to increase their success in procurement and grow business opportunities (NMSDC, 2009).

Topics for discussion

Can the social economy be the means to assist the movement of socially disadvantaged people into the formal economy?

Look at the case studies of social enterprises in the fall 2006 issue of *ReVista* or a similar collection of examples. What are the common themes and what are the main differences?

Related reading

A. Amin (2009) 'Extraordinarily Ordinary: Working in the Social Economy', *Social Enterprise Journal*, 5(1), 30–49.

ReVista, Harvard Review of Latin America, fall 2006, 6–31 (available at: www.drclas.harvard.edu/revista).

9 Housing and Housing Markets

The housing industry – building, buying, selling or managing residential property, together with the equity tied up in housing – is likely to be a significant part of a local economy. However, housing systems typically have a strong national imprint – forms of provision, design and construction, finance and regulation are typically strongly national in character. For example, Singapore has a history of public land acquisition using powerful legislation, and development of extensive areas of high-rise flats by the government's Housing and Development Board. In contrast, in much of Latin America failures in state housing provision mean that housing policy largely takes the form of tolerating informal settlements developed on 'illegally' occupied land (Jenkins *et al.*, 2007).

To begin at the beginning, businesses need labour, and labour needs somewhere to live. Houses need land. Demand for housing land is strongest in those places where economic growth is strong. Land is not the only expense in providing or obtaining a house. Housing needs a good deal of capital investment. Access to housing that is affordable is difficult for people relying on low and irregular incomes. These few short sentences encompass several key challenges for regional and local economic development. The policies and practices that are implemented can be related to the typologies that we developed in Chapters 1 and 4. However, as the discussion will show, there are often contradictions, different outputs from similar aspirations and important debates about what works.

Housing tensions in global cities

Major urban areas that see themselves as global cities competing for new investment are expensive places to live. High market prices for housing and housing land squeeze lower-value uses. In such circumstances economic development policies are likely to work with the market to facilitate intensification and higher-end development. A supply of luxury housing is part of the 'quality of life' offer to an economic elite. Curran and Hanson (2005: 461) suggested that a 'monovision induced by the lure of the global city designation' can lead to 'benign neglect' of other sectors. They described the situation in New York, where about 250,000 people still worked in manufacturing in the early 2000s. Yet the existing industrial infrastructure was often presumed by officials to be unsuited to modern needs, generating what Weber (2002: 532) called a 'narrative of obsolescence' around factories and warehouses, facilitating their conversion to more lucrative residential uses or renovation into loft-living artists studios and live–work spaces. The once heavily industrial neighbourhood of Williamsburg, Brooklyn, part of New York City, has seen many of its small manufacturing businesses displaced since the late 1990s. Furthermore, when wanting to expand or develop their businesses, or relocate due to rising rents and landlords that favour residential development, a 'lack of appropriate industrial space severely constrains manufacturers' choices' (Curran, 2007: 1433).

The perception that a 'global city' needs to be sanitized by removal of manufacturing industry sometimes extends to the removal of 'unsightly' persons, such as homeless people. Cities are putting on their best face to attract business and middle/upper class residents and consumers (Harvey, 1989; Mitchell, 1997, 2003), and to some that means hiding the homeless. Since the early 1990s, cities in the USA have enacted a raft of laws aimed at curbing the behaviour of homeless people. Mitchell (1997, 2003) argued that these laws, such as those mandating 'no loitering', 'no sleeping', 'no eating', and so forth have been devised to aid local economic development and encourage urban investment. The rights of homeless people seem to pale in comparison to '"our" [i.e. housed citizens'] rights to order, comfort, places for relaxation, recreation and unfettered shopping' (Mitchell, 1997: 321).

Mitchell's logic is that cities deal harshly with homeless people, as it is perceived that those with income to spend and invest will choose to go elsewhere if they actually have to see a homeless population that they find distasteful. Since the mid-1980s, city-centre redevelopment projects, processes of gentrification, the construction of shopping and entertainment districts, are all sustained and 'protect(ed) through anti-homeless laws' which maintain the illusion of a middle- and upper-class community with readily available opportunities for consumption, devoid of the poor and absent of poverty (Mitchell, 1997: 324). Should homeless people infringe on this image, by their mere presence, then the consumers will supposedly leave the city for suburban attractions and dwellings, urban investments will decline accordingly, and the city will plunge into a downward spiral of disinvestment, lower tax revenues, blight and decay.

Although challenges to anti-homeless laws such as those illus- trated have been made, many have proved unsuccessful (Mitchell, 1997: 308). In 2006, however, federal courts in Los Angeles ruled that 'arresting homeless people for sleeping, sitting or lying on side- walks [pavements] and other public property when shelter is not available was cruel and unusual punishment', and thus unconsti- tutional (Archibold, 2006: 9). In Los Angeles, such behaviours had resulted in punishments ranging from a $1,000 fine to six months' imprisonment. The judges ruled that such laws were unjust since there were between 10,000 and 12,000 homeless people in the city, and provision of 9,000–10,000 shelter beds. This disproportion- ate number of homeless individuals in relation to shelter beds is common across the UAS (see Box 9.1). However, the court further maintained that similar anti-homeless laws in other US cities were acceptable because they were less onerous, since they were limited to specific locations and certain time periods (Archibold, 2006).

In summary, there is evidence that some approaches to local eco- nomic development that concentrate on attracting and retaining investment believe that homelessness harms a city's competitive- ness by making it less attractive to shoppers, tourists and investors. However, punitive policies targeting the homeless are unlikely to resolve the problem, while at the same time they will make life even more difficult for very vulnerable people. It is better to have in place means of providing adequate housing for all, and to manage in a sensitive way the problems of people who are 'hard to house', such as those with a history of mental illness or drug or alcohol abuse. While such social welfare actions generally fall beyond the scope of economic development agencies, they are likely to be more effec- tive ways of treating even the economic aspects of homelessness than the kind of harsh 'anti-homeless' laws seen in many cities in the USA.

are likely to adversely affect international competitiveness. Barker (2004), after a major review of housing in the UK, also argued that a very high level of owner-occupation can hamper flexibility in labour markets and thus affect competitiveness. Her report concluded that under-provision of affordable housing and rising house prices have significant macroeconomic effects.

The problem of providing housing in places where business needs it was dramatically illustrated as China's economy went into rapid growth. During China's period of industrialization and state socialism, housing provision was linked to employment. Housing investment was directly linked to planned industrial development or employment in local government, universities or similar public institutions. 'Housing was planned in terms of housing needed for the people who would work in the institution' (Wang and Murie, 1999: 66). This meant that people could live near their work, an arrangement many today see as positive in environmental terms, and major employers could oversee housing for the labour they used. However, as Wang and Murie showed, it also created inefficiencies. Enterprises had to devote management time and other resources to housing, and because the location of housing was linked to the institution there was little flexibility when things changed. Wang and Murie described a cycle of houses being built then demolished to create more houses on the same site through higher density. When housing was not available new workers had to be given temporary accommodation in other buildings. As demand tended to exceed supply, corruption and conflicts between employers and employees were not uncommon.

The system could not have housed the labour in the places and in the numbers that China's growth after the 1980s required. There was privatization and housing reform, but also some continuities. In particular, the system known as *hukou*, which had been introduced in the 1950s, continued (Wang 2004). It was a system of residential registration, which linked rights and services to place of residence. Its effect was to restrict the migration of poor people from the countryside to the urban areas. However the boom in urban low-skill jobs after the reforms made it necessary to tolerate such migration. Nevertheless, it was still difficult for the migrants to access housing, particularly through renting of public sector apartments (Huang, 2003). A key factor in overcoming these blockages has been the highly deregulated development process in what are officially rural areas beyond the urban boundary. Such supposedly rural 'villages' have been intensively developed and have been important sources of affordable accommodation for these 'unofficial' urban residents, as well as for industrial development (see Box 9.2).

Thus unregulated development (though regulated residence) along with informal provision has been the means of matching labour and housing during China's rapid growth through foreign direct investment. Are there forms of smart planning and regulation that operate under different development and governance conditions? One challenge for housing and planning systems is to ensure that there is an adequate supply of land in suitable locations, so that housing development can proceed to meet the needs of workers and their employers. However, planning systems can also be used in an exclusionary way, restricting housing provision. Interestingly, Bramley *et al.* (2004) found that in 'green belt' areas in Scotland, industrial development was more likely to be permitted than housing. In other words, the councils administering the planning policies were more willing to accommodate jobs and businesses than to ensure that housing demand was being met.

Hague (2007) reviewed the way that planning policies operate in Europe. He noted that 'the compact city and the containment of urban spread has been promoted on a pan-European scale and as a consciously European construct' (Hague, 2007: 20). However, he also noted significant national differences in planning policies and land policies. In Scandinavia, for example, strategic land use plans had allowed growth to take place in corridors. In Stockholm, for example, 'corridor planning has allowed Sweden's most important economic region to grow without sacrificing the environmental quality that makes it such an attraction to its highly skilled workforce' (Hague, 2007: 26). In contrast, plans that impose a 'green belt' around the edge of a city to prevent the settlement growing are likely to displace housing to locations that are distant from jobs and to make housing more expensive: see, for example, C. Hague (2005b) who showed such effects in Scotland around Edinburgh and Aberdeen. Furthermore, Hague noted that Ireland had experienced very strong growth in the 1990s and at the start of the twenty-first century, at a time when councils there operated a permissive approach to housing development that had resulted in sprawl. However, with hindsight, it is clear that there was massive over-provision of housing in Ireland as part of a speculative 'bubble' which burst in 2008.

Box 9.2: The Chinese model of housing migrant workers in 'urban villages'

In the 30 years since China's economic reforms began, Shenzhen grew from a small town near the border with Hong Kong into a metropolis of 8 million people. China's first Special Economic Zone (SEZ) was created there in 1980. Traditional villages in the Shenzhen area have changed from agricultural communities into 'urban villages' (*cheng zhong cun*) where, 'Due to their unique locations and the collective ownership of land (non-state ownership), cheaper private rental housing in those villages become the main source of accommodation for poor migrants' (Wang *et al.*, 2010: 84).

Within the SEZ, processing plants, industrial workshops and factories were rapidly developed by direct foreign investment from Hong Kong and elsewhere. Large numbers of migrants from throughout China arrived to get jobs. However, these rural migrants 'did not have the right to rent public housing or buy commercial housing. High housing prices and rents also prevented migrants from gaining access to new, properly built housing estates' (Wang *et al.*, 2009: 959).

→

Meanwhile, Asian 'development states' Hong Kong and Singapore have made substantial use of development of new towns as a means to accommodate urban growth and reduce overcrowding in older districts. The new settlements mainly comprise high rise apartment blocks which provide public rental and subsidized housing. In summary, planning and housing policies depend strongly on national legislation and institutions, but from an economic development perspective it is important that the system can ensure a supply of housing and house types in locations from which people can access jobs. Weak planning and regulation point to problems of oversupply, congestion and environmental damage. Overly restrictive planning – or housing systems that fail to provide housing for all – are likely to result in inefficiencies within regional and local labour markets.

International donor agencies such as the World Bank have been trying to promote owner-occupation since the 1980s. The

From 1979 to 1992, the municipal government concentrated on the development of new areas and local villages were left to find their own ways to adapt to the dramatically changing environment. 'Very limited planning control was applied in these villages. At the same time, the government gradually took land away from farmers, and, in response, farmers shifted their attention from food production to property renting' (Wang *et al.*, 2009: 959). Income from renting spare rooms to migrants was commonly invested in adding extra rooms, e.g. by building upwards. The homes of better-off families became multi-storey apartment blocks (Fig. 9.1). At intervals the government issued new regulations in an attempt to control the rampant development process. For example, in 1993 the amount of floor space that a household could construct was capped at 450sqm, but development continued unabated. As Wang and his colleagues (2010: 962) wryly observed, 'Households tried every trick to maximize building areas on their land. The reduced plot size pushed up the construction density and building height'. Then the government 'tried to reinforce the regulation by suspending approval for house building applications in the mid-1990s. As a result, unauthorized house building occurred on an unprecedented scale. All new buildings were over the legal size and height limit'. Some buildings reach 20 storeys. (Sources: Wang *et al.* (2009); Wang *et al.* (2010).)

theoretical case to support this stance was made in an influential book by de Soto (2000). In its simplest terms, de Soto's argument is that the poor have homes which are a potential asset that can be used to raise loans and facilitate business activity. However, in poor countries where much of the housing is 'informal' and 'illegal' the poor have no formal legal title to their home; this absence restricts their capacity to use their property as collateral. Their assets are 'dead' capital. De Soto argued that over a period of two centuries, property systems had improved in the West in ways that enabled capital to be made available for economic investment.

Like social enterprises that were discussed in Chapter 8, these arguments suggest that the way to lift people out of poverty is to use opportunities created by markets. Similarly, Social Compact (discussed in Box 8.4) used house values, among other 'hidden' assets, to boost investment in inner-city Detroit. However, when the US sub-prime mortgage market collapsed in 2008, precipitating a

crisis that would also severely damage the city's automobile industry, the price of some houses in Detroit plunged to less than $1,000.
Banks were left with thousands of vacant homes, which cost money
to maintain and keep secure, and for which there were virtually no
buyers. Clark (2008) quoted the example of a house that had sold
in 2001 for $88,000, but then had been sold again for only $33,500

Figure 9.1   **Residential development in Shenzhen**

in 2006. The new buyer was unable to keep up the mortgage repayments. The bank foreclosed the mortgage (one of over 37,000 foreclosures in Detroit in 2008 up to the end of September), and in October 2008 was trying to sell it at a 'rock-bottom price'. Half of the city's home sales in 2008 were for prices less than $10,000. Clark (2008: 6) quoted Robin Boyle, professor of urban planning at the local Wayne State University, as saying that Detroit had been a US leader in efforts to encourage home ownership amongst the poor through sub-prime mortgages.

Area regeneration and housing

Areas of run-down housing and mixed land uses are often a focus for local economic development interventions. However, there are sharp debates about the value of such 'place-based' approaches. Critics argue that public funds are better targeted at people rather than places. Crane and Manville (2008) summarized the positions. Supporters of 'people-based' approaches argue that most of the poor do not live in poor areas, and not everyone in a poor neighbourhood is poor. Thus area targeting is inefficient in its use of scarce resources. Furthermore if welfare support is somehow tied to the place of residence, there is a probability that the poor will remain in their area rather than seeking opportunities elsewhere. In addition, the main (though often unintended) beneficiaries of property-based approaches to area regeneration are usually landowners.

Thus Crane and Manville (2008: 3) posed the question: 'should we simply give poor people money or housing vouchers, or should we also, for example, locate new facilities in their neighbourhoods, or try to induce development where poor people live?' In answer they pointed out that there are 'spatial market failures' which result in neighbourhoods with 'underinvestment and inadequate provision of public spatial goods, including safety, education, transit, community identity, political networks and the spatial externalities of geographically linked labour and housing markets'. While individual poverty may be best tackled by benefits or vouchers, the case for a place-based approach is that targeting areas where poverty is concentrated can be an efficient option. If the rise in land values created through interventions can be clawed back to finance the programmes, this is again a benefit.

There are also environmental sustainability arguments in favour of area regeneration if the alternative is new build on greenfield land. Very often such areas have services in place that can be used more efficiently, avoiding the costs of new service and infrastructure provisions. Similarly, access to such areas is generally good: they may, for example be near the central business district. Economic development agencies are likely to view such areas as offering opportunities that can be unlocked by some imaginative interventions that can turn around the fortunes of the neighbourhood.

Tax Increment Financing (TIF) is a place-based area regeneration approach that has been widely used in the USA. Municipal authorities, often at the behest of local stakeholders, undertake a survey of local property conditions. The survey evaluates whether the property in the local area is blighted. A number of locally approved criteria are used in this assessment, such as levels of vacancy, age and physical condition of building structures, perceived obsolescence of properties and their usages, or lack of maintenance. However, identification and eradication of blight does not have to be the rationale for TIFs; municipalities can set other criteria depending on legislation passed by the US state in which they are located.

The property analysis typically concludes that an area would not develop 'but for' the financial assistance made available by designation as a TIF district. The municipal council then decides which lots and properties to include in the TIF district, and passes legislation designating the area as a TIF. Different locations vary the rules and regulations about what money can be spent on within a TIF and how long the TIF designation will last. For example, in the City of Chicago in Illinois, where TIFs have been allowed since 1977, around 160 TIF districts were in operation by 2010, each with a 23-year duration.

During the period of the TIF district's operation, property tax monies raised within the boundaries of the TIF district are divided between the municipality's general funds and a specific TIF fund, known as the increment, which goes exclusively into the particular TIF area. Some states mandate that TIF funds cannot be used for residential purposes, whereas other allow greater flexibility in spending. Commonly approved projects include infrastructural and physical maintenance of properties, rehabilitation of deteriorated facilities, surveys and site studies to encourage relocation or expansion of businesses, job training, small business grants and loans, financing costs, and so forth. Often a municipality will use TIF funds to purchase property for subsequent resale. Money is also commonly spent on streetscaping and other beautification projects, repair of sewers and other infrastructural maintenance, provision of green space and other investments perceived to be in the public good that will subsequently encourage private economic developers to invest within the TIF.

Over the duration of the TIF, the amount of money directed into the municipality's general funds stays the same. This is usually stipulated as a dollar amount equitable to the level of property taxes being collected at the moment of TIF designation rather than as a percentage of tax revenues. As a result, increases in property tax revenues accumulate in the increment over the duration of the TIF while the amount of money being directed into the municipality's general funds remains unchanged. However, designation does not necessarily mean that tax money will accumulate in the increment. If the TIF is successful and the increment builds as businesses prosper, land values increase and property taxes are raised, then that money, which would otherwise not have been generated, is reinvested in the locale stimulating further economic development.

As TIFs are used throughout the USA, arguably they aid large national chains rather than locally owned businesses. A major company such as Walmart is familiar with TIFs and has the resources to apply for TIF subsidies in numerous municipalities. They may be able to apply for TIF financing in one location, freeing up internal finances to invest elsewhere. A small, independent business owner, by contrast, may not be able to access increment funds as regularly, as easily, or to offset costs incurred elsewhere. In one case in Addison, Illinois, discussed in Box 9.3, this property-led approach was found to have deliberately targeted low-income households, leading to demolitions and displacement.

Another major US programme sought to combine place-based and people-based approaches. Housing Opportunities for People Everywhere (HOPE) aimed to transform deprived neighbourhoods into mixed income neighbourhoods. It recognized that that place can compound the poverty experienced by individuals. If people who are out of work live in a neighbourhood where many others are also out of work, then they are likely to be cut off from the kind of informal networks (and perhaps even formal ones too) which can help in finding a job. Similarly, employers may be reluctant to hire people who come 'from a bad address'. Local schools are also likely to suffer from a poor reputation, and crime can thrive in the vacuum left by legal means

Box 9.3: A TIF displacing low-income housing in Addison, Illinois (USA)

Addison, Illinois, is a municipality of approximately 36,000 residents, about 75% of whom are white. It is in the suburban commuter belt just over 20 miles west of Chicago. In 1994, Addison designated two TIF districts in residential areas. At the time, both locations were undergoing demographic change as the white population declined and the Hispanic population increased. A report from a local consultancy identified the two locations as suffering from conditions of blight. Addison's officials designated the TIF districts and began condemning property. Over 30 buildings were demolished and city authorities began acquiring parcels of land for future redevelopment.

However, local residents challenged the TIF designation under the 1968 Fair Housing Act. They argued that the municipality had targeted the areas for TIF designation because of the Hispanic residents, and that many of the criteria for determining blight, such as physically deteriorating property, overcrowding and insufficient parking, were assessed on the basis of white Americans' suburban lifestyles rather than any quantitative measurement.

Furthermore, it transpired that in other locations in Addison, those which were predominantly occupied by whites, 'Some of the [property maintenance] code infractions that made these areas eligible for TIF designation were interpreted only as minor code violations, such as repairing a hole in a [window] screen, painting rust spots on an awning, removing dust on window sills, replacing toilet paper roll holders, repairing cracks in linoleum floors, and removing stains from porcelain bathroom fixtures' (Reingold, 2001: 227).

Similarly, disputants demonstrated that the shortfall in parking availability was partly the result of a designation five years previously that prevented on-street parking between 2 a.m. and 5 a.m. The dispute was settled out of court with the US Department of Justice fining Addison around $25m. and demanding that the municipality compensate residents who had been displaced by the demolitions. The municipality was also required to replace the housing that had been demolished and provide more car parking facilities. (Source: Reingold (2001).)

of gaining income and esteem. After reviewing such factors, Berube (2005: 2) summarized that the research literature showed that 'area-based interventions must produce real changes in neighbourhood conditions to improve residents' life chances significantly'.

Such thinking on the need to de-concentrate the housing of the poor to improve their job and educational prospects underpinned the HOPE VI, the sixth iteration of the programme, which was launched in 1992. The overall goal was revitalization of public housing in three areas: physical improvements, management improvements and social and community services to address resident needs (HUD, 2008). The basic premise was that 'introducing a social and economic mix of people to a poor area can tackle severe and long-standing concentrations of deprivation' (Gardiner, 2006: 20). It was a two-pronged strategy: some of the poor were to be helped to relocate to middle-income neighbourhoods and new, mixed-income housing would replace the old public housing. HOPE VI sought to move public housing away from being seen as segregated, isolated projects housing only the very poor (primarily African-American women and children) so that being in public housing had itself become a barrier to upward mobility. Further, by redeveloping the worst public housing, HOPE VI intended to ameliorate conditions in their adjoining neighbourhoods. These areas, 'though typically less poor than the public housing, still had very high rates of poverty, unemployment, high school dropouts, crime, and other social ills, few services or stores, and even fewer jobs' (Popkin *et al.*, 2004: 7).

HOPE VI was well funded with $5.8bn (Gardiner, 2006). The money was allocated as grants to individual Public Housing Authorities (PHAs), which are city-level institutions. Fundamentally, HOPE VI was structured to encourage PHAs to shift their role from housing owner and manager to facilitator of housing opportunities. PHAs were required at least to partially outsource to private agencies such functions as security, management and ownership of housing. Under HOPE VI, PHAs sought to lever investment funds from private housing developers to merge with US Department of Housing and Urban Development (HUD) grant funds. For-profit management schemes were assumed to be more efficient. One of the first HOPE VI projects to be approved and implemented was at Centennial Place in Atlanta, Georgia. It is explained in Box 9.4.

From an economic development perspective, some of the statistics associated with HOPE VI look impressive, persuading the

---

Box 9.4: A Hope VI project – Centennial Place, Atlanta, Georgia (USA)

Centennial Place arose on the site of the former Techwood Homes public housing project which had been built near the Georgia Institute of Technology in 1937. Centennial Place exemplifies many of the goals of HOPE VI in that it was a joint venture of public HUD funds, federal and state tax credits, and private developer funds. Techwood's original 1,195 units of public housing were demolished and replaced by 900 units of mixed-income housing that included 40% market rent units, 40%public housing and 20% tax credit units (these are available to people with low incomes that are above the threshold that would qualify them for public housing). Centennial Place is 'New Urbanist' in style, with townhouses and garden apartments featuring New Urbanism's signature front porches as well as an overall plan emphasizing green spaces and 'walkability' (Congress for the New Urbanism, 2009; Grant, 2006).

The development reflects HOPE VI principles of encouraging resident self-sufficiency and discouraging isolation of the very poor by requiring all residents to be either employed or in job training, and by its mixed-income status.

---

government in England to develop its own version of the programme in 2005, which it called the Mixed Communities Initiative. Between 1990 and 2000 unemployment fell by 10 per cent in HOPE VI neighbourhoods, and average local incomes rose two-thirds faster than the town or city averages (Gardiner, 2006: 20). However, the fall in unemployment was because new residents, more likely to be in jobs, now live in the mixed-income housing that replaced public housing in these neighbourhoods.

The 'people-based' part of the programme allowed actual homes to be replaced by 'Housing Choice vouchers'. These provide rent assistance from the PHA for former public housing occupants to use in the private rental market. However, Gardiner (2006: 21) quoted research by Popkin *et al.* (2004) that found that only 10 per cent of residents who were moved so that their estates could be demolished had found new HOPE VI homes, and that the figure will never rise over 30 per cent. This failure of new developments to adequately house former residents, even with their vouchers, is one of the most serious criticisms of the programme. Since not all rental units accept Housing Choice vouchers, former estate residents have difficulty finding housing, and often must search over a wide area. Again markets were shown not to operate on purely rational economic criteria but to be fashioned by social and cultural presumptions. This scattering does disperse the poor, which is one of the aims of the programme, but it also fractures social networks. Notwithstanding the criticisms of HOPE VI, Popkin *et al.* (2004: 3) were of the view that:

> There is no question that the program has had some notable accomplishments. Hundreds of profoundly distressed developments have been targeted for demolition, and many of them are now replaced with well-designed, high-quality housing serving a mix of income levels. HOPE VI has been an incubator for innovations in project financing, management, and service delivery. Some projects have helped turn around conditions in the surrounding neighbourhoods and have contributed to the revitalization of whole inner-city communities.

Thus HOPE VI can be interpreted as a successful programme of area regeneration, creating a phoenix-like revival in some very depressed neighbourhoods, and levering in private capital and know-how, through a project-based approach to governance. However, changing a neighbourhood is not the same as changing the economic prospects of the people who used to live there. The real test of a programme such as HOPE VI should be the impact it has on the livelihoods of the poor: do they move into better housing and get jobs – or are the single mothers and their children simply 'de-housed', left with vouchers that they cannot use and cut off from their established social networks from which they drew support? Bennett *et al.* (2006), for example, question HOPE VI in Chicago on these grounds.

Housing and poverty reduction

Housing is a major problem for poor people. Not only is housing difficult to afford, access and maintain, but lack of housing can be a barrier to access employment. Furthermore, people who lack a house, or who have shelter but no formal address, are unlikely to be contributing to local taxes. Fiscally weak municipal councils then struggle to deliver services or to provide effective conditions for local economic development, so the cycle is perpetuated. Furthermore, the poor are often excluded from discussions about their housing, as the example of HOPE VI shows. However, better housing for the poor can be a means to boost a local economy and increase participation in labour markets; and savings and investment schemes can have local economic benefits.

How can a local economic development initiative help both private investors and the poor seeking housing? In Mumbai, India, local and international NGOs and the World Bank successfully collaborated to fund the Oshiwara housing scheme to assist poor people (see Box 9.5). The Oshiwara experience shows that very poor people can improve their housing conditions and create economic opportunities. The key is in the skills of the agencies and the way they build confidence and manage risk. For example, in the Oshiwara case, the confidence of the World Bank and the credibility of the organizations with which it dealt, was an important building block. Similarly, the private landowners knew the Indian Alliance could deliver things they wanted but could not achieve themselves. The involvement of the bank in the second phase of the project was because the bank had seen the success of the first phase, and because of its confidence in the guarantees provided by Homeless International.

The Oshiwara example also demonstrates how housing can be linked to jobs and skills development, so that there are economic development gains and not just better houses at the end of the process. By getting rehoused the poor were also creating income-generating opportunities. As with all these examples, the case is unique and specific factors and institutions were vital to the outcome – for example the Indian Alliance is a very able, experienced and well-connected institution. However, the opportunistic, experimental and holistic way of thinking that was evident in the Oshiwara case is the essence of what is needed to create economic opportunities in challenging situations.

Economic development and education

Poverty is a multifaceted problem, and low incomes are likely to be associated with other forms of deprivation. As we saw above, this insight is at the heart of the debates about the relative merits of people-based and place-based approaches. Of all the public goods that go with residence in a particular neighbourhood, education

Box 9.5: Involving the private sector in rehousing slum dwellers: the Oshiwara housing scheme, Mumbai (India)

The Oshiwara housing scheme in Mumbai involves the private sector in a number of ways in resettling poor families. The intention is to house over 3,000 families over two phases. The key to the project is the work of the Indian Alliance, which is an umbrella body linking three major NGOs representing the poor (the National Slum Dwellers Federation, the Society for the Promotion of Area Resource Centres and a network of women's collectives called Mahila Milan).

Private landowners approached the Indian Alliance seeking help in developing their land. The Alliance had experience and expertise that the owners lacked when it came to dealing with resettlement. The Alliance also knew their way through the government bureaucracy that structures the design and implementation of such a project. Also the Alliance could access World Bank subsidies. The World Bank's Mumbai Urban Infrastructure Project provides subsidies – in the form of development rights that can be sold in the open market – to the landowner giving their land for resettlement and to the developer. Therefore a partnership with the Alliance made commercial sense.

The Alliance negotiated with private contractors and employed them on parts of the housing scheme. Ten private contractors provided pre-financing for 30% of the project cost. The Alliance also negotiated contracts that a proportion of labour or subcontracting had to be drawn from local slum communities. The contracts also required development to standards approved by slum communities during previous projects.

There was also involvement of commercial banks. One of the largest banks in India agreed to invest £2.4m. into the second phase of the work. Homeless International, a UK-based NGO, guaranteed the loan.

In both phases of the development a small percentage of the houses were sold on the open market. This provided an element of cross-subsidy to the slum dwellers, and added to the private sector involvement. (Source: McLeod and Hughes (2006).)

is probably the most important, since it impacts on the next generation. Since schools in poor neighbourhoods are often seen to be poor, education is a major challenge for intergenerational equity. One innovative, and increasingly influential, US effort to transform the educational opportunities of low income groups is the Harlem Children's Zone (HCZ), a bottom-up, third sector approach, which is summarized in Box 9.6.

Although a non-profit organization, HCZ is incorporated. Its moniker is a registered trade mark, and it operates more like a business than a charity, planning corporate style development strategies with strict targets and demands for accountability (Tough 2004, 2008). HCZ programme proposals come complete with economic impact assessments, sophisticated financial analyses and overview from staff in a managerial hierarchy (Colby *et al.*, 2004). This links back to discussion in Chapter 8 about social enterprises and their mode of operation across traditional market–social purpose dualisms.

Schools are vital community institutions, though their importance is often not recognized in economic development work. The quality of schools is likely to influence the decisions of parents about

---

Box 9.6: Harlem Children's Zone, New York City (USA)

Founded in 1997 and covering around 100 blocks, Harlem Children's Zone (HCZ) is a geographically targeted development programme that serves over 7,500 of New York City's most disadvantaged children. With plans to reach 15,000 children and 7,000 adults by 2011, the 'Harlem Children's Zone Project is a community-building strategy ... that is intended to improve the health and well-being' of residents in Harlem (Nicholas *et al.*, 2005: 245).

HCZ was conceived to improve the health and life opportunities for the children of those families still struggling in Harlem as the area gentrified in the 1990s. It was designed to generate economic opportunities for the community and educational and medical benefits for local children.

Harlem has a poverty rate of around 40%. The Harlem Children's Zone (2008) makes it clear that poverty is an economic development issue: 'Poverty now costs the U.S. about 4% of its gross domestic product annually in lost production, decreased economic output, and increased social expenditures. As today's poor children enter tomorrow's workplace, under-educated and ill-prepared, the cost

→

where to live. Recent assessments of school reorganization in Atlanta (Hankins, 2007) and Chicago (Lipman and Haines, 2007) suggest that the state provision of public education is becoming a tool in area regeneration approaches to economic development. One of HCZ's major efforts was to provide improved schools for local children. This led to criticism as HCZ chose to establish charter schools. These are privately operated, but retain public funding, and bypass teachers' unions to offer higher, performance-related, wages to non-union teachers, albeit with lower job security. In Harlem, the selection process that placed children in the charter schools was challenged by parents, particularly as waiting lists grew (Tough, 2004).

Programmes like charter schools have begun to replace traditional public schools in many US urban areas. In US cities, declining state financing and disinvestment created notorious public school

---

to America's future competitiveness in the world marketplace is incalculable'.

The HCZ approach to local development and tackling poverty, 'sidestep[s] the macroeconomic solutions ... better wages, a national jobs program, a bigger earned income tax credit' and instead focuses on local-scale programmes with a direct and measurable impact, such as developing tutoring programmes to improve reading skills and giving children access to pre-school education (Tough, 2004: 44). Recruitment has often been through door-knocking, visiting laundromats and grocery stores to access people typically overlooked by traditional development programmes. Parents who enrol children are eligible to win prizes such as store gift certificates or rent payments (Tough, 2004).

HCZ operates a community centre, charter school, affordable housing, after-school tutoring, children's music classes, anti-obesity clinics and parenting classes (Tough, 2004, 2008). It employs over 650 people and has the vision of integrating a holistic network of support for people, providing 'medical, educational, environmental, social, and legal' services from birth until college-age (Nicholas *et al.*, 2005: 246). The operating budget for 2005 was $36.3m. and by 2009 was $40m., much of it raised from philanthropic donations, and largely spent on education, supplementing public school programmes and operations (Pines, 2005).

systems that cater overwhelmingly to low-income households. Middle- and upper-class students, via their parental choice, opt out and attend private schools. The provision of new public–private charter schools, or similar institutions such as renovated 'small' schools and college preparatory academies, has become a tool of urban economic development. Neighbourhoods can be targeted for growth in land values and promotion of real estate interests by locating a new school therein. Area regeneration and property speculation can be steered by determining the location of new schools, or recent gentrification and investments secured by opening new public–private schools. For example, proponents argue that Chicago's *Renaissance 2010* plan to transform public schooling boosts options and opportunities for the city's children, and deny that the pattern of school closings and openings will promote gentrification. In contrast, critics such as Lipman and Haines (2007) maintain the policy is part of wider efforts to remake Chicago as an investment-friendly 'global city'. Their critique is summarized in Box 9.7.

Summary

While housing and schools may not be seen as mainstream economic development issues, this chapter has shown their importance in a variety of contexts. Again it has been possible to draw a distinction between different approaches, based on the typologies that were created in Chapters 1 and 4. However, the discussion and examples have pointed to some differences in approach that reflect local situations and institutions. Thus China, Hong Kong and Singapore all chased inward investment as development states, yet the highly regulated situation in the latter two, with strong government housing agencies providing much of the housing, contrasts with the unregulated and seemingly 'unregulatable' entrepreneurialism of China's farmers who built 20-storey housing blocks for new rural migrants.

Another important theme in this chapter is the strength and weaknesses of people-based versus property-based approaches. The major US programmes TIF and HOPE VI have been used to exemplify these debates, though there are similar initiatives in other countries that could be interrogated in similar fashion. These approaches stand in contrast to the bottom-up and inclusive

Box 9.7: Schools as a tool of local economic development: Chicago's Renaissance 2010 programme (USA)

In 2004 Chicago adopted *Renaissance 2010*, a plan to close 'failing' schools and open new ones. The proposal was formulated in 2003 by the long-standing business lobby the Commercial Club of Chicago. Corporate stakeholders in the city immediately offered $50m. to aid the implementation of *Renaissance 2010* (Lipman and Haines, 2007).

Given two weeks' notice that they would close in early 2004, 20 of the first 22 schools targeted by *Renaissance 2010* were in neighbourhoods with large African-American majorities in the southern part of the city, most notably the historically significant area known as Bronzeville (Lipman and Haines, 2007). Concerned local people asserted at public hearings that such measures would accelerate increases in house prices and displacement of area residents. Subsequent patterns of school closures suggested that areas most impacted were ones in which house sales and real estate development had been most marked in the first few years of the twenty-first century. One African-American neighbourhood on the western edge of Chicago, North Lawndale, was targeted for *Renaissance 2010* school restructuring. In this location, 'described in real estate sections of local newspapers as a "hot" area … [recent investments included] a 1,200-unit residential development … a 300-unit residential development with houses selling for $250,000 to $600,000, a new shopping center, and a $47 million film center' (Lipman and Haines, 2007: 488). Many of the school closings are in African-American and Latino areas where public housing projects have been demolished and former tenants relocated, often many miles away.

In their place come new and rehabilitated high-price houses and the new *Renaissance 2010* schools. One teacher described the programme in the local newspaper, the *Chicago Tribune*: 'It's becoming increasingly clear that this is not an education plan, it is a business plan. It is a real estate developer plan that has nothing to do with education' (Sadovi, 2009: 13). (Source: Lipman and Haines (2007).)

initiative in Mumbai (Box 9.5) led by an NGO. Similarly the example of the Harlem Children's Zone (Box 9.6) again demonstrates the capacity for a form of local economic development that combines social concerns with business acumen, a theme emphasized in discussion of social enterprises and the social economy in the previous chapter.

In the end the fundamental point for regional and local economic development is that land and housing need to be made available to accommodate workers whose labour will sustain and develop the economy. However, land and location are often fiercely contested, and forced relocation of existing residents or homeless people raises deep ethical questions. Economic development agencies need to ensure that planning authorities are aware of the full range of housing needs that land allocations in plans should accommodate. It is also important to link housing of the poor to skills development and job creation, and to see housing development and upgrading as an economic opportunity.

Topics for discussion

Discuss the proposition that 'The experiences of urban villages in China can be useful to policymakers in other fast urbanizing regions' (Wang, Wang and Wu, 2009: 970).

Debate the case for and against place-based approaches to economic development.

Related reading

Y. P. Wang, Y. Wang and J. Wu (2009) 'Urbanisation and Informal Development in China', *International Journal of Urban and Regional Research*, 33(4), 957–73.

Y. P. Wang, Y. Wang and J. Wu (2010) 'Housing Migrant Workers in Rapidly Urbanizing Regions: A Study of the Chinese Model in Shenzhen', *Housing Studies*, 25(1), 83–100.

R. Crane and M. Manville (2008) 'People or Place? Revisiting the Who Versus the Where of Urban Development', *Land Lines*, 20(3), 2–7.

In places across the USA and around the world, there have been debates over the impacts of the world's largest retailer, Walmart, on economic development. Opponents of the 'big box' store argue that jobs are low-paying, offer poor health care and pension bene- fits and are rarely full-time, while the store displaces other retail options (Lichtenstein, 2009). Also, Walmart's large-scale and low- cost offerings push greater efficiency, and often job losses, up its supply chain, so that new jobs in retail may be offset by losses elsewhere (Fishman, 2003).

However, retailing can help people who have been unemployed get jobs. At Meadowhall, a large shopping centre in Sheffield, Eng- land, The Source is an innovative £5.5m. training and development centre that opened in 2003 as a partnership between British Land (a developer) and Sheffield City Council. By 2006, over 500 people had received job-skills training, with most attendees being from groups such as the long-term unemployed, those affected by homelessness, former drug users, ex-offenders, single parents and people with autism (King Sturge/Business in the Community, 2006). The Source wants Meadowhall's retailers to offer their staff the opportunity to under- take accredited vocational training, and also offers first aid courses, health and safety training, technology courses and apprenticeships.

Crucially, The Source is not a bolt-on training project but it is an integral part of the shopping centre itself. The manager of the shop- ping centre is involved in the operations of The Source and similarly the manager of The Source is a part of the overall management team of the centre. A similar organization, Working Links, runs a simu- lated shop in Middlesbrough, another English town with high levels of deprivation. The 'shop' has tills and stock where unemployed people can gain experience through role play. In this way they learn about customer service, handling cash, maximizing sales, awkward customers and working within the bounds of legislation such as that which restricts the sales of goods such as alcohol and tobacco prod- ucts to young people. Because the trainers are working with people whose confidence is often low, they give one-to-one attention and only work with six people at a time (Macdonald, 2006: 25).

Retailing is also a sector which the self-employed can enter rel- atively easily. Though getting suitable premises is a hurdle, street traders or other entrepreneurial types can often find ways to get round such problems. As the former Soviet bloc unravelled in the early 1990s, for example, street trading was an important first step in creating a market economy. Box 10.1 provides a vignette of what happened in St Petersburg: similar stories could be told of the underpasses and entrances to metro stations in many of the larger cities.

Street markets, some more formal than others, are important places for small retailers to do business. They add colour and life to the street, potentially a 'spillover' benefit, though the congestion they generate can be a problem. Informal trading can be a particularly important means of access to income for women. The NGO called Women in Informal Employment: Globalizing and Organizing (WIEGO, 2009) works to improve the status of the working poor, and especially women, in the informal economy. It has helped to form a global alliance of street vendor organizations, called StreetNet International.

However, there are frequently tensions around regulation of street trading and informal markets. While money laundering can be undertaken more easily in informal markets than under more formal business conditions, the main rationale for crackdowns on traders is often about restoring amenity and making the city tidy. Hansen (2002: 62) reported on the experience in Lusaka, Zambia, where street vending had 'achieved anarchic proportions' by 1998, turning much of the city into 'one huge outdoor shopping mall where thousands of street vendors were selling all manner of goods'. There were problems not only of traffic congestion, but also of public health and thieving. Companies began to relocate from downtown to escape the chaos. In 1999, the authorities launched pre-dawn raids that demolished the informal market structures and removed more than 2000 street vendors from their place of business. A new, purpose-built, city market had been open, but largely vacant, for two years. Furthermore, said Hansen, the government was encouraging international investors to develop new shopping malls in and around Lusaka's city centre.

Though informal trading is important to local livelihoods, approaches to economic development that prioritize attraction of significant foreign investment may seek to remove such 'disorderly' forms of economic activity. However, there are other ways of tackling the problems. A 'smart' approach to regulation involves working sympathetically with the traders while ensuring that basic standards of environmental health, for example, are met, and there is fair access to stalls in return for a fair rent if the stall is on public property (rather than rental income leaking to the criminal end of the

Box 10.1: A new economy: kiosks in St Petersburg (Russia)

Following the collapse of the Soviet Union in 1991, local economic development in St Petersburg saw the emergence of a proto-capitalist trading network, built around almost 10,000 commercial retail kiosks. '[M]obile, ephemeral, small-scale [and] low-cost', kiosks were typically set up on sidewalks by their proprietors. Locations next to public transportation hubs were particularly prized, with an average of 2.5–3 kiosks serving every one thousand commuters (Axenov *et al.*, 1997: 420). These informal retail venues were, 'tolerate[d]' by local authorities and 'largely unregulated by the state' (Axenov *et al.*, 1997: 421). Commodities sold at St Petersburg's kiosks in the mid-1990s varied from soft drinks and imported consumer goods, to alcohol, tobacco, cleaning products and other everyday necessities such as food and clothing. Local entrepreneurs owned and operated kiosks, often supplying wholesale goods to other kiosk vendors. With official statistics unavailable, Axenov *et al.* (1997) estimate that kiosks, and their associated businesses such as transportation and importing, may have employed up to 90,000 people in St Petersburg in the mid-1990s.

Acting like businesses in a more formal capitalist economy, over the course of the decade kiosks began to agglomerate and became major retail destinations for customers. As the Russian institutions began to stabilize, 'mini-marts' were developed to replace the informal economy of the kiosks: 'The municipal authorities [would] dictate the removal of all the kiosks [in an area, such as a block] and grant the right to [a] private developer to construct commercial pavilions or other fixed-space trading facilities [on] the site' (Axenov *et al.*, 1997: 429). Initially, however, these mini-marts were less popular than kiosks. Although they provided more permanence, customers faced queues, and mini-mart retailers were fixed in place and unable to move, as the kiosks did, to find a new clientele. The mini-marts were also helpless in the face of new kiosks locating alongside and out-competing them.

By 1995, more formal shops were beginning to challenge the kiosks, as were regulations against money laundering. Efforts to streetscape and modernize St Petersburg also put pressure on the kiosks, but they persisted into the twenty-first century. In June 2006, however, in a measure ostensibly to prevent the sale of counterfeit goods, particularly CDs and DVDs, the governor of St Petersburg ordered all kiosks at Metro stations to close (Dranitsyna, 2006).

informal economy spectrum). In Port of Spain, Trinidad, a successful scheme along these lines has been implemented in Charlotte Street, a busy downtown thoroughfare. It kept traders in business and maintained the popularity of the street as a market on certain days, while also reducing the traffic gridlock that had been a problem.

Edge-city retailing: a challenge for smart planning and regulation?

The form and location of retail development is responsive to market demand and new development is usually planned and undertaken by developers sensitive to expectations of their tenants, shareholders and bankers. The shopping mall was invented in the USA in the mid-1950s. The mall idea succeeded because 'sales breed sales'. In other words, there are agglomeration benefits to traders who are located close to other traders. Put simply, shoppers come to look, stop and have a coffee, see other shops, and buy some more goods. In a very large mall, a developer will break the line of sight so that customers do not actually get to see how far they need to walk to access all the shops. Landscaping, seats, piped music, maybe even live entertainment are provided to keep the shoppers there. Friedberg (2002: 444) described a mall as a 'selling machine' adding the observation that many are now 'mini-theme parks'.

Malls typically require large sites (with relatively low land costs) and good accessibility. Flat sites are preferred that have high visibility from highways. Part of a mall's offer to shoppers is that it is easy to reach, usually by car, so that it is relatively convenient to take away large volumes of purchases. Such sites are most likely to be found at the edge of a city, preferably close to a highway network that gives the mall a large potential catchment area for shoppers. Similar considerations apply with respect to retail parks where a number of medium or large shopping units typically are built around an extensive car parking area. Malls are private spaces that usually close at night and employ security guards during opening hours to exclude people who are seen as detrimental to the shopping experience of mainstream clients. Such practices have been widely criticized by academics, but defended by developers and traders as a means of protecting their assets.

Developers seeking to create new shopping centres often stress the economic benefits they will bring to the area. There can be no disputing the fact that such centres are major employment nodes, and also support associated jobs, e.g. in deliveries, advertising in local newspapers, etc. However, they also create competition to other traders in the region, and this may mean some loss of jobs and create vacant property. Against that, supporters of such centres argue correctly that they are likely to bring new trade into the area – i.e. they enhance the competitive position of the area where they locate vis-à-vis adjacent authorities. At the same time they aim to offer lower prices, which in aggregate will have the effect of boosting disposable income within a local economy.

A key part of the economic development benefits of major shopping malls is that they usually trigger other forms of development nearby, notably offices and business parks. Garreau (1991: 4) described how shopping moved out of US cities in the 1960s and 1970s, a phenomenon he called 'the malling of America', though he also argued that the decentralization dynamic is about much more than retailing. Business and households aspire to be out of town, and in the USA, and other countries where land is plentiful, that is where they have gone. The single-family detached home, the atrium in the new corporate headquarters, the shopping malls, the jogging tracks and the freeways are the components of this emergent townscape. Garreau (1991: 4) coined the phrase 'Edge Cities' to describe them. They have all the functions that a city had but they are much more spread out. To Garreau, a confident embrace of the edge-city phenomenon is the best medicine for those who would foster local economic development. However, there is a counter-argument that such places typically make people car dependent, and thus are not efficient in terms of energy or environmentally-friendly. Nevertheless, the mall phenomenon has now colonized much of the world and the start of the twenty-first century saw a major boom in shopping mall development in India, such as those described in Box 10.2. In part this was a response to a growing middle-class that was becoming more consumerist. However, it also represented a shift in the way that retail developers operated. The results have been a scale of investment that has fuelled regional and local economies.

Developments such as R-Mall in the Mulund suburb of Mumbai have become important sales outlets for manufacturing companies that have themselves been expanding rapidly. Marketing is vital to the success of any business, and the sales environment of the malls can offer competitive advantages to companies able to trade from there. Similarly, the global brands seeking to trade in unfamiliar

Box 10.2: The mall boom in India

Gurgaon was a suburb of New Delhi, which quickly became the 'shopping mall capital of India' in the space of a couple of years. Each mall in Gurgaon is about 300,000 sq. ft. in size, with the anchor stores typically between 60,000–80,000 sq. ft. The City Center Mall on Mahatma Gandhi Road has become a place to go for eating out, shopping and cinema. The Metropolitan Mall has a multiplex cinema theatre, underground parking and a food court.

In Mumbai, 25 malls were under construction in 2004, with US$87m. invested. The anchors in the Mumbai malls already trading were US and European chains such as McDonald's, Lacoste, Pizza Hut, Benetton, Subway, Marks & Spencer and Mango. However, it is important to note that their success had 'spawned the emergence of successful Indian chains such as Pantaloon, Globus, Shoppers Stop, Giant, Lifestyle and Big Bazaar ... Foreign mall operators cannot enter India as foreign companies are not allowed to own real estate in India. Companies like Nike, McDonalds [*sic*] and Reebok sell at mall outlets through their Indian subsidiaries or franchisees' (Bist, 2004).

Bist further noted that Indian malls were following a process of segmentation, 'each trying to project a particular environment, a specific image. In Mumbai, for instance, is Crossroads, the country's first mall (opened in 1999), a chic, ultra-modern collective of international brands including Swarovski, Lacoste, Tag Heuer and Marks & Spencer and eat-outs such as Pizza Hut, Subway and McDonalds [*sic*]. At the other extreme is R-Mall in suburban Mulund, proudly displaying homegrown retail labels such as Big Bazaar (household items), Hakoba (ladies' wear), Planet M (music), Food Bazaar (groceries), Weekender Kids (children's wear) and Pantaloon (men's readymades)'. (Source: Bist (2004).)

markets are likely to be reassured by their familiarity with malls as outlets. However, Bist (2004) rightly sounded a note of caution, stressing the risks of oversupply of malls as developers rushed to build. In the USA, for example, many first-generation malls now stand empty and when 'big box' retailers such as Walmart or Home Depot have moved elsewhere, they have left behind large, vacant premises that other retailers find unusable. Successful shopping malls need to have a good location and to get the infrastructure right – transport, water and electricity. Malls are large consumers of water and energy and, in situations where supplies of either are scarce or unpredictable, there will be problems, though some of these can be avoided, for example, by malls having their own electricity generators.

Oversupply and obsolescence as new competitors enter the market are likely to occur in situations where there is little attempt to challenge a market-led development process. There are also concerns that edge-city retail development is problematic on environmental and social grounds. If car use is essential to access the centre, then this will contribute to CO_2 emissions, while also excluding non-car users from using the centre and possibly putting shops out of business that such groups can reach. Thus smart planning and regulation approaches seek to work with the market but steer developers towards what are seen as more sustainable solutions. Graz, Austria, offers one example of just such an integrated planning approach. When the private company that owned the Murpark shopping centre wanted to expand, it worked with city officials to develop a mobility management strategy to ensure that the expanded centre was easily accessible by public buses and a city tram line. As the larger centre necessitated changing the existing zoning plan of Graz, the city made permission to develop conditional on providing a sustainable transportation infrastructure (Kampus, 2008). In addition to the public transit provisions, a direct link to a nearby motorway and a park-and-ride cardeck with around 500 parking places were also constructed and, to further reduce car usage, the cost for parking a car at the Murpark shopping centre includes one day's use of Graz's entire public transportation network.

Sustaining city-centre retailing

Sustaining city-centre retailing in the face of edge-city development is a typical aim of planning that looks to encourage use of public transport for environmental and social reasons. Similarly, revitalization of a town centre as a shopping destination may be an important part of an area regeneration strategy. Retail areas that were developed before the second half of the twentieth century may not be able to offer ample car parking adjacent to the shops, while the size and layout of older shopping units may make them ill-suited to modern retailing methods. Access for delivery vehicles may also be physically difficult or restricted to certain hours by regulators seeking to avoid congestion. As retailing has moved to a 'just in time' system, so as to optimize the use of floorspace and storage, and to ensure products are fresh, these problems have become more significant.

Such problems can afflict a town centre as a whole and undermine its competitive position. A drab and depressed town centre projects a negative image that is unlikely to attract investors. While retailing is not the only use in a town centre, it is a definitive use. Two terms are used to assess the health of town centre retail. Vitality is a measure of how busy a centre is at different times and in different parts. Viability measures a centre's capacity to attract ongoing investment for maintenance, improvement and development (Department of the Environment, 1994).

Monitoring can be done in various ways, depending on the resources available and the local situation. At the most basic level, it is useful and easy to monitor shop vacancies (preferably disaggregating into types of unit and, ideally, floorspace). Simply talking with, and listening to, retailers can also be a valuable means of collecting information about trends, challenges and opportunities. Analysis of the composition of the local retailing sector is also important, particularly if this is done in a comparative way with similar places within a region or nation. For example, is the town over-represented or underrepresented in various sectors such as sports goods or bridal shops, and if so are there gaps in the market that potential entrepreneurs or investors could fill?

The physical aspects of a shopping area are also easy to monitor, and should also be a focus for maintenance and improvement. For example, how accessible are the shops by different modes of transport – walking, public transport or cars and delivery vehicles? Are car-parking restrictions or charges likely to deter shoppers? For example, in town centres parking regimes that allow commuters to arrive before the shops open, park their cars for the day and then leave in the evening may put pressure on spaces for shoppers. Thus, in a congested centre, a 'no parking restrictions' regime is unlikely to aid shops and shoppers, especially during the working week. Similarly, though shopkeepers tend to want drivers to be able to ride past their shop and make a purchase, in general pedestrianized shopping environments are likely to be preferred by consumers, as long as they are well designed, easily accessed and have attractive shops. In this vein, the quality of street furniture, paving and lighting are all part of the shopping environment that can be monitored.

Retro-fitting new retailing uses into an existing town centre building or even a gap site is a challenging task. It requires refurbishment and restorations of buildings for new uses, and imaginative developments to accommodate cars and new retail floorspace. One of the main difficulties is often assembling a site. A patchwork pattern of land ownership in a developed town centre can make it difficult to put together enough land, with the right relations between the different parcels. In these circumstances, public authorities may exercise powers of eminent domain (see Chapter 5), and enter a partnership with a commercial developer. The returns are that a prime city-centre site offers the prospect of a very wide catchment and a huge number of potential shoppers passing through. High-quality downtown malls can also help to sustain the quality of the city centre as a whole as a shopping venue, in the face of scompetition for out-of-town malls.

One reason why town centres struggle to compete with out-of-town malls is because a mall will have a single owner able to ensure a uniform quality, and to target provision of extra attractions (e.g. performers or themed areas) which create positive externalities for traders. The management of a mall is unified. In contrast, an integrated approach to management and marketing is harder in a traditional town centre where there are many different owners and traders. It was this realization, together with competition from other centres, that led to the movement for town centre management.

Town centre management seeks to build partnerships between city-centre businesses and the local council responsible for delivering public services to the centre such as policing, garbage collection, street cleaning and lighting, etc. As in any partnership, the aim is to work together for mutual benefit. However, town centre business interests are often surprisingly diverse. For example, not all town centre businesses are involved in retailing. Furthermore, businesses can be competitors, but also operate in very different ways with very different mindsets. Think, for example, of the differences between a small family-owned shop where livelihoods depend on that one shop and the local branch of a chain store. Similarly, the owners of the property are likely to be pension funds or other investors, with a different set of attitudes to those of the traders or local politicians. In addition, one weakness of town centre management is that when a centre is improved through, for example, investment in new street furniture, all the traders in the centre stand to benefit, regardless of whether or not they have made a contribution towards the costs. In the jargon, such beneficiaries are called 'free riders', and the risk is that if everyone acts that way, maximizing their self-interest in the narrowest way, then no improvements will be made.

A Business Improvement District (BID) is a form of place-based regeneration that tries to overcome such disadvantages. Though BIDs are normally business-led, the initiative often comes from a public body concerned with local economic development. BIDs operate within a legal framework that enables a levy to be charged on property owners and/or tenants of commercial properties. The money raised is then committed for projects and activities to improve the area from the point of view of the local businesses. The essence of a BID is typically a form of partnership arrangement through which the public–private sector cooperate to undertake projects and deliver services that will benefit the local economy.

The earliest examples were in the late-1970s and early-1980s in the USA and Canada, where local businesses began to agree to pool finances for landscaping, garbage collection, beautification schemes, street maintenance, and other similar projects. Ward (2007: 793) described a case in Milwaukee, USA, where BIDs developed 'as both a critique of existing city government policies and practices, and an understanding that more could be done collectively by downtown business and property owners' (see Box 10.3).

The common practice within a BID is for local businesses to voluntarily offer to pay additional taxes on themselves, raising taxes in a specific location with the proviso that these same businesses paying the additional taxes would be able to determine how and where this money was to be spent. The BID money can be used as collateral against which additional loans can be sought or can be spent directly on local projects. When the money raised is spent directly, it is done so in a geographically targeted manner to stimulate economic development in a small, specifically designated area. The success of BIDs in the USA had led to their adoption throughout the world in places as far-ranging as Belgium, Japan, Serbia, Jamaica, New Zealand and the UK.

Following the passage of enabling legislation, the enactment of a BID is a two-stage process. First, business owners in an area vote to create a BID. They then lobby municipal officials to draw the boundaries of the BID, define its operation, and make it law (Hochleutner, 2003, cited in Ward, 2006). BIDs are often concerned with

Box 10.3: Business Improvement Districts, Milwaukee (USA)

Like many Great Lakes urban areas in the USA, Milwaukee (population 600,000) is a former manufacturing centre which was hit hard by deindustrialization, the closure of factories, and associated population decline, in the second half of the twentieth century. As such, it typifies a 'rust belt' city searching for economic development strategies to retain its standing in the US urban hierarchy and secure future growth.

In 2007, Milwaukee operated around 30 BIDs, the first one having been designated in 1988. In designating BIDs, municipal officials developed alliances with local business leaders to select areas for designation as BIDs. Ward (2007: 790) described the city's BIDs as having an 'in-between' status, being neither fully public nor fully private entities and often providing the types of services formerly supplied by the city through public funds.

Milwaukee's BIDs have three main functions. First, the funds raised are used to encourage economic development through maintenance of the streetscape, through investment in infrastructure, furniture and paying for clean-ups and repairs. Second, the BID sought to promote the District through brochures and other marketing devices. Third, the BID lobbied municipal officials, hired security guards and installed surveillance equipment and made connections with other stake-holders in the area. Ward (2007: 790) called this last function 'policy advocacy'.

Most of these BIDs focus on the city centre and state law mandates that each is overseen by a minimum five-member board, the majority of whom must own or occupy property within the designated BID. The city's most centrally located BID, covering 640 acres and initiated in 1997 is Downtown Milwaukee BID no.21. It had a 19-member board, and its 2008 budget was $3m. ($2.85m. coming from the additional tax levies and the remainder in contributions from other area occupants). It funded, among other things, 'Public Service Ambassadors', people who dressed in casual uniforms walking throughout the BID area offering advice and information to shoppers and other visitors (Ward, 2007: 792). (Source: Ward (2007).)

the aesthetics of a small area, funding projects such as installing Christmas lights or supporting the operation of a tourist information facility (Zukin, 1995). However, BIDs can be controversial. In some locations, BID finances have been used to renovate parks, add street furniture and then hire security guards to patrol an area to deter usage by homeless people or other groups deemed bad for business by commercial property owners within the BID boundaries. One criticism of BIDs, therefore, is that they have accelerated the privatization of public space, replacing police officers with private security guards and envisioning streets as places to be managed for the good of local business interests and middle- and upper-income groups. For example, Zukin (1995) critically assessed a park restoration project in New York by the Bryant Park BID in this way. To her the work of the BID was 'controlling diversity while re-creating a consumable vision of civility' (1995: 31). Ward (2007: 801) argues that although BIDs are ostensibly public–private partnerships, in practice they hand control of parcels of a city to business elites, and that this can be to the detriment of usages and users who are seen by this business community to add little economic value to a place.

Food and economic development: farmers markets and fair trade

Superstores typically anchor their business on selling food. However, the edge city–superstore model of retailing has been challenged not only by policy-makers seeking to give more emphasis to environmental and social sustainability. The whole food production and supply system is being redesigned in a movement that has been led by policy-makers and practitioners (Sonnino, 2009: 426). There has been a reaction against 'the global, industrial and corporate-led food system' (Pothukuchi, 2009: 350; Wiskerke, 2009). A range of factors have triggered endeavours to develop local food networks: use of pesticides in agriculture, ecological destruction, climate change and obesity are just some of them.

As Sonnino (2009: 426) summarized them, the new, alternative strategies:

> create new economic opportunities for thousands of small farmers and retailers who would not survive the expansion of the global food system. They contribute to individual and community health by responding to the different food and nutritious needs of socially and culturally diverse

populations. And they are beginning to re-design the urban and peri-urban environments (as well as the linkages between them) with important gains for the general quality of life of the millions of people who live in and around fast growing cities.

This amounts to a significant decentralization of the governance of food, which was previously dominated by national governments or supranational states like the EU (Wiskerke, 2009: 376).

Attention to food strategies tends to emphasize their 'alternative' nature, as is the case in the sections that follow. However, the importance of understanding supply chain networks and removing barriers to innovation, rather orthodox business concerns, are also important. For example, Hingley *et al.* (2010) showed how ethnic minority-controlled foodservice businesses in the UK's West Midlands failed to achieve their full potential because of poor network integration. Gatekeepers such as wholesale traders remained very resistant to notions of linking local and regional supply and demand. Instead they were tied to overseas agencies and their produce. Similarly, there were disconnections between white rural growers and Asian wholesalers and retail businesses. Findings of market failures such as these point to a role for fairly conventional forms of 'pro-business' interventions to help the food industry better realize emergent market opportunities. For example, Hingley *et al.* (2010) recommended production, technical and marketing support at the grower and intermediary levels.

One aspect of the consumers' revolt against agri-business and its retailing forms is food miles, a shorthand for 'how far food travels between its production and the final consumer' (Weber and Matthews, 2008: 3508). The concept was developed in the UK in the mid-1990s as an indicator of sustainability and aims at more accurately representing the environmental impact of food production by incorporating calculations about the energy consumption and carbon emissions produced by transporting food to consumers. In the UK, for example, around 95 per cent of fruits and vegetables are imported from abroad, and commonly reach British consumers through the use of high-energy-consuming and high-emissions-producing air transportation (Thottathil, 2008).

Farmers markets are perhaps the best-known and most market-focused example of these agri-food innovations. One of the reasons consumers are drawn to local farmers markets is to reduce food miles (Stagl, 2002), The essence of a farmers market is that fresh local produce is sold, often by the producer, direct to consumers in a nearby urban area. Farmers markets are credited with increasing social interaction and contributing to a spread of environmental values, as well as economically helping farmers (Griffin and Frongillo, 2003; Stagl, 2002). They can be seen as embodying the principles of eco-modernization.

However, there can be controversy over just who should benefit. For example, in the farmers market of Tomah, Wisconsin, resellers, who buy produce in bulk elsewhere and sell it at the market, faced criticism from traditional farmers. A local farmer who sold at the Tomah market wanted the city to restrict the market to farmers, claiming that resellers often offered out-of-season produce, sold at too-low rates, and in effect deceived shoppers who came to the market to support local farms (Etter, 2010). A May 2010 vote by Tomah's city council supported letting resellers continue to sell at the farmers market, despite the local opposition (Froelich, 2010). The US Department of Agriculture (2009b) reported that 63 per cent of US markets have some rules restricting market access to local farmers.

Furthermore, Weber and Matthews (2008: 3510–11) contended that a focus on food miles does not accurately reflect the variation in energy uses and carbon emissions of different foods. Fruit, for example, often has a high food mileage from site of production to consumption, but the production of red meat requires greater transportation of animals and feed in the production process overall, although its final movement from slaughter to retail is, on average, less than that of fruit. The mileage from production site to consumption site, Weber and Matthews (2008) concluded, produces only 4 per cent of total emissions generated during food production. Other measures, such as the total emissions over the lifecycle of the food rather than a focus on transportation, may better demonstrate the environmental impacts of food production.

A drive towards local food production systems in rich countries potentially threatens livelihoods of those employed in similar jobs in poorer, food-producing countries. The Fair Trade movement is a practical pro-poor international approach to regional and local economic development. As Box 10.4 shows, action at the government level can lead local practice and use globalization to deliver benefits in regions across the world.

Food deserts

Tackling food deserts requires pro-poor practices. Food deserts are areas with poor access to healthy and affordable food, so a food desert has no accessible grocery stores that carry healthy food items such as fresh fruits and vegetables. Frequently, these areas are home to the poor and to racial minorities. Typically, the options available in food deserts are fast-food restaurants or so-called convenience stores that carry mainly packaged and processed foods. Any fresh foods available in such stores often are priced higher than they are in large grocery stores, or are of poor quality (Block and Kouba, 2006). The US Department of Agriculture (2009a) found that 2.2 per cent of Americans live more than a mile from a supermarket and do not have a vehicle.

Box 10.4: Fair Trade policy in Wales

The Welsh Government Assembly (WGA) adopted a sustainable development strategy. It included commitments to maintain environmental quality and biodiversity, produce healthy and economically sustainable communities, engage residents in decision making, and act in a manner that promotes sustainable development 'at a global as well as a local level' (Munday and Roberts, 2006: 537). In 2005–6 the WGA initiated a project to make Wales the world's first Fair Trade nation (Townley, 2009: 1027). Officials worked with Fair Trade Wales, an association including NGOs such as Oxfam, businesses and community groups.

A publicity campaign was launched to raise awareness about what Fair Trade entailed and how it would benefit Wales. It centred upon goods certified by Fairtrade Labelling Organizations Limited (FLO), particularly fruit and tropical agricultural produce. The FLO helps farmers in the global South set prices that 'cover the costs of sustainable production'. It also ensures that producers provide 'decent working conditions for hired labour' (FLO, 2010). In Wales, particular efforts were made to have public and private institutions buy tea, coffee, sugar

→

Food deserts are caused by a set of overlapping issues. Major grocery stores have been reluctant to locate in poor neighbourhoods. Overstressed urban budgets have cut transportation lines, often leaving the low-income residents who cannot afford cars without a way to travel to other neighbourhoods to shop. Corner stores charge more for produce and the combination of higher prices or a longer travelling time means that many in these neighbourhoods opt for the cheapest, closest food, which is often nutritionally poor fast food. These problems contribute to rising obesity and other health problems among poor Americans, particularly minorities (US Department of Agriculture, 2009a).

There are many initiatives aimed at addressing the problems of food deserts. These range from creating incentives for major grocery stores to locate in poor neighbourhoods (essentially an area-regeneration 'gap-funding' style approach) to more small-scale or local solutions. The giant grocery firm Walmart made use of food desert arguments to bolster its bid to build a second supercentre

---

and biscuits (cookies) that had Fair Trade certification, and ensure that all caterers had access to Fair Trade goods.

By 2008 every county in Wales had a Fair Trade group and had worked to achieve Fair Trade status. In addition, due to a nationally promoted 'Fair Trade Fortnight', schools, religious institutions, labour unions, universities, caterers, businesses and retailers had all markedly increased their use of fair trade products. Awareness about Fair Trade had also risen among the general public such that those buying at least one Fair Trade product annually rose from 45% in 2006 to 77% in 2008 (Richardson and Wilson, 2008: 5). Direct connections had been made with coffee producers in Uganda, beeswax producers in Cameroon, and craft manufacturers in Zimbabwe (Townley, 2009).

Statistics showed that Welsh consumers were both more knowledgeable about and more likely to purchase goods with the FLO's Fair Trade label than their counterparts elsewhere in the UK (Richardson and Wilson, 2008). The overall aim of the Fair Trade initiative is to simultaneously 'ensure social and economic development and wellbeing of the people of Wales ... [while] supporting producers in the global South' (Townley, 2009: 1029). Wales announced that it had achieved Fair Trade Nation status on 6 June 2008.

store in the city of Chicago (Guy, 2009). Elsewhere in the city, local entrepreneurs have been recognized for opening independent grocery stores in underserved communities (Gray, 2009a, 2009b).

Community-supported agriculture (see Box 10.5) is another innovative alternative to conventional food production and distribution and the problems of food deserts. Some community-supported agriculture initiatives invite subscribers to contribute with labour on the farm and some offer other community-building programmes.

In cities in the developing world, urban agriculture can be a critical survival strategy Bryld (2003). It can provide food security, build incomes, and create environmental advantages through

---

Box 10.5: Alternative food production and distribution: Englewood, Chicago (USA)

Chicago-based Growing Home is a social enterprise that intends to 'bring about social change' as well as advance the cause of local and organic produce. To this end, Growing Home trains homeless and previously incarcerated individuals in the skills of organic and sustainable agriculture. It has located one of its urban farms in the Englewood neighbourhood in south Chicago, a community plagued by drug and gang-related problems, as well as high unemployment. Englewood is a food desert. The community is the site of many vacant lots and the operating businesses are often 'corner stores' that sell convenience foods and liquor.

Growing Home intends to use urban agriculture as a trigger of community development and empowerment. The plot of land that Growing Home's Englewood garden is located on was donated to the enterprise by the City of Chicago for $1, under the stipulation that the land remain a community garden over the term of the lease (99 years). The site is generally respected by community members, left alone by local gang members, and serves as a place to acquire new skills. Growing Home's founders consider it especially important that the garden provides an opportunity for the neighbourhood's poor and African-American residents to interact with nature. It sells its produce on a subscription basis to customers all over Chicago who pay in advance for a seasonal or yearly share of a local farmer's harvest. Growing Home also operates a farmers market in Englewood.

composting waste, nutrient recycling and increasing green space. However, urban agriculture can also pose a potential health hazard when compost is poorly managed or when agricultural chemicals are misused. It can also contribute to land competition in places where housing options are already limited. Moreover, urban agriculturalists face challenges due to lack of secure tenure, theft and soil impoverishment. Thus, again, issues of regulation need to be built into any development strategy. For example, Bryld recommended local governments create programmes to legalize and recognize urban agriculture, in part by providing services such as composting and soil preservation education.

Support to urban agriculture therefore is important. However, it needs to be integrated with other steps to make a food-planning strategy. Approaches to alternative food systems in Europe and North America owe much to social enterprises and market initiatives. While they fit well with styles of governance in 'hollowed out' states, conscious public sector policy-making has more chance of delivering integration through a linked set of interrelated measures. This is the approach taken in Belo Horizonte (see Box 10.6), a city of around 2.5 million in Brazil where, over a period of 15 years, an integrated set of actions led by the city authorities made Belo Horizonte 'the city that ended hunger' (Lappé, 2009).

Summary

The focus of this chapter on retailing and food has challenged conventional perceptions of the concerns and scope of regional and local economic development. Orthodox retail development has delivered increases in efficiency, most obviously manifested in superstores and edge city malls and retail parks, which have been important sources of goods and jobs. However, alternative practices have come to the fore, which prioritize concerns for the vitality of town centres, environmental sustainability, health and social inclusion. The different approaches to regional and local economic development sketched in the typology in Chapter 1 are therefore reflected through the landscapes of malls and big-box retailing (pro-business competition), and innovations such as BIDS (area regeneration), farmers' markets (eco-modernization) and fair trade (pro-poor).

The exploration of retailing and food has also re-emphasized issues of governance and scale. Retailing has been globalized, with

---

Box 10.6: Neighbourhood Food Policy in Belo Horizonte (Brazil)

In 1993 the municipal government in Belo Horizonte set up a Secretariat for Food Policy and Supply (Secretario Municipal Adjunta di Abastecimento). The goal was to increase access to healthy food for all. The programme has six main strands of work: subsidized food sales, food and nutrition assistance, supply and regulation of food markets, support to urban agriculture, education for food consumption, and job and income generation.

In 1994 the first Restaurante Popular was opened. Like the other three that had followed by 2008, it was a cafeteria serving cheap, healthy food and employing 80 people. The first one was downtown near the main public transport hubs. The second (dating from 2004) is close to a concentration of hospitals. The third is in a low-income suburb. The fourth (planned in 2008) is for a suburban area with the highest poverty indicators.

The food and nutrition assistance programme is targeted on at-risk groups: children and youths, the elderly and the homeless.
→

---

superstore chains operating in many different countries, internet selling and the proliferation of standardized units such as shopping malls across what were once diverse cultures in retailing. However, globalization is also being used by consumers to counter some of the dominance of the orthodox model, for example through fair trade and ethical consumer practices. Governments may have to work with other stakeholders, NGOs and private and stakeholder partners, but they can still have an impact, as the examples from Wales and Belo Horizonte showed.

Last but not least, regional and local economic development in retailing and food has been practice led. Certainly there are ideas behind the practice, not least ideas coming from ecology and from health sciences. Similarly, there are debates, but the debates are largely about what works (for example, in town centre regeneration or in respect of farmers' markets). The tone is pragmatic. This is a field where theory trails in the wake of policy and practice.

It works through schools and daycare centres, health clinics, nursing homes, shelters and charities. It includes a school-meals programme, and a 'food bank' that seeks to reduce food waste and improve access to food for marginalized groups not covered by other programmes.

Partnerships with private food suppliers have brought food to previously neglected neighbourhoods. Prices and quality of basic food and vegetables supplied through the programme are regulated. A licensing system is used to ensure that low-income neighbourhoods get served and that some prices are set below market rates.

Participatory involvement and environmentally sustainable methods are at the heart of the urban agriculture component. There are four main projects: 'Community Gardens', 'School Gardens', 'Workshops for Planting in Alternative Spaces' and 'Pro-Orchard' (fruit trees in communal and school spaces).

There are also workshops on healthy eating targeted at children, parents and teachers, and training programmes for vocational qualifications in food. While a range of challenges remain, and the food policy has still not been made mainstream or permanent, Belo Horizonte's food strategy has received substantial praise. (Source: Rocha and Lessa (2009).)

Topics for discussion

Are Business Improvement Districts a good tool for local economic development?

What are the achievements and potential of 'food planning' as an approach in regional and local economic development?

Related reading

K. Ward (2006) '"Policies in Motion", Urban Management and State Restructuring: the Trans-Local Expansion of Business Improvement Districts', *International Journal of Urban and Regional Research*, 30(1), 54–75.

Special issue of *International Planning Studies*, 14(4), 2009, 'Feeding the City: The Challenge of Urban Food Planning'.

11 Leisure, Culture and Tourism

The possibility of the mass of the people having leisure time and enough disposable income and good health to enjoy it is relatively modern, and still by no means a global phenomenon. A classic sociological text was written (Veblen, 1912) that identified a 'leisure class' who were so defined because of their lack of engagement in useful employment. The rising affluence and changed working conditions of the decades that followed saw a modicum of leisure become recognized as something of a civil right. More recently it appears that the intensification of work has stimulated an intensification of leisure activity. There are still important differences between countries and classes in leisure time, but leisure, tourism and cultural industries have become entwined with the processes of globalization. They are increasingly important economic sectors. Zukin (1995: 1–2) put it succinctly: 'With the disappearance of local manufacturing industries and periodic crises in government and finance, culture is more and more the business of cities – the basis of their tourist attractions and their unique, competitive edge'.

While Zukin was primarily addressing the situation in the old industrial countries, it is clear today that the growing middle classes in rapidly developing Asian countries are also using their disposable incomes to buy leisure products and experiences. The booming shopping malls of urban India (Box 10.2) are just one indicator. The creation of the Indian Premier League (IPL) cricket competition/business is a dramatic illustration of a commercial leisure product that is a new economic driver. It is both local and global, with players from many countries and global TV coverage. In a matter of months the IPL overturned the traditional international relationships in the sport that had long been politically and culturally dominated by the UK. Similarly, the 2008 Beijing Olympics and the 2010 soccer World Cup in South Africa were about much more than games.

Leisure, tourism and cultural industries are important for regional and local economic development because they offer the prospect of growing markets. For example, new forms of tourism have developed tapping into niche markets made viable in part by their increasingly global reach. Examples are:

- winter tourism;
- agri-tourism (e.g. staying on farms, picking fruit, riding horses);
- food tourism (unique and memorable eating and drinking experiences);
- eco-tourism (by ecologically aware people to environmentally important sites);
- extreme tourism (travel to dangerous places or participation in dangerous activities);
- heritage tourism;
- gay and lesbian tourism or 'gaycation', in places offering tolerance and gay culture;
- health tourism (to access health care);
- sailing and boating;
- pop-culture tourism (linked to film and TV locations, associations with celebrities, etc.);
- religious tourism;
- staycations (people staying at or close to home and taking vacations there);
- war/military history tourism (e.g. battlefield tours); and
- wildlife tourism.

All these subsectors are intensely place based but also global in a way that makes places themselves brands. Hollywood is the obvious example. Landry (2000) argued that culture, leisure and creativity constitute a basis for economic development. While there is competition and there are risks, using leisure and tourism as a development strategy means swimming with the tide and not against it. Zukin (1995: 8) quoted data showing that during the early 1990s in the USA employment in 'entertainment and recreation' grew more than in health care, and six times more than in the car industry. However, like retailing, the leisure and tourism industries have often been dismissed in terms of their job creation potential because many of the jobs are temporary, seasonal, require low skills and pay poorly. Furthermore working antisocial hours, at times when others are relaxing, is almost by definition, part of the job.

The wide array of job types in leisure and tourism leave such generalizations open to challenge. Furthermore, if we focus particularly on the cultural industries that serve so many leisure needs, a different picture emerges. Landry (2000) claimed that the cultural industries employ 3–5 per cent of the workforce in world cities (e.g. London, New York, Milan, Berlin), and also help to sustain tourist industries. Echoing Florida's 'creative-class' thesis (Chapter 2), Landry (2000) saw culture as closely linked with creativity, and so he argued that its influence on urban competitiveness is even greater. He suggested that international companies are likely to put their inward investment into places able to offer a vibrant cultural life. Further, he contended that places that engage positively with culture also demonstrate a creative approach to problem-solving, and hence have been able to achieve economic development benefits that would otherwise have been improbable. Similarly, Zukin (1995) argued that art galleries, museums, restaurants and similar cultural and recreational sites provide a set of places where mobile business elites meet and exchange ideas.

Global competition for sport and mega-events

One very visible aspect of globalization has become the competition between cities to stage major international sporting events (Cochrane *et al.*, 1996). The hope is that the events themselves will be successful, but furthermore that hosting them will raise the global profile of the city or country providing the venues. Thus in terms of the typology in Chapter 1, competition for such events is most likely to be part of a strategy prioritizing 'pro-business competition to attract inward investment'.

For example, Qatar's rapidly growing economy at the start of this century was based on oil, but their output was peaking. Tourism offered a potential way to diversify the economy of this small Gulf state, Doha, Qatar's capital city, bid unsuccessfully for the 2016 Summer Olympic Games. More significantly, by bidding to host the 2022 soccer World Cup Finals (arguably the world's top-ranking sports event), Qatar was able to get its name into the global sports media throughout the two-year bidding process, and so begin to challenge the dominance of Dubai as the leading Arab-speaking tourism destination. The decision to award the 2022 World Cup to Qatar surprised many. It was accompanied by suggestions that those who decide on where to host global sports events are also aware of the impacts of their votes on businesses in their own country. For example, in 2010 France wanted Qatar to increase its order for five Airbus 380 aircraft. Seven days before a 22-man committee of the Fédération Internationale de Football Association (FIFA) voted on where to hold the 2022 finals, Qatar Airlines announced that it would definitely consider increasing its Airbus order. The French President, Nicolas Sarkozy, had put 'pressure on Michel Platini to vote for Qatar's 2022 bid' (Scott, 2010: 8). Platini, a distinguished former French international player, was part of the FIFA committee.

The economic development benefits and risks of such strategies need to be carefully considered. Gratton *et al.* (2000) developed a typology of major sports events that is useful in reaching economic development decisions about competing to host such spectacles. It is as follows:

- Type A: irregular, one-off major international spectator events generating significant economic activity and major media interest (e.g. Olympics, Football World Cup).
- Type B: major spectator events, generating significant economic activity and part of an annual domestic cycle of sports events (e.g. Formula One Grand Prix, Rugby Union Internationals, Test Match cricket, Open Golf, Open tennis champion ships).
- Type C: irregular, one-off major international spectator/ competitor events generating uncertain economic activity (e.g. world and continental championships in all sports).
- Type D: major competitor events generating limited economic activity and part of an annual cycle of sports events (e.g. national championships in most sports).

The message is that not all 'major' sporting events are necessarily important in terms of their likely impacts on a local economy. By definition most events in any one year are in categories B, C and D. The benefits from Type D events do not cover the costs in economic terms and thus the rationale for bidding for such events has to be other than an economic development one. Type A and B events generate the largest economic benefits, and so there is fierce competition between cities wanting to host Type A events. However, most Type B events use the same venue each year, or cities are not invited to bid for them. Therefore the tricky decisions are those for Type C events. Gratton *et al.* (2001) offered guidance in respect of Type C:

- the economic impact of competitor-driven events is relatively easy to forecast, the real uncertainty is for spectator-driven events;
- spectator forecasts for Type C events can be subject to large margins of error, and there is a tendency to make overoptimistic forecasts. The same event can pull very different crowds in different cultures depending on the national interest in the sport in question.
- the more senior the event and the longer the event, and the more affluent the competitors are, then the larger the economic impact is likely to be.

If a one-off or irregular event involves construction of major new infrastructure, there are obvious concerns about future use. These can be compounded by the tendency for business to drop off anyway once the event has finished. For example, the 2000 Sydney Olympic Games was centred on a 760-hectare site that had once been used by industry and the military. Although new stadia and rail connections were constructed, thinking about the post-games legacy only really began after the event (Marrs, 2006). Sue Holliday, Director-General of the New South Wales State Planning Department at the time, stated that many businesses established in the run-up to the Games failed soon afterwards. 'The economy of the whole city declined as soon as the games ended. Tourists stopped visiting in such large numbers and there was a very big slump' (Holliday, cited in Marrs, 2006: 13). The SuperDome, a 21,000-seat venue built for the basketball and gymnastics competitions, went into receivership in 2004, leaving the taxpayers with the costs of maintenance. It reopened in 2009 as the Acer Arena to host conferences, dinners, receptions and other events.

Although there are signs that the Sydney Olympics site has seen some recovery since the dip that occurred immediately after the games, there remain grounds for being sceptical about the economics of sports events as drivers of regional and local development. Crompton (2001) was critical about the methodologies used in economic impact studies of public investment to support private sports teams and events through construction of stadia or related facilities. He argued that spending by visitors does not necessarily boost the incomes of local households. For example, a visitor filling up a car with petrol is mainly passing the money to government and the oil companies, not boosting the income of nearby residents. This notion of 'leakage' from a local economy is a familiar one, but it is typically disregarded by evaluations that stress visitor spending. Similarly, Crompton suggested that impact studies tend to translate increases in spending into jobs, whereas local businesses are unlikely to take on extra staff just because there is an occasional sports event in their vicinity. He also said that spending by local spectators should not be counted, as that does not bring new money into the economy from outside. Furthermore, some people are intending to visit a place anyway and decide to time their visit to coincide with the sports event. As they would have made the visit eventually, Crompton argues their spending should not be attributed as a gain from the event itself.

Globalizing leisure and attracting investment

Chatterton and Hollands (2002) pointed to the way that large, multisite breweries and leisure companies expanded their operations through the development of brands and themes. Arndorfer (2003: 179) noted that the themed restaurant idea began in Chicago in 1971 when a local restaurateur decided to give patrons in a gentrifying neighbourhood a 'dining experience' generating 'an offbeat, casual vibe', and adding 'hanging plants [and] modern art' to the décor to create a restaurant defined as much by its theatricality and entertainment as it was by its menu. For example, Irish-themed bars (Box 11.1) spread rapidly throughout the world in the 1990s. In the USA, Arndorfer (2003: 178) argued, such venues 'had a strong appeal among young professionals, tourists, and conventioneers' and as a result became highly successful in the American leisure and catering industries.

Box 11.1: A mainstream nightlife venue: Fado Irish Pub, Chicago (USA)

The Fado Irish Pub in Chicago is just one entertainment venue within an area that, as recently as the late 1970s, was a transitional location of warehouses, offices and factories located between the exclusive residences of Chicago's 'Gold Coast' and its low-income Cabrini Green high-rise public housing estates. Fado is located among major national and international chains like Hard Rock Café, House of Blues, Rainforest Café and McDonald's.

Chicago's Fado (Gaelic for 'long ago') opened in 1997 and is one of this chain's fourteen Irish-themed pubs in the USA. The Irish Pub Company arranges for all the bar's fittings, except some tables and chairs, to be shipped directly from Ireland.

In this three-floor pub, which Arndorfer (2003: 173) described as depicting 'Ireland as Disney would "imagineer" it', Gaelic words and Celtic-style font adorn the walls, as do period black and white photographs, statistics and graphs detailing Irish industrial output of the mid-twentieth century, anachronistic advertisements for biscuits and cigarettes, and murals mimicking stained glass and exhibiting Irish saints. The mezzanine level is a replica ship complete with masts, sails, oars, nets and barrels and depicts the legendary sixth-century voyage to the Americas by St Brendan, an Irish monk.

The Irish Pub Company aimed to incorporate within the same building several different styles of Irish pub. There are elements of a rural cottage pub, an urban Victorian bar, a grocery store local pub, a theatre bar, and so forth. When Purty's Kitchen Bar in Dun Loaghrie, Ireland, remodelled, the Irish Pub Company bought the bar and incorporated it into the Fado design, reducing its length by around one-third and reconstructing it 4,000 miles away in their Chicago building.

Television screens show European football and Gaelic Athletic Association events, and the menu features a range of choices from US mainstays such as chicken wings, to hybrid dishes such as potato pancake quesadillas. Arndorfer (2003: 181) feared that due to Irish-themed pubs, 'Ireland the country' may be 'doomed forever to live in the shadow of Ireland the brand'.

Chatterton and Hollands (2002) focused on the UK, so their findings may not apply in other countries. They argued that as local authorities sought to attract inward investment from corporate chains of pub and entertainment providers (especially the large ones who are likely to be the most commercially sound and reliable), so the balance of power shifted away from traditional regulators like the magistrates and the police. For example, licensing hours became liberalized. The power to regulate increasingly passed to the private producer who operates through pricing, dress codes, CCTV and bouncers. However, deregulation of the cultural economy in the search for corporate investment to spur local economic development and to revitalize a town centre, carries risks. Drink-fuelled indulgence is likely to have negative impacts on the image of the place. Noise and disturbance may make it harder to attract residents.

Getting the regulatory balance right involves tricky decisions, and the boundary line will vary from place to place. Too strict regulation makes a discouraging environment. Too little and the night-time economy may drive out other investors. Montgomery (2007: 214) cited Manchester as 'a good example of coordinated policies on planning, policing and liquor licensing'. This involves a range of measures to reduce noise and disturbance (e.g. extensive acoustic measures in buildings, establishment of maximum noise levels, etc.), early morning street cleaning, plus high-profile police targeting of 'crime hotspots'. The details are specific to the city, but the message applies far more widely. It is that a night-time economy needs to be regulated in a coordinated way by the public sector to ensure that it is a valuable part of the city's economy.

Nevertheless, much of the dynamism that drives the cultural industries in particular is very bottom-up. Fashion and changing tastes make leisure and culture high-risk commercial propositions. The creative chaos on the margins of the economy provides the milieu for innovation and commercial success. Key qualities of successful place competitiveness seem to be reflected in this culture – diversity, empowerment, creativity, strong identity, the use of informal networks, a willingness to break the rules. Corporate culture then adapts and incorporates new fashions, and then switches its investments as the fad fades.

It is not surprising then to find that young adults have been important drivers of the new evening economy of urban centres. Both formal and underground economies, such as music, dancing, drinking and illegal drugs, can become significant sectors of an urban economy. In the 1980s in Manchester, England, streetwise young people, who left school to find that there were few mainstream job opportunities open to them, played a vital part in a boom period of music and clubbing that raised the city's profile internationally and stimulated economic development (see Box 11.2).

In many ways Manchester's music scene was an example of how tacit knowledge, spillovers, networks and synergies can create an environment in which innovation can flourish. It demonstrates the principles of what Leadbeater (2005: 15), drawing on the work of Eric van Hippel at the Massachusetts Institute of Technology, called a 'user innovation revolution'. As users are innovators too, innovation becomes a very democratic process. Leadbeater (2005) for example described how in the 1970s, a group of young bike riders in California wanted to ride mountain trails on racing bikes. It could not be done. So they put together the more sturdy frames

---

Box 11.2: Youth culture and innovation: music in Manchester (England)

In the 1980s, Manchester, the world's first industrial city, was in a very depressed condition. Many jobs had been lost as traditional manufacturing industries closed. Unemployment was high, especially among young people. The demise of the cotton industry had left the central part of the city with a stockpile of empty warehouses, many with impressive facades. The supply of these former industrial or retail buildings far exceeded the demand to use them, so they were cheap and easy to rent. They were colonized by a youthful generation of entrepreneurs and commandeered for use as nightclubs, bars, record shops, cafés and restaurants. Thus Affleck's Palace, a former departmental store that had closed became a Mecca for teenagers shopping for kind of cheap clothing that was the 'cool' negation of orthodox adult tastes.

In 1978 Tony Wilson, a local entrepreneur and TV presenter formed Factory Records. The success of this venture in challenging the big international record companies inspired 20–30 other small record companies to start up in the city. There was also a mushrooming

→

from traditional town bikes, gears from racing bikes, balloon tyres and brakes from motorcycles. Working in their own garages, they made these bikes. Leisure and manufacturing merged. By 1976, there were a few small firms run by enthusiasts in Marin County, just outside San Francisco. They were basically making these new types of bikes for their friends. The first commercial mountain bike came out in 1982, and within a few years such bikes were being made by the big companies and sold in mainstream markets. Leadbeater and Miller (2004) call it *The Pro-Am Revolution* ('pro-am' is a tem for a golf competition where professionals and amateurs are paired into teams to compete against other pairs.).

Almost by definition, economic development agencies cannot plan for the kind of spontaneous eruption of ideas and practices that drove Manchester's music scene or the invention of the mountain bike. However, they can help to create the preconditions in which innovation is more likely to happen. In the case of

---

of small independent companies making programmes for local radio and TV. The city became identified with 'indie-music', the 'independent' record labels that were part of the punk-rock reaction to the way that rock music had drifted from its roots and become controlled by corporate business. In punk anyone could be a musician.

An empty building became The Hacienda, a nightclub that first opened in 1982 and soon became the flagship for Manchester's rise to international status in youth culture. Bands strongly identified with the city, notably Oasis, the Happy Mondays, the Smiths, and the Stone Roses became global stars. Manchester became 'Madchester', a term capturing the anarchic, rebellious and hedonistic ethos of its music and youth lifestyle.

Shaun Ryder of the Happy Mondays said that in the early 1980s there were some 200 to 300 'cool geezers' involved as drivers of this alternative economy as owners of record companies, night clubs, fashion outlets, or journalists. By the mid-1990s the scale of the operation had increased with much more extensive networks of businesses, buildings, and places. In 1994, *City Life*, a Manchester entertainment magazine, claimed a readership of '"80,000 high-profile, intelligent and affluent people", of whom 57 per cent were under 29' (Taylor *et al.*, 1996: 273). (Source: Taylor *et al.* (1996).)

Manchester, for example, an economic development agency, the Central Manchester Development Corporation, played a notable role in assisting the reuse and temporary use of empty buildings through a mix of grants, tax incentives and property management (Taylor *et al.*, 1996). Similarly, some of the networks that developed around the music scene in the city fed into wider partnerships for regeneration.

Cultural clusters

Creative clusters are centres that combine production and consumption of cultural products. The idea of clusters and agglomeration economies, discussed in Chapter 3, is very strong in the cultural industries. The high-risk nature of much cultural production is a key driver of clustering. Larger companies are likely to outsource the risk of creating new cultural content (e.g. designs, music, computer games etc.) but the distributors and the providers both need to be 'in the loop', so that they can quickly know about the latest ideas or market opportunities. As Montgomery (2007: 306) noted, intertrading and subcontracting amongst a network of enterprises in a 'distribution–production–consumption value chain' is the essence of a successful cluster. Furthermore, consumption of the cultural products (e.g. a theatre performance) is likely to trigger 'derived consumption' in the form of food and drink, or maybe provide a general boost to tourism, as people come to take in a show as part of a break in another city. Montgomery (2007: 307) further added that 'most cultural quarters tend to operate at the modern, design and media end of the cultural spectrum'.

Again it is important to stress that not every town will be able to support a successful cultural quarter. 'Cultural quarters only work where there are venues, workplaces for cultural producers and working artists', said Montgomery (2007: 348). Intervention by a local economic development agency can help to provide the kind of small work places that can be the seedbeds for the growth of cultural industries. Existing arts venues might serve as magnets around which smaller, newer enterprises might be drawn. Similarly, marketing can help promote the cluster and attract new investment.

Leisure-led regeneration

In situations of serious decline and economic restructuring, regeneration initiatives based on leisure and tourism may be the last alternative when others have failed (Jones and Munday 2001). Any reconstruction, reclamation or conservation project is likely to create some jobs in the phase when initial works, often in construction, are undertaken. However, the real challenge in terms of local economic development is to be able to create long-term job opportunities that can be funded through visitors. A significant scale project may also hope to create spin-off benefits for employment in local services such as hotels and shops. However, there are likely to be problems of forecasting visitor numbers in a competitive industry dependent on fashion and where direct comparisons with existing attractions are often difficult to make. There can also be tensions between the economic aims and community sustainability. As always happens in regeneration, the outcomes are a new situation, not a reversal to a pre-existing one. In the 1990s, Stoke-on-Trent, England, focused much of its economic development efforts on generating a leisure and retail complex called Festival Park. Many in the city, however, found the resulting development to be far from welcoming (see Box 11.3).

Where leisure attractions are the drivers of regeneration they have to ensure that they capture visitor spending. Jones and Munday (2001) looked at a World Heritage Site based on the industrial landscape of mining and iron-making in Blaenavon, an extremely deprived part of Wales. They argued that in very depressed economies such as Blaenavon efforts should also be made to support business start-ups. Furthermore, to lever more spending in the area, the general environment and facilities needed to be upgraded. These authors also advocated building links between contractors and suppliers to strengthen the local business base. They suggested that the public sector procurers should split large contracts and in other ways facilitate the involvement of local business in the work. Where a long-established local culture has not favoured entrepreneurialism, there is a risk that the implant of a major tourism attraction will not see the opportunities for spin-offs grasped by local residents who are in need of the jobs and benefits such activities could bring.

Box 11.3: Leisure-led regeneration: Festival Park, Stoke-on-Trent (England)

Festival Park in Stoke-on-Trent is located on a former steel works where the majority of industrial operations ended in 1978. The land was reclaimed for Britain's 1986 National Garden Festival, one of a series of such events in the 1980s and 1990s which aimed to regenerate former industrial sites in economically depressed locations (Thomas and Hague, 2000). For the Garden Festival, much of the contaminated land area was remediated, stabilized and landscaped, a task that required the removal of over 1.4 million cubic metres of material, including slurry, concrete and industrial waste. National and city government bodies, in partnership with private companies, financed the Festival which, from the outset, was understood to be a stepping stone towards redevelopment. Areas of the Festival site were earmarked for future development as 'offices, warehousing, industry and leisure facilities', although the initial plans to prohibit retail to prevent competition with traditional city centre shops were subsequently reversed (Thomas and Hague, 2000: 124).

Following the Garden Festival, the 64-hectare site, less than 1 mile from the town centre, was again redeveloped and in 1989 opened as Festival Park. It contained national chain retailers, a cinema, a 10-pin bowling alley, a swimming pool/water park, a ski slope, fast food restaurants, a hotel and a number of other leisure facilities. Housing was subsequently added to part of the site, which also incorporates a series of nature trails through replanted woodland. Festival Park is a major contributor to the local economy and provider of jobs. However, studies by Hague *et al.* (2000a, 2000b) demonstrated that the stores and leisure activities offered were perceived to be exclusionary. People over 35 and local residents without disposable income felt that the area offered little in the way of entertainment that they sought, and that which was available was seen by some as too costly. As access to Festival Park was via a multilane highway, this privileged car users. Signs prohibited bicycles and motorcycles from certain areas and public transportation options were limited, infrequent and, pointedly, generally ended service before the cinema and restaurants closed for the evening. Car traffic became congested at peak times with few entrances and exits to the parking areas and, at night, young drivers, primarily men, would meet to race cars illegally.

Tourism itself is a highly competitive industry and there are plenty of examples of once-thriving tourist towns that are now facing severe economic difficulties as leisure patterns and preferences have changed. No place can afford to stand still, but many did so and paid the price as visitor numbers tailed off and properties became vacant, creating a spiral of decline. Many seaside towns in particular saw their tourism as purely seasonal, based on people coming to use their beaches and other facilities in the summer months. It is increasingly clear that even places by the sea need a year-round business plan, with clear ideas about what opportunities they can offer to attract businesses and leisure trips in the off-season months. One of the most famous, and controversial, examples of just such a strategy was Atlantic City's decision in the 1970s to open casinos (Box 11.4). When it was enacted in 1977, the New Jersey Casino Control Act envisioned casino gambling as 'a unique tool of urban redevelopment for Atlantic City' that would 'facilitate the redevelopment of existing blighted areas, and the refurbishing and expansion of existing hotel, convention, tourist and entertainment facilities' (Goodman, 1995: 19). The casinos promised multiplier effects that would generate thousands of new jobs for local residents and new customers for local retailers, restaurants and businesses in Atlantic City.

By the 1990s Atlantic City's casinos had generated about 40,000 new jobs, but most of these went to people living elsewhere who commuted to work and, as a result, the city's high rates of unemployment persisted (Thompson, 1997). A second problem was that casinos soaked up almost all the tourist trade in the city. People came to visit the casinos and rarely ventured beyond these massive complexes to engage with non-casino businesses (Goodman, 1995). Thus other retail business and employment in Atlantic City continued to decline despite the presence of gambling (Kindt, 1998: 134).

By the mid-1990s, Goodman (1995: 20) explained, 'Atlantic City became virtually two cities – one of extravagant casinos, largely manned by an outside workforce, and the other, a city of boarded-up buildings and a predominantly minority population that suffered massive unemployment and was given easy access to gambling'. Ultimately, the story in Atlantic City is one of moderate success. Urban planner James W. Hughes commented 'the casinos did provide a lot of state revenue to do a lot of housing projects, but

Box 11.4: Casinos as a driver for regeneration of a rundown seaside town: Atlantic City, New Jersey (USA)

In the mid-1970s, after decades of losing jobs and population, the seaside resort of Atlantic City, around 125 miles from New York City, turned to casinos to stimulate economic development. Strictly regulated in the USA at the time, legal gambling centred on Las Vegas some 2,500 miles away. In 1977 the state of New Jersey passed the New Jersey Casino Control Act which legalized gambling in Atlantic City. The Act established an independent New Jersey Casino Control Commission to regulate the operation of casinos and a Division of Gaming Enforcement.

Atlantic City's first casino, Resorts International Casino, opened in 1978 and within nine months the company's US$77m investment had been repaid (Thompson, 1997). Over the next three years, eight more casinos were built and, on average, the casinos were 100 times more profitable per square foot than a shopping centre (Sternlieb and Hughes, 1983). By 1982, the casinos in Atlantic City employed around 30,000 workers and were making $15m. per month in profits.

They were also paying $117m. per year into New Jersey's budget because a central aspect of the New Jersey Casino Control Act were taxation regulations and other surcharges which mandated that a portion of casino revenues had to be paid to the state for use in social programmes, such as care for the elderly and disabled, economic development projects, and job creation strategies (Sternlieb and Hughes, 1983; Thompson, 1997). Casinos were taxed at 8% of their winnings, with this income distributed throughout New Jersey via the Casino Revenue Fund. A second levy, the Alternative Investment Tax, 1.25% of casino gross revenues, was channelled into regeneration programmes in Atlantic City. However, as the public authorities became increasingly reliant on these sources of revenue, they also relaxed their regulation, so that by 1994 almost all the original limits on the gambling had been rescinded.

In 1984 New Jersey formed the Casino Reinvestment Development Authority (CRDA) to fund housing and community facilities (Hague, 2001: 20). Around $500m. in tax revenues had been utilized by 2001 to finance, amongst other things, a health centre, youth clubs, an aquarium, a baseball stadium, day care centres, landscaping, and facilities for the elderly. CRDA also contributed $175m. for casino and hotel expansion, and developed housing for sale at market rates.

it's taken twenty years to get there' (quoted in E. Hague, 2001: 21). This conclusion serves to emphasize the need to take a long-term approach to the regeneration of seaside towns, and also to be prepared to invest in housing and related social facilities as necessary complements to an economic development strategy.

Cultural and environmental conservation

Eco-tourism is one of the manifestations of an eco-modernization approach to regional and local economic development. Wearing and Neil (2009: xiii) defined it as 'travel to relatively undisturbed or protected natural areas fostering understanding, appreciation and conservation of the flora, fauna, geology and ecosystems of an area'. It is thus a classic 'glocal' process, connecting local places and communities into global markets. It also seeks to negate the traditional 'economy or environment' dualism. The growth in this niche tourism market has made eco-tourism an even more attractive economic development proposition. However, there are also some fairly obvious questions to be asked about the greenhouse gas emissions resulting from a trip to experience the conservation of a rain forest that will help absorb CO_2 and mitigate risks from climate change. There are also issues about the impacts of such tourism on local ecosystems and on local communities. For example, species conservation in national parks has often been controversial in terms of its impacts on the way that local groups have used the land. Yet, innovative eco-tourism projects can balance local lifestyles and wildlife habitats with economic development.

Eco-tourism delicately balances environmental and local economic needs. The Kipepeo project, described in Box 11.5, is particularly interesting as it sends its produce onto the global market allowing people to view its exotic butterflies near their own place of residence and not necessitating travel to Kenya to see them. Both Kipepeo and the Il Ngwesi project have pro-poor aspects built in, though the divisions in opinion amongst the Maasai about the latter show how complex the calculus of costs and benefits can be once general policy is translated into action on the ground.

Environment and culture are often closely interwoven and their interplay can be the basis for a form of eco-tourism. For example, in Taiwan, the Hakka Tung Blossom Festival is now organized each

---

Box 11.5: Eco-tourism in Kenya

The 2009 documentary film *Milking the Rhino* details a local economic development strategy in rural Kenya. The development model followed is one of 'community-based conservation' (CBC) in which residents agree to provide land for eco-tourism facilities and in return operate conservation strategies that maintain wildlife populations. Filmmaker Jeannie Magill describes CBC as 'a bottom-up approach to conservation ... that utilizes natural resources in such a way that the people that are living with those natural resources benefit and the biodiversity of the area is increased' (interview by Prescott, 2009).

The six-room Il Ngwesi Lodge in northern Kenya, the first of its kind in Kenya, was built in 1995 and the first paying guests arrived in 1996. Community owned and operated by the Maasai, the eco-lodge is constructed of local materials and uses solar power. To attract tourists, the Il Ngwesi Maasai set aside 80% of their traditional pasturelands for conservation to encourage the growth of elephant, rhinoceros, giraffe and lion populations. The local Maasai are divided over the project, particularly as it has resulted in more intense grazing on other areas of land.

→

---

year by the ethnic Hakka communities in the hill region of Miaoli County. The Hakka people originally came from the Chinese mainland and are a minority within Taiwan, mainly living in remote mountainous regions, which is where the tung trees blossom with beautiful white flowers in late spring and early summer. The festival is now seen as a catalyst to better integrate the people, tourism and local industries. It involves a range of cultural events including concerts, dancing and competitions, but there is also a focus on tung blossom products. The wood is used for making matches, clogs and toothpicks, while the seed oil is used in waterproof clothing. Several local councils and private enterprises work together to deliver the festival. Information about the progress of the blossom is provided on a website, connecting a remote region into a global network of destinations. There are brochures explaining tourist routes and scenic spots, as well as the location

For some, the wild animals are not as productive as cattle, goats or other livestock. Supporters of the Il Ngwesi CDC project counter that the fees generated from the tourists enable land purchases and future community development.

Proceeds from this CBC development strategy have established an HIV/AIDS awareness programme with seventeen employees; funded infrastructure repair; paid teachers' wages and students' school fees; and, supported a local mobile banking facility.

Kipepeo is another project in Kenya. The Arabuko-Sokoko Forest covers over 41,000 hectares on Kenya's north coast. It is the largest single block of natural coastal forest left in East Africa. However, it is under pressure from tourist development and local subsistence farmers short of land. In 1993 the East Africa Natural History Society and the National Museum of Kenya developed a project for butterfly farming that was aided by a small grant from the United Nations Development Program. Local farmers in the area were taught how to breed and care for the butterflies. Kipepeo (Swahili for butterfly) has grown into a community-based enterprise that supports local livelihoods while also helping to conserve the forest. Kipepeo sells butterfly and moth pupae and other live insects, as well as honey and locally produced silk cloth. (Sources: Antoniou (2001: 98–9); Kipepeo (2009); Simpson (2009).)

of shops selling tung blossom products (Hakka Tung Blossom Festival, 2009).

Conservation of the built environment can also be the basis for tourism. While every place has some potential to celebrate its heritage, a form of global competition has developed to get placed on the UNESCO list of World Heritage Sites. Under an international convention signed in 1972, a committee of experts reviews nominations from countries for places to be designated as World Heritage Sites. The committee also publishes a list of World Heritage in Danger. UNESCO provides modest funding mainly to developing countries to assist with conservation once a site is given World Heritage status, but that status can also often be a catalyst for drawing in other funds. To be accorded World Heritage status, sites must be of 'outstanding universal value' and meet at least one of 10 selection criteria. These criteria essentially demarcate the breadth of the concept of heritage, encompassing, for example, monuments, buildings, sites or landscapes, geology or the culture of people (UNESCO, 2009). Český Krumlov, described in Box 11.6, is a small town that used World Heritage status to power its local development.

Český Krumlov's heritage assets had existed for centuries, but it took an enterprising local administration to seize the opportunities presented by the collapse of the Soviet Union and capitalize on those assets through imaginative management and a visionary approach. The town's leaders grasped that with the advent of the market economy, the potential existed to attract investment. To realize that potential they had to have appropriate financial instruments, levering resources from both the public and the private sectors, but also ensure that there was supporting infrastructure such as hotels, coach parks, and a work force trained both in heritage management and for the hospitality industry. Becoming

---

Box 11.6: Using World Heritage in a tourism strategy: Český Krumlov (Czech Republic)

Český Krumlov is a historic town in southern Bohemia with a population of about 15,000. It grew around a deep meander in the Vltava River at the edge of the Sumava mountain range that runs between Austria and Bavaria. During the Cold War years it was a rather neglected place, on the edge of the Soviet bloc, dangerously close to the borders with Austria and West Germany.

In medieval times it had been home to the Rosenburg family when they ruled over one-seventh of Bohemia. The legacy of an age of wealth followed by centuries of relative isolation from development pressures is a townscape rich in Gothic, Renaissance and Baroque buildings, with an intricate pattern of cobbled alleys and spaces (Figure 11.1). It is dominated by a spectacular clifftop castle with thirteenth-century origins. The quality and integrity of this townscape was recognized when UNESCO made it a World Heritage Site in 1992.

After 1989 the local council, as in other Czech towns, became the owner of a considerable stock of property, much of it with potential

→

a World Heritage site is just the start – the challenge is to manage the site in such a way that it stimulates the local economy without destroying the very same asset that draws tourists. Sensitive policies and interventions are needed to ensure adequate protection and that new development is good development that enhances rather than detracts from the experience of the place. Land-use planning controls are important here, with effective mechanisms for their enforcement.

The idea of working with communities is now central to the UNESCO approach but there is clearly the risk that preservation of heritage areas can mean resisting new development and potential improvements in the livelihoods of local residents. Yet cultural heritage can be used to create economic opportunities for poor people. Box 11.7 described such a project in rural India where folk festivals, arts and crafts both aid economic development and protect local traditions.

---

value but also serious problems of disrepair. These included some 300 historic buildings, mostly in very poor condition, as well as many flats in prefabricated units, energy infrastructure, vacant plots and 1500 hectares of forests. The challenge was to protect the historical town centre, while gaining the benefits from tourism and fostering new local enterprises.

The council took the view that it could not finance the refurbishment itself, and that it would look to privatization and joint ventures. A town bylaw was used to privatize some 70% (by value) of all town properties, giving the right of first refusal to local small businesses and residents. The Český Krumlov Development Fund was established in 1992 as a limited liability company, with the town council as the sole owner, but operating as a normal commercial entity, and engaging in 'arm's length transactions'. Fifty of the most commercially attractive properties owned by the council were transferred to the fund, and a feasibility study was done for their future use, recognizing their importance to the national cultural heritage. A tourism development plan was also produced to help create investment opportunities so that the town would become a centre for cultural tourism and conference tourism. The outcome has been very successful.

Figure 11.1   **Český Krumlov**

Box 11.7: Cultural heritage as a basis for tourism and economic development: Jaipur Virasat Foundation (India)

The Jaipur Virasat Foundation (the JVF) was set up in 2002. It operates in rural regions and the towns of Rajasthan in India. 'Virasat' is the tradition of the people, a set of values and way of life rooted in the past. The vision of the JVF is to use Virasat as a force for real progress for the poor and marginalized people. It is 'a replicable model for inclusive growth based in traditional knowledge and values that lie with the majority of the people' (Jaipur Virasat Foundation, 2009: n.p.).

The JVF has worked to raise awareness and respect for Virasat across Rajasthan, encouraging popular participation in Virasat activities, drawing huge audiences to some events. It has created new cultural tourism products for the region, notably the Jaipur Heritage International Festival, the Jaipur Literature Festival and the Rajasthan International Folk Festival. These are annual events that showcase local talent but project them to a wider audience. In this way new recognition has been won for the traditional arts and crafts of the area and new demand for the products of local workers. A state-wide membership organization, Rajashtan CAN, a non-profit organization, has been set up to upscale these culture-based development activities, and develop tourism and the crafts trade. For example, there is an annual crafts bazaar. JVF also puts an emphasis on actively involving young people and building their pride in their culture. (Sources: Jaipur Virasat Foundation (2009); Singh (2009).)

Festivals can be used in many different contexts and can be targeted at very diverse audiences – from famous international festivals such as those at Salzburg or Edinburgh to very local events that mainly serve to strengthen cohesion within a community and provide inspiration and hope to local people. The value of this latter type of festival should not be underestimated; many are used to create new opportunities and encourage creativity and, as we have already seen, a culture of creativity and innovation is important for economic development. For example, the Craigmillar Festival Society was a leader in setting up a community arts festival led mainly by women in a deprived neighbourhood of Edinburgh in the 1960s. It developed into an annual event and proved to be a catalyst for other activity such as action on housing, childcare and jobs. Eventually there was success in getting a small local industrial estate and for a period the Society was able to act as a conduit for local funding through EU and UK programmes (Crummy, 1992). The problems, as Craigmillar's experience showed, are in sustaining energies in a voluntary organization and sustaining funds from public sector grant programmes. Even more important, despite the energy of the Craigmillar Festival Society, the area remained one of the most deprived neighbourhoods in Scotland. Community arts can only take a community so far: skills, job markets and housing markets shape the prospects of any such district.

Summary

Leisure and tourism are increasingly significant aspects of regional and local economies. The chapter has not sought to cover all the forms of leisure and tourism. The list is too extensive, but it does testify to the innovative capacity that has been evident in the industry since the 1990s. As with the rest of the book, our aim has been to exemplify and test out our typologies about policy approaches and governance styles in regional and local economic development by exploring what practice is doing. They again prove useful at a general level, though not surprisingly, real situations do not always fit neatly within our abstract categories.

Competition for major events has become one of the defining features of the contemporary world and a key marker both for locations seeking global city status and leading cites ranked in the second or third tier. While business is clearly seen as a beneficiary of such captive markets once they have been secured, it is too reductionist to class this as 'pro-business competition'. Much of the machismo involved in such competition is from political leaders: global corporate business can work with whoever wins. Similarly, the capacity of an institution such as the world's soccer federation, FIFA, to accumulate huge income from its World Cup should be recognized. There is a real risk that in creating the large development projects required for hosting such events, and in consenting to the conditions imposed by the international bodies, whether the International Olympic Committee or UNESCO, the short-term and long-term costs to local residents and existing businesses get marginalized. Critiques of the lack of a 'legacy' from big events have prompted a concern to link them with area regeneration, as is the case for the London Olympics in 2012.

National and regional/local governments (albeit with private sector partners) are usually key drivers of such competitive approaches. Similarly, they are likely to lead regeneration approaches, with projects and grants key governance mechanisms. The commercial nature of the leisure industry, and the extent to which fashion shapes opportunities for revenues, poses challenges for regeneration approaches. There is certainly potential for a major new facility (an art gallery or museum, for example), to lever other investment into a local economy. However, the revenue side of the main facility may be difficult to sustain once the novelty wears off and newer competitors enter the market. One feature of the success of the casino-led regeneration of Atlantic City was that there were no nearby competitors and it fed directly on a strong commercial income stream. However, the nature of regeneration is that it changes a place, and that will again create winners and losers, as the Festival Park example showed.

The eco-modernization approach might usefully be stretched to encompass other forms of cultural conservation, which seek to find new global markets as a means to sustain places and practices that otherwise are under threat. A global 'connexity' model, linking local places into new and often innovative networks and supply chains seems central to this practice, along with a governance style that requires smart planning and regulation if success is to be achieved. NGOs and social enterprises seem to play a leading role in eco-tourism and strategies that aspire to conserve traditional cultures (as distinct from marketing pastiche versions of such cultures, laced with stereotypes of dress, food, etc.).

Some eco-tourism or cultural conservation projects also have a distinct pro-poor agenda, as indicated by our examples. Without such a dimension there is the risk that in saving the planet for future generations, they sacrifice the livelihoods of poor and marginalized groups in this generation who live in the area affected by the project.

Topics for discussion

What are the ingredients that make a successful cultural quarter?

Eco-tourism is an attractive idea, but what needs to be done to ensure that its development meets environmental, economic and social needs?

Related reading

J. Montgomery (2007) *The New Wealth of Cities: City Dynamics and the Fifth Wave* (Aldershot, UK and Burlington, VT: Ashgate), 299–358.

S. Wearing and J. Neil (2009) *Ecotourism: Impacts, Potentials and Possibilities,* 2nd edn (Oxford, UK: Butterworth-Heinemann), 36–60.

12 Place Marketing

As place competition has increased so also has place marketing and place branding. Some argue that the practice is not really new. Ward and Gold (1994: 2) showed that seaside resorts have a long history of producing posters and pamphlets advertising their 'golden sands, invigorating climates … [and] welcoming hotels'. In the USA there is a long tradition of promoting towns. The activity gave rise to a new word, 'boosterism'. It was typically led by a local business grouping, which subsequently added support from other quarters to create a 'growth coalition' (Logan and Molotch, 1987: 62). Meanwhile, in the UK in the 1960s, the old industrial city of Newcastle-upon-Tyne began to project itself as 'the New Brasilia' and 'The Milan of the North', as it embarked on a major programme of comprehensive redevelopment. In general, though, the promotional aspect of regional and local economic development in those days was concentrated on advertising the land and property aspects of a place, its industrial estates and access to the highway network. It has become more sophisticated and widespread.

Economic restructuring and deindustrialization in the 1970s and 1980s coincided with a new level of competition between places – for foreign direct investment, to protect their town centres from out-of-town competition, and to halt the drift of people and jobs out of the cities. Reimaging and place marketing became definitive features of the new, more entrepreneurial form of urban governance and old industrial cities. Wigan, a coal mining town in the north-west of England was immortalized in *The Road to Wigan Pier*, George Orwell's account of grim working-class life in the 1930s. In the 1980s its city council created the Wigan Pier Heritage Centre in a decaying canal-side warehouse. Pittsburgh was a classic example of reimaging as part of an urban regeneration strategy. The story of its transformation from a city of declining heavy industries to a 'liveable' city is told in Box 12.1. Of course Pittsburgh had another reality that was not featured

247

Box 12.1: Reimaging an industrial city: Pittsburgh (USA)

Pittsburgh was a steel-producing city with a range of other heavy industries. It was notorious for its grime and air pollution. However its steel industry could not compete with cheaper overseas producers and between 1979 and 1987 more than 67,000 steel jobs were lost together with 63,000 heavy manufacturing jobs. The population had been over 700,000 in 1950, but now plunged below the 400,000 mark.

A public–private partnership convened a commission to seek a new way forward. One result was a series of marketing campaigns by a range of bodies – the Greater Pittsburgh Office of Promotion, the Urban Redevelopment Authority, the Neighbourhoods for Living Centre (marketing the residential neighbourhoods), and Penn's South West Association (a non-profit regional economic development body).

These produced a wide range of brochures, information packs and videos, singing the praises of a city that was transformed from a smoky industrial place to a high technology economy where the University employs more people than does the largest surviving steel company. Typical points made in the publicity material were air quality that matched that of 'the green rolling hills of Louisville, Kentucky', safety from personal crime, affordable housing, and a greater density of golf courses per capita than any other US city. Between 1975 and 1987 over 100,000 jobs were created, mostly in education, health care and research. In 1985 the city received the national accolade of 'the most liveable city' in the USA. (Source: Holcomb (1993).)

---

in the promotional exercises. It was a divided city, with high levels of black unemployment and infant mortality (Holcomb, 1993). Holcomb (1994) argued that increasing competition between places required not just the transformation of traditional industrial cities into 'post-industrial' service centres, but also a reimaging of place and a remaking of the built environment. Thus once-industrial cities have been remade to fit an image of what are seen as the desirable features of a post-industrial city, and for the major cities, a 'global city'.

Place identity

Griffiths (1998) argued that place marketing strategies have to speak not only to external audiences but also to internal ones.

The message to investors, migrants and high spenders also needs to create internal legitimation for regeneration polices and foster social cohesion. Kearns and Philo (1993: 3) made a similar point, arguing that the economic logic of selling places includes a subtle form of socialization, that sought to convince local residents 'many of whom will be disadvantaged and potentially disaffected, that they are cogs in a successful community and that all sorts of "good things" are really being done on their behalf'. Such tensions over new images are rooted in conflicting interests, but also different senses of place identity. Identity is how you see yourself: image is how others see you. Place identities – what residents think are the essential character of a place – are formed through a mix of meanings, experiences, memories and actions. Ultimately they are personal; the meaning of a place to each of us depends on our own experience of it. But they are also fashioned by social structures and shared experiences, so there can be common ground about what makes a place unique. However, there are likely to be a number of

---

Box 12.2: A contested street name: King Boulevard, Chattanooga (USA)

In 1981, the city of Chattanooga, Tennessee, proposed renaming Ninth Street to Martin Luther King Boulevard, to commemorate the civil rights leader assassinated in 1968. The proposal was controversial. One white property owner in the area, named T. A. Lupton, alleged that such a renaming had 'racial overtones' and would limit his ability to rent office space to businesses (Dwyer and Alderman, 2008: 3). Indeed, Lupton even suggested that renaming the street to honour King would cause him to have to withdraw from participation in a federally funded urban redevelopment programme tabled for Chattanooga's city centre. However, others threatened to push federal authorities to withdraw their financing *unless* the street's name was changed in memory of King.

City leaders first bowed to pressure to retain the Ninth Street name, but subsequent protests by prominent members of the African-American community led to King Boulevard being designated in 1982. Lupton continued to argue that the street renaming would damage the area's potential to develop economically. However, he constructed the office buildings he had initially threatened to shelve, albeit by building a private road and giving the new properties the address 'Union Square'. (Source: Dwyer and Alderman (2008).)

different identities for any one place, with different social groups (e.g. young people, old people, long-term residents, new residents, small local firms or international companies, etc.) seeing the same place in different ways. Indeed, something as apparently mundane as a street name can in fact become a focus for conflicts over the identity of a city, as the example of Martin Luther King Boulevard in Box 12.2 shows.

Issues of place identity are likely to be particularly difficult and economically damaging in locations where there has been conflict and rapid change, such as in the Vietnamese city of Vinh (see Box 12.3). Shannon and Loeckx (2004: 131), discussing Vinh, argued that its 'identity must be almost nearly invented anew'. In Vinh, issues of identity infused practical decisions on how to develop and redevelop a city. The team from UN–Habitat undertook 'layered narratives' surveys with locals to develop understandings

---

Box 12.3: Tradition and transition in city planning: Vinh (Vietnam)

Vinh has a long history as a settlement. For centuries it was on Vietnam's southern frontier, then became the provincial capital of north-central Vietnam under French colonialism. It suffered damage in wars thereafter, and was substantially rebuilt with Soviet and Chinese assistance when the French withdrew in 1954, only to suffer further damage from US air raids during the Vietnam War. Once more the city was rebuilt as a socialist city, beginning in 1974, and using architects and planners from the then East Germany. Blocks of flats, designed in central Europe were constructed using low-quality materials and with poor technical detailing, and without regard to the climatic differences. Vinh was twinned with East Berlin. As Shannon and Loeckx (2004: 131) observed, 'The legacy of the socialist city is the monumental scale urbanity... combined with an international model of industry and celebration of the collective realm'.

In Vietnam's transition economy, Vinh and the province it is in, Nghe An, are competing with other secondary cities in Vietnam for foreign investment. Shannon and Loeckx (2004: 131) commented that 'the time has come to establish marketable distinctiveness that can

→

of the diverse histories of the city. They also identified the city's 'contested territories' ('industrial roles, ecological constraints and urban challenges') in the drive for modernization and development (Shannon and Loeckx, 2004: 125). A series of 'visions' were created to 'develop a unique identity, capitalizing on the sociocultural, geographical and historical potential of Vinh, its immediate surroundings and Nghe An province' (Shannon and Loeckx, 2004: 133). However, the outcomes were frustrated by politicians and officials in Hanoi. Shannon and Loeckx (2004: 145) commented that 'The fantastical thinking that Vinh can transform itself overnight into an orderly, individualistic-driven market system is irresponsible and results in irrelevant urban visions. Seductive imagery is not the solution for one of the city's most important urban sites'.

Vinh exemplifies many post-conflict situations where new building has been essential for economic reconstruction and has broken

---

draw capital'. However, given the legacy of East German buildings and the lack of a beautiful natural setting, 'Vinh's identity must be almost nearly invented anew' (Shannon and Loeckx, 2004: 131).

On the edge of the city gated 'European-style' villas are emerging, bringing 'eccentric splashes of colour to the otherwise grey city' (Shannon and Loeckx, 2004: 132). The city authorities continued to convert farmland into sites for industry, despite existing industrial parks being only half occupied. Similarly, proposals developed by a UN–Habitat team for demolition and upgrading of the Quang Trung Housing Estate, 'the single most dominating urban design/architectural work in Vinh', were 'significantly compromised' (Shannon and Loeckx, 2004:142, 143). The Ministry of Construction in Hanoi ruled instead that a national showpiece scheme should be developed in which the estate would become almost entirely 'market housing' with most of the present residents shifted to a new 'low-cost' housing project on the edge of the city.

Shannon and Loeckx (2004: 133) were critical of the way that the contemporary planning of the city 'is neither local nor global. There is no meaningful consideration of the local and an underestimation and political incapacity to convincingly deal with the global'. (Source: Shannon and Loeckx (2004).)

with past traditions. It also shows the problems of transposing solutions from different countries and cultures that are inappropriate for local conditions. Not only did this happen in the years after 1974, but officialdom and the entrepreneurs building on the edge of the city today seem in awe of a 'global' model of urban development, that is imagined to be necessary to attract inward investment.

Of course, other identities are possible, not least those that connect with a strong environmental narrative about a place. Sendai, Japan, as outlined in Box 12.4, attempted to use a 'green' place identity as a framework for a range of development policies. In Sendai, culture and history was the basis for a widely shared understanding about what makes a place special. This identity could then be a positive, structuring force in conceiving and delivering local development. Central government policy had been based on 'survival

---

Box 12.4: Using place identity for local mobilization and to set a policy framework: Sendai (Japan)

Sendai (population 1 million), 300km from Tokyo, developed from a seventeenth-century castle town to an early twentieth century industrial centre (Murakami and Wood, 2006: 447). After most of its central area was destroyed by wartime air raids in 1945, rapid industrialization and urbanization followed. Car ownership rose steeply, urban sprawl ensued and, in 1964, Sendai was designated as a 'new industrial city' as part of central government policy to encourage industrialization (Sato, 2006: 461). Population reached 545,000 in 1970.

Faced with rapid development, Sendai's citizens and local government wanted the city to retain its character. In 1962 the mayor set out a 'Healthy City Declaration' (Sato, 2006: 463), taking on board citizen concerns about environmental damage caused by economic development. A local masterplan was produced, though in Japan's centralized governmental system it was not legally enforceable. However, it was a channel through which the citizens and the administration could 'reconsider [what] the identity of the city should be' (Sato, 2006: 463).

→

through industrialization' (Tanaka and Murakami, 2006: 452). The environmental and historical themes in 'City of Trees' was a counter-narrative to the industrial identity which the city was beginning to acquire. As Healey (2006: 476) noted, in Japan landscape design and imagery are linked to 'deeply ingrained cultural and spiritual values'.

The 'City of Trees' was described by Tanaka and Murakami (2006: 459) as a 'Grand Concept', and a 'slogan' that gave a 'clear, comprehensible image'. It was developed in an iterative manner. However, they also stressed that 'key phrases alone are not effective ... a concrete concept must form the basis for real plans' (Tanaka and Murakami, 2006: 459). They also argued that it takes effort to establish grand concepts, and that informal governance helps to develop innovative ways of thinking and acting. In summary, the place identity forged for Sendai, with its echoes of a pre-industrial landscape, was an attempt to 'promote a distinct idea of the city'

The 1973 'City of Trees' plan was published by the Sendai Developer Committee, a voluntary organization whose office was in the city's Chamber of Commerce and Industry (Tanaka and Murakami, 2006: 453). The Committee had been set up in 1971 to co-ordinate major projects, and brought together leading public officials from different levels of government, local business leaders and academics. It had proved difficult to reach agreement on issues and a consultant, Professor Yoshizaka, was asked to develop the basis for a shared vision. His team engaged in a wide public consultation process.

Although the plan was not statutory, and was not immediately reflected in projects, the 'City of Trees' philosophy proved very influential. 'The memory of the city of trees and a winding river with green banks,' comments Healey (2006: 476), was 'kept alive through the hugely destructive wartime fire bombing and a strategy of re-planting which now provides the city with shade and pollution-cleaning greenery'. Most post-1973 development plans, therefore, 'shared the ideals of the "City of Trees" and were able to keep the vitality of the central commercial districts, and the new tree-lined boulevards began to attract many visitors as well as local people for various community-led festivals' (Tanaka and Murakami (2006: 458). (Sources: Tanaka and Murakami (2006); Sato (2006); Healey (2006).)

that would maximize the benefits and minimize the damage of national industrial development. 'As a result the city now attracts commuters from Tokyo because of the quality of its urban environment (Healey, 2006: 477) and its access to the 'bullet train'.

In summary, identities of a place are partly inherited and hard to change. Things like the local climate, nature, history, cultural heritage and the fame of a local sports club have fashioned them. However, there are other aspects that can be shaped by regional or local action. These include things like provision and maintenance of open space or cultural facilities, the schools, regeneration of run-down areas, the quality of a town centre etc.

Using design of the public realm in urban competition

As the discussion above has shown, the built and natural environment can be components of place identities. Regional and local economic development policies that centre on pro-business competition to attract investment, or on area regeneration are likely to go further and actively try to use architecture and design to project an image of the place to investors and potential residents. For example, in England, the Urban Task Force (2005) led by the architect Sir Richard Rogers, unequivocally identified the poor quality of the urban environment as having contributed to the exodus from English towns and cities. Their report suggested that good urban design would redress this. The role of urban design in local economic development was prescribed as follows:

> An attractive, well-designed environment can help create a framework for promoting economic identity and growth ... it can ensure that the city does not stagnate, by continually recycling buildings and spaces to perform new economic functions compatible with the city's business needs. In the twenty-first century , it is the skilled worker, as well as the global company, who will be footloose. Cities must work hard to attract and retain both. (Urban Task Force, 2005: 16)

Similarly, the Commission for Architecture and the Built Environment (CABE) argued that good design could benefit economic development by, amongst other things, raising the prestige of places and raising confidence in development opportunities (DETR/CABE, 2001). Such rhetoric focuses on competition, rather than inclusion.

For example, Crilley (1993: 233) noted that 'Architecture, as much as expensive city marketing campaigns, is mobilized to transmit a catching, idiosyncratic image of urban vitality', Crilley said that this generalization holds for all levels of the urban hierarchy. Paris, a world city, commissioned a number of *grands projets* in the 1970s and 1980s. Examples include the Pompidou centre (Beaubourg), the Opéra-Bastille, Ieoh Ming Pei's pyramid at the Louvre, the science park at La Villette, and the Musée d'Orsay. All were defiantly anti-pastiche and assertive of innovation. The most dazzling of all was the Grande Arche de la Défense. It constitutes the terminus of the visual link between the Louvre, the Arc de Triomphe and the new business centre of La Défense. Kearns (1993: 88) quoted a description of the Grande Arche: '[t]he facades of this open cube appear with a bright and smooth surface, symbolising a micro-chip, showing the lines of communication – an abstract graphic work inspired by the most brilliant invention of modern electronics'.

Neill (2003) described how Berlin changed from being associated with industrial production to become a major centre linking East and West in the enlarged European Union. He focused particularly on Potsdamer Platz, the heart of pre-Second World War Berlin that was then divided by the Berlin Wall. After reunification, and to accelerate the mutation of Berlin into its new European role, land here was sold by the government of Berlin at discount prices to Debis, a subsidiary of Daimler-Benz, for development of a major office and business complex. Berlin gained 'a new corporate heart' as the world's leading architects worked on Europe's largest building site.

There have been similar iconic developments in major cities around the world. They are usually commissioned by governments who use architectural competitions, judged by international juries of professionals. The governance approach is thus top-down. The architecture seeks to dazzle through extravagant renditions of modern, international building styles. For example, the China Central Television building, completed in 2009, occupies a 10-hectare site in Beijing. It has two 'L-shaped' towers (234 meters and 194 meters high) that are joined together at the top and the bottom, but at an angle. An international competition was held in 2002 and won by the Dutch architect Rem Koolhaas and his company OMA, who worked on it in partnership with the East China Architecture and Design Institute.

Such 'flagship projects' are so high profile and prestigious that they are expected to have catalytic and spillover effects, creating a momentum sufficient to attract other developments to the area or city. This was the case in Chicago where millions of dollars were invested in a new city centre 'Millennium Park', as described in Box 12.5.

A notch down the urban hierarchy from Chicago, Berlin or Paris we find Birmingham, aspiring to be a European City, with its convention centre and extensive public arts in the civic spaces at the centre of the city. These have been ways of redefining the negative image that attached to Birmingham, which owed much to 1960s infrastructure such as the inner ring road and the shopping and office complex of the Bull Ring and the Rotunda. Pedestrianization and sculptures have redefined the heart of the city. Loftman and Nevin (2003: 88) analysed Birmingham's 'pro-growth' city centre regeneration and its use of flagship projects, tracing the story from the 1980s to 2002. They argued that these prestige projects

---

Box 12.5: A flagship development: Millennium Park, Chicago (USA)

In 2004, after almost seven years of construction, the City of Chicago unveiled Millennium Park. A multimillion dollar revitalization of around 25 acres (10 hectares) in the city centre that had been rail tracks, car parks and locomotive yards, Millennium Park was more than just a park. It was a central element of the policies under Mayor Richard M. Daley to renovate the shore of Lake Michigan as a 'lakefront tourist and leisure landscape' (Gilfoyle, 2006: 350). It included an underground car park, bicycle storage amenities and a commuter rail station; new fountains designed by Jaume Plensa; a massive stainless steel sculpture entitled 'Cloud Gate' by Anish Kapoor (its shape earning it the moniker 'The Bean' – a local term that soon became shorthand for Millennium Park as a whole); a concert performance area and footbridge designed by Frank Gehry; a 1,500-seat theatre built deep into the ground with an entrance at street level; and, other walkways, gardens and plantings.

→

succeeded in making Birmingham an 'international business and leisure city' instead of 'a manufacturing city', but concluded that in many respects the impacts of such development on poor residents of the city, who are dependent on 'basic' local authority services, have been negative.

Place marketing and branding

Marketing evolved in the 1970s to embrace forms that sought to influence attitudes – 'image marketing' – focusing less on claims for the product and more on associating the product with a range of positive feelings among target groups. This paved the way within the marketing industry for the development of place marketing. However, Ashworth and Voogd (1994) stressed that places as products are not the same as more conventional commodities. For example, what is 'consumed' may not match the precise spatial boundaries of the place itself – e.g. those drawn to the city may locate in the

---

Seen from the air or on a map, the layout of Millennium Park looks like the floor plan of a house comprising corridors, rather than the wide open spaces of older public parks like New York's Central Park and London's Hyde Park. The design seems deliberately restrictive, with limited entrances to each section of the park enabling sections to be closed off and, at the right price, rented out for private events. It was developed on public land but with private sponsorship of its various parts, and ran well over time and budget.

Millennium Park was intended to stimulate the real estate market in central Chicago, particularly to act as a catalyst for the nascent trend of converting city centre commercial office space into high priced flats and condominiums. 'City officials', comments Gilfoyle (2006: 170), 'insisted that Millennium Park would give "added luster to nearby commercial properties, particularly those for overseas investors", thus enhancing the city's tax coffers in the years ahead'. Such investments did indeed follow, from both local and international property developers and speculators and Millennium Park has become a major tourist attraction. It is a central icon of the 'new' Chicago of the twenty-first century. No other city in the USA, suggests Gilfoyle (2006: 341, 345) 'incorporates public art with distinctive urbanism like Millennium Park'.

surrounding suburbs. The same physical assets, facilities or place attributes are being simultaneously marketed to different customers for different purposes.

If a place has poor facilities and a poor image, marketing alone will not solve the problems. Ashworth and Voogd (1994) identified three other situations, each requiring a different strategy:

- poor facilities with a favourable image – improve the product, rather than promote it;
- a favourable image and good facilities – only market to the level required to maintain this situation; and
- good facilities with an undeserved poor image or a weak/non-existent image – promotion and marketing required.

One aspect that can damage a city's image and make it less competitive is crime (UN–Habitat, 2006: 147). At best, capital has to be diverted into security, at worst investors fear their assets might get stolen, and employees become reluctant to leave or go to work in the dark. This means that safety is often a part of the place marketing package, as occurred in Mexico City in 2002, but statistics and bad publicity can undermine such efforts, as happened in Philadelphia in the 1990s (see Box 12.6).

As well as being honest, place marketing needs to analyse the 'offer', the target market and the competition. The Creative Coast Alliance (TCCA), based in Savannah, Georgia, for example, has a mission to create, grow and attract knowledge- and technology-based economic development through both existing companies and new businesses. Savannah has traditionally been a tourist town and its Savannah Economic Development Agency (SEDA) works with big-box stores and other established manufacturers to create jobs. In setting out to attract smaller, creative and technology companies, Savannah established the Creative Coast Initiative, with TCCA as a semi-autonomous agency. Working with companies that employ between five and 10 people, TCCA hosts networking and social events and encourages small and mid-size companies to relocate to Savannah. One success story for TCCA is Smack Dab Studios which moved from Atlanta to Savannah in 2006. The company subsequently grew from employing two or three people to 13 to14 and, soon after, other companies that worked closely with Smack Dab also relocated to Savannah (Haile, 2008). TCCA's targeted approach has also led to strategic connections with local 'business angel' investors and the Georgia Institute of Technology's business incubator programme.

The fact that Savannah remains a tourist centre is not a problem: it is large enough and sufficiently well established to sustain that while adding a new marketing stream targeted at creative industries in the region. One of the advantages that big cities have is that they can typically offer a range of these 'products' – they can be a place of research and learning, but also a centre for culture and have an airport. Smaller communities are unlikely to be able to offer all these things, and so have to be more focused in their own place-marketing, or combine with others as a region to offer more. There are situations where competition is best advanced through cooperation with others.

'Differentiate or perish' is a mantra to place-marketing professionals. A visit to the website of the Creative Coast Alliance (www.thecreativecoast.org) gives some insight into how they have tackled this. Lots of other cities are likely to be chasing 'creative sector' jobs, so what does Savannah have to offer that is special? The unique qualities are projected through a style that is deliberately informal, young-sounding and confidently self-mocking: 'talent to spare', 'we speak geek', whacky design student friends', 'drunk on creative juice' and 'quirky people'.

By presenting itself in the imagined linguistic style of a 25-year-old aspiring computer-graphics designer, TCCA is seeking to brand itself and by extension the place it is marketing. The website design itself stops somewhere short of embodying the brand, being rather more formal and traditional in layout (though the combination of blues, greens and white and the font give it a certain 'cool' feel). Branding is part of the way of bridging the gap between the identity of a place and its image. Thus branding has to be built on authentic qualities of the place. It should not be something invented so as to fit only an aspiration: there must be some basis in reality.

Thus branding is about content (and for commercial products it appears that some notion of values is an important part of a brand). But it is also about communication of a reality. Basic things like the name of a place are part of the brand. From an economic development viewpoint it does not help if the name is something conjured up by bureaucrats after a rationalization of local government, and only meaningful to them. Similarly, while the name is likely to be fixed

---

Box 12.6: Crime and place image: Mexico City (Mexico) and Philadelphia (USA)

In 2002, Giuliani Partners Group, the consultancy company operated by New York City's former Mayor, Rudolph Giuliani, was hired on a US$4m. contract to bring 'zero tolerance' policing to Mexico City. The publicity surrounding such initiatives, and visual presence of police officers on the streets, generated the impression that the city was safer and thus more attractive to potential residents and investors. Four years after Giuliani Partners arrived in Mexico City, although Giuliani himself claimed a crime rate reduced by 8% (and by 28% in the city centre), local residents told Mountz and Curran (2009: 1036) that Giuliani's policing strategies 'did nothing' and were largely superficial exercises with little presence beyond the historic central area. Mountz and Curran (2009: 1039) conclude that 'The implementation of zero tolerance as a policy rests on the image of government that zero tolerance provides, an assurance to capital that its interests are valued and will be protected. Plan Giuliani was more important as public spectacle than as actual policy'.

→

---

already, that may or may not be an asset. It will be known locally, but may, for example be difficult for foreigners to pronounce (in which case it can be written out phonetically for them, e.g. on the website or promotional materials). Logos are used to project a brand, though some can be ambiguous. Slogans spell out key messages. Style always matters: colours, fonts, graphics, photos etc. need to have consistency with the brand and express the key message.

When coordinated, a city's place branding can be part of a wider economic development strategy. The strategy of the Wildwoods, discussed in Box 12.7, sought to target families rather than to compete with the casinos of Atlantic City and the Victorian bed and breakfasts of nearby Cape May. A clear brand has been developed that is not just a slogan, though there is one: 'It's cool! It's Retro! It's Wildwood' (Doo Wop Preservation League, 2009). Rather the brand is rooted in the place and its buildings and is reinforced through the operation of the local planning system and the investments of enthusiasts and local businesses.

In another example, in the 1970s, Philadelphia marketed itself as the USA's 'safest large city'. This claim was based on crime statistics that had been falsified since the 1950s (Brownlow, 2009: 1695). For almost 50 years Philadelphia's Police Department consistently downgraded and under-reported crimes, particularly rapes and sexual assaults committed against poor, primarily African-American, women. This enabled Philadelphia to boast of its supposed safety to potential investors and new residents. 'Downplaying crime had become part of a culture to make the city of Philadelphia seem more crime-free than it actually was, a form of salesmanship to lure tourism and business' (Hockenberry, 2003, cited in Brownlow, 2009: 1696). The erroneous crime statistics and, with them, the marketing of safety, Brownlow (2009: 1696) noted, 'invited economic success', and indirectly generated business, stimulated high-income housing developments, new restaurants and entertainment venues. Only after a young, upper class, white woman was raped and murdered in the late-1990s did Philadelphia's manipulation of crime data became apparent (Brownlow, 2009). For Philadelphia and other US cities, concluded Brownlow (2009: 1681) 'safety (or, at least, perceived safety) is of central importance to urban economic development, whereby to be a competitive city is to be a safe city (or, at least, that is perceived to be safe by the consuming public) and vice versa'.

In a new settlement on a greenfield site, the branding can be comprehensive and consistent. A striking example is Thames Town, some 30km from downtown Shanghai, but 'an authentic (sic) British-style town' (Thames Town, 2009). It is part of a very coherent development strategy. In 2001 the Shanghai Municipal Government launched a strategic development concept called 'One City Nine Towns'. The plan was for the suburban districts to link major economic projects and the construction of major transport infrastructure, and develop as major centres in their own right, reversing the situation of an expanding city centre and scattered suburbs. The target is to create 'an industrialized, urbanized and modernized city-town cluster, as well as an urban economic rim' (Thames Town, 2009). One of the new centres is Songjiang New City, and Thames Town is a one square kilometre area jointly developed by Shanghai Songjiang New City Construction and Development

---

**Box 12.7: Place marketing through architecture and music:
The Wildwoods, New Jersey (USA)**

The Wildwoods, New Jersey, is a beachside vacation resort. In 1997
local business leaders, motel owners, restaurateurs and architecture
preservationists, formed the Doo Wop Preservation League (DWPL).
This independent group proposed that the Wildwoods' economic
development strategy be based around kitsch 1950s architecture
(primarily of motels) and the period's 'Doo Wop' style of music
popularized by performers such as the Ink Spots. Pitching their efforts
as 'souped up preservation', the DWPL renovated a 1950s restaurant
into a Doo Wop Museum, complete with the Jitterbug Malt Shop that
sells milkshakes, and signage from disused and demolished businesses
in a Neon Sign Garden. A subsequent strategy has been to preserve
the original architecture and décor of two main streets as the 'Doo
Wop Motel District, the largest concentration of mid-[20th] Century
commercial architecture in America' (DWPL, 2009: n.p.). Although
DWPL efforts to designate hundreds of buildings as together combining
a National Historic District have been unsuccessful, individual motels
have been designated historically significant at both state and national
levels.

→

Co., Ltd, and large real estate corporations. The streets and the
buildings look like those of an English market town, 'Reviving
the spirit of the true-blue English lifestyle' in this 'quaint town'
(Thames Town, 2009).

Marketing of eco-places

While most place marketing is down to support competitiveness
and regeneration strategies, there are a growing number of practices that promote places as adopting an ecological approach to
development. As in much of the eco-modernization approach,
the Scandinavians played a leading role. James and Lahti (2004)
described the origins. In 1980 the economically depressed Finnish town of Suomussalmi became the first eco-municipality in

In 2005 the DWPL and Wildwood Crest Planning Board devised a 10-point plan for development of lodging in the resort area. It aimed to reduce the number of motels being demolished and replaced by condominiums. The DWPL proposed allowing motel expansion and renovation to add modern facilities to existing structures, additional parking spaces, gift shops, and alteration of existing zoning laws to initiate a 'Mixed Resort Use' category.

Current and new businesses are encouraged to renovate or construct their premises using the DWPL's 'How To Doo Wop Handbook' design guide. One suggestion is that well-established businesses, such as national chain restaurants, redesign their signage into 1930s–1950s styles. The Mayor's office supports the Doo Wop architectural design standards, although compliance with them is voluntary. Developers are encouraged to submit architectural plans to the DWPL for review, though the DWPL views are not legally binding. This strategy has led to the construction of 'neo-Doo Wop' properties that replicate or even outdo the original buildings with their kitsch additions, such as heart-shaped swimming pools or neon signs depicting Martini glasses. Other developers have transformed motel buildings into condominiums while retaining and restoring the original signage and building exteriors. The plastic palm trees at the StarLux Motel (Figure 12.1) should not be missed! (Sources: Hirsch (2008); Doo Wop Preservation League (2009).)

Scandinavia. Three years later, Övertorneå in Sweden, badly hit by the economic recession and with 20 per cent regional unemployment, followed suit. New enterprises were developed: organic farms, beekeeping, fish farms and eco-tourism among them. It became 100 per cent free of fossil fuel use in its municipal operations. Public transport is free and cars run on ethanol. In 1990 at a conference in Orsa, Sweden, municipal officials, environmental experts and others formed an association of eco-municipalities. By 2004, there were 60 members. James and Lahti stressed the central part that public involvement plays in eco-municipalities.

Since then similar bottom-up initiatives have sprung up in 'green places' elsewhere. There is a network of Transition Towns. 'A Transition Initiative (which could be a town, village, university or island, etc.) is a community-led response to the pressures of climate

Figure 12.1   **StarLux Motel, Wildwoods, New Jersey (USA)**

change, fossil fuel depletion and increasingly, economic contraction' (Transition Network, 2010). As the website explains the process is driven by a small but growing group of people, who then begin 'an EDAP (Energy Descent Action Plan) process. This is a community-visioned and community-designed 15–20 year plan that creates a coordinated range of projects ... with the aim of bringing the community to a sufficiently resilient and low CO_2-emitting state'. Implementation follows.

While initiatives like Transition Towns work with existing settlements, a number of specially designed new settlements are being marketed as 'eco-cities'. For example Masdar City in Abu Dhabi is claiming it will be the world's first carbon-neutral city, using new solar technologies (Alternative Energy 2010). The governance structure behind this project could hardly be more different than that in Transition Towns: the project is funded by the ruler of Abu Dhabi, Sheikh Khalifa bin Zayed Al Nahyan.

Dongtan on Chongming island at the mouth of the Yangtze River near Shanghai is already under development. The Sino-Singapore eco-city Tianjin is another top-down planned project getting underway as this book is being written (Channel News Asia, 2010).

Inclusive cities

Jensen-Butler (1999) argued that a measure of equity within a city is necessary to avoid a negative image. The main pro-poor form of place imaging is the idea of 'inclusive cities'. The concept covers social inclusion (*all* residents, regardless of race, ethnicity, gender or socio-economic status), political inclusion (civil rights, liberties and participation), cultural inclusion (celebrating diversity) and, of course, economic inclusion though 'equal opportunities for business and access to employment, and... pro-poor economic policies' (UN–Habitat 2010: 56). In a survey of 27 cities across Asia, Africa and Latin America, UN–Habitat (2010: 149) found that economic inclusiveness was linked (in descending order) to:

- coordination and planning at all levels of government;
- promotion of political will, free expression and other human rights by organized civil society;
- government-induced employment;
- fiscal incentives for business along with contractual and legal certainty in the general business environment; and
- freedom of the press and multi-party elections.

In 2010 the Commonwealth Local Government Forum and the Commonwealth Association of Planners were working together to create a Commonwealth Network of Inclusive Cities that would be based on knowledge exchange and support amongst practitioners. A meeting of a Pilot Network in Ahmadabad resulted in two issues being identified as priority topics: migrants and local economic development.

This emergent work is based on the idea of the 'Right to the City', which was elaborated by Lefebvre (1968, 1973, 1990) and developed by Mitchell (2003). The fundamental and very practical idea is that city living offers the 'urban advantage', a range of services and opportunities that every person should be able to access. In addition, as part of a new contract between governments and citizens, there should be rights to participate in the governance of cities.

These may sound very generalized concepts, distant from the practice of local economic development. However, as several of the case studies in the book have shown, place-based economic development policies are frequently imposed from above, take no account of the needs of poor and marginalized groups, and in some cases exclude them from sources of housing and income. Land and property are commodities with the ability to command a market price, and thus place a crucial filter on who can gain access. As UN–Habitat (2010: 90) observed, everywhere access to these benefits that urban living can bring 'is determined by various 'organizations and institutions – including, crucially, the formal land and labour markets as well as public utilities. The problem in developing countries is that most of these institutions are weak or dysfunctional' or lacking altogether. The result is that private interests are able to claim more than their fair share of the benefits of the 'urban advantage'. The main losers, said UN–Habitat, were young slum dwellers, particularly women, who were forced to live and work in informal, insecure conditions.

The idea of the 'Right to the City' has been taken up most enthusiastically in Latin America. Where 'the nature of state action or its failure to act has determined the exclusionary nature of urban development in Latin America, combining property speculation, widespread vacant urban land, environmental degradation, widespread gated communities, and above all the proliferation of precarious informal settlements' (Fernandes, 2007: 210).

Summary

Place marketing, branding and the use of flagship architectural projects have become an important practice when regional and local economic development policies seek to boost place competitiveness in the race to win new investment. Similarly, reimaging of places is an important part of creating new markets for land and property in area regeneration and attracting new businesses and members of the 'creative class'. To be credible, such approaches need to have some basis in reality, which may necessitate as a start-up the kind of physical redevelopment and social replacement that they then seek to sustain. Place marketing needs to be targeted, clear about what qualities of the place are the product that will appeal to its target, and also take account of the competition. Duplication of what others are already doing better is probably a waste of money. The challenge is to differentiate, while also maximizing the reach to potential 'customers'. While attention needs to be paid to residents' perceptions of place identity, to maintain legitimacy, the reality is that exercises of this type are usually undertaken through top-down forms of governance and public–private partnerships, with experts playing a decisive role, for example as designers and evaluators of anything from logos to iconic buildings.

Growing concerns about the environment underpin a range of practice-led initiatives that promote towns and cities as 'ecological'. Some of these are very bottom-up and see that route as fundamental to success, since governments are seen as unwilling or unable to take the lead. Such approaches tend to focus on ways to change the way existing settlements operate, and in the process to create new 'green' jobs as well as making places more resilient in the face of environmental hazards and the likely impacts of energy shortages. However, where major new eco-cities are developed, the approach is more likely to be top-down and to share some of the same features, and even the same architects, of the kind of iconic buildings that are designed to make 'global city' statements on urban skylines.

Finally, we have noted the rising interest in the idea of the 'Right to the City' and its translation into 'inclusive city' practices, many of which have been anticipated through case studies in earlier chapters. This approach holds out the vision of a shared sense of identity with the city, and a regional and local economic development practice that works to enhance the economic inclusion of the poor, women, ethnic minorities and other marginalized groups.

Topic for discussion

How might your town or neighbourhood brand itself as a 'transition town'?

Related reading

The 'Transition Initiatives Primer' (Brangwyn and Hopkins, 2008) is available at: www.transitiontowns.org/TransitionNetwork/TransitionPrimer

Look at the websites of regional and local development agencies and consider who they are targeting and what the place they are marketing has to offer that differentiates it from competitors.

13 Skills for Regional and Local Economic Development

This chapter retains the focus on policy and practice, but from a different angle. The previous chapters have presented many short examples of practices from many different places. To complement that breadth this chapter looks in more depth at the story of Pilsen, one neighbourhood in Chicago. In this way, the context and interconnectedness of a series of local economic development interventions can be analysed. The focus on Pilsen is then used in the second part of the chapter to highlight skills that can be used in regional and local economic development work. Skills are acquired during a career, though they may not be written down and reflected upon. Egan *et al.* (2004) argued that there are generic skills – skills that cut across traditional professional boundaries and are needed in a wide range of place development tasks. Similarly, Hague *et al.* (2006: 10) argued that 'Skills such as creativity, a capacity to challenge assumptions and grasp the big picture, and governance skills such as communication and negotiation may not be entirely new. What is different is that today they are essential'.

In the real world events do not come along neatly packaged into chapters like a book. Things are messy and edges between housing, transport, conservation, place marketing and any number of other things are blurred. Stakeholders have different agendas and disagreements are the norm not the exception. Power is all-pervasive, yet also multidimensional. A constellation of power bases and interests shape economic development decisions and actions, such as class, gender, ethnicity, the power of the market, the genius of individuals, the legacy of the past, strong or weak institutions or many other factors. Most day to day regional and local economic development simply does not get written about in books or learned articles, and may not even make it onto the internet. This is especially likely to be the case where the efforts for development are led by low income groups themselves with little access to formal agencies endowed through legislation, salaried staff and investment funds to develop and implement policies aimed at regional and local economic development. Yet it is our view that these 'hidden voices' are in fact critical to evaluating the success of such programmes.

Pilsen, Chicago: the front line of a global city

Pilsen is about 3 miles south west of Chicago's Loop central business district. It is a place where the contradictions and processes of economic development in a global city become apparent. It is no coincidence that Chicago's Economic Development Office is called without irony 'World Business Chicago' (WBC). Like several institutions that exercise power in the city, it is chaired by the city's mayor. In 2009 WBC was recognized by Site Selection Magazine as being one of the leading US economic development bodies. Similarly, *Foreign Direct Investment* magazine named Chicago as having the best foreign direct investment (FDI) promotion strategy of any North American city. Rita Athas, Executive Director of WBC said 'World Business Chicago is fortunate to be able to showcase the city's tremendous resources, including its access to the world, diverse and talented workforce and unparalleled quality of life' (World Business Chicago, 2009a). The city has undertaken major projects such as Millennium Park (see Box 12.5) to promote the status of its downtown. Chicago was ranked eighth in a list of global cities in 2008. It was especially highly rated for human capital and as a top global destination for higher education and claims to be an international 'green' leader (World Business Chicago 2009b). Quite clearly then the overarching economic development narrative in the city is one of pro-business competition to attract and retain inward investment. In terms of governance, Chicago is a 'development state', a city with a long tradition of a strong mayor and a Democratic Party political machine that runs the city.

Within what WBC called this 'top tier business location' (World Business Chicago 2009b) is Pilsen. From the 1870s until the 1940s, the neighbourhood's houses were mainly occupied by eastern

European immigrants who named the area after the Czech city of Plzen. They lived amongst light industrial buildings, small work-shops and local shops. Since the 1950s, the demographic profile of Pilsen has changed markedly, due to another wave of international migration. Today's residents trace their origins to Central and South America, primarily Mexico. In the 2000 US Census, Pilsen's popula-tion of around 44,000 was almost 90 per cent Hispanic and almost 50 per cent foreign born (Hague *et al.*, 2008: 1). The neighbour-hood is now one of Chicago's major Spanish-speaking communities (Grammenos, 2006), in a city where 'international connections' are marketed as an asset by WBC (World Business Chicago 2009b). Thus Pilsen is both a part of the global city, but in other respects apart from it, with housing and economic activities that do not fit the self-image of an international business centre.

Environmentally, Pilsen is old-fashioned. It suffers from land con-tamination and, where manufacturers are still active, continuing air pollution. Only two coal-burning power plants remain within Chicago – one is in Pilsen, the other is a couple of miles west of the neighbourhood. Consequently, Pilsen residents have higher than average rates of asthma and other illnesses associated with a pol-luted urban environment (Mead, 2007).

Pilsen's accessibility to the Loop, high numbers of immigrants and low income families mean that it is seen by the City of Chi-cago as an area with potential and need for development. How-ever, local economic development in Pilsen has become a complex and controversial issue with debates centring around several of the themes covered in this book – ethnic minority businesses, eminent domain, place marketing, housing, transportation, creative indus-tries clusters, premises for industrial use and area-based regen-eration programmes such as Tax Increment Financing (TIF) and Empowerment Zones (EZs).

Established communities have longer and different memories than do city officials or investors from outside. Thus today's issues in Pilsen are viewed by many residents through memories of previous conflicts, not as instruments in a policy for positioning Chicago in the rankings of global cities. In the 1950s two major redevelopments impacted on Pilsen and its residents. Eminent domain powers were used to create a campus for the University of Illinois, Chicago on land adjacent to Pilsen. Many houses were demolished and their res-idents were displaced. Grammenos (2006) noted that many Latino households moved into Pilsen as their old houses were cleared away. Around the same time, hundreds of houses in Pilsen itself were demolished to make way for a major highway that also cut through industrial properties. These experiences still shape attitudes of local residents when faced with proposals for radical changes in their neighbourhood. Thus, from the 1980s onwards, real estate interests, politicians, community residents and non-profit organizations have lined up for and against different development strategies. In particular, the period from the late-1990s until 2009 saw some major controversies, each of which shed light on the approaches to local economic development hypothesized in the typology in Chapter 1.

Chicago's Empowerment Zone

Area regeneration has been the main approach adopted in Pilsen, primarily through the establishment in 1994 of one of the USA's first federal EZs. The EZ programme is a local economic development tool that geographically targets severely distressed areas. In governance terms it fits ideas of the 'project state'. US EZs were initially funded by US$4bn over 10 years and aimed to generate public–private partnerships, reduce poverty, and integrate community organizations into the planning process for their localities (McCarthy, 1998; Keating and Krumholz, 1999). EZs aimed to offer 'an inclusive strategic planning process that included local government(s), community organizations, local businesses, and, ideally, residents within the proposed zone-designated area' (Oakley and Tsao, 2006: 445; 2007). Tax incentives and favourable loans were provided to businesses to encourage employment and business development. The programmes pursued were intended to utilize federal monies to generate community development partnerships, include residents in neighbourhood development strategies, encourage environmentally sustainable practices, stimulate job creation and enable maintenance of infrastructure to revitalize depressed locales. Thus although primarily a regeneration programme, the EZ idea also made reference to inclusion, environmental sustainability and strategic planning. This confirms that our typology needs to be interpreted with some flexibility.

In Chicago, the 14-square mile EZ was divided into three 'clusters', i.e. separate, non-contiguous sites (Merrion, 2006). Pilsen was in one of these. Gittell, *et al.* (1998: 538) said that 'Each cluster met separately to determine community priorities and develop programme ideas. Organizations outside the clusters also contributed programme priorities. As a result of competition within and across clusters, few actual programmes were firmly in place in Chicago's proposal. Instead, Chicago's strategic plan contained what some termed a laundry list of project ideas'.

Organizations awarded EZ funding for capital projects are expected to make every effort to hire EZ residents to work on capital projects and upon project completion as permanent hires. This reflects recognition of the need to integrate property-based and people-based strategies. However, during 2007 there were only 14 construction hires and 39 permanent hires across Chicago's three zones (Housing and Urban Development, 2009). Indeed, Merrion (2006) notes that Pilsen and the other areas within Chicago's EZ actually fared worse than other depressed areas of the city, losing more jobs and businesses. Although some non-profits received grants, few companies utilized the federally available funds or took advantage of the tax breaks for hiring local residents. After ten years of operation, Merrion (2006: 3) explained that critics believed 'the city lacked a strategy to nurture businesses and create jobs', and that Chicago's EZ was a $100m. 'dud'.

Transit, labour markets and housing markets

In 1998 the Chicago Transit Authority (CTA) reduced service on the 'Blue Line', the elevated rail route that connects Pilsen to the central business district Loop. In particular, night and weekend services were cut. The CTA said this was due to low usage levels. However, the reduced services made it difficult for Pilsen residents to commute home from major sources of jobs at the O'Hare Airport and office complexes, and the downtown hotels, restaurants and other businesses. Furthermore, within Pilsen there lingered a feeling of transport racism as the communities most affected by the CTA decision were largely poor and non-white.

A coalition of community groups and stakeholders formed the Blue Line Transit Taskforce (BLTT). They staged a series of studies and protests, including a demonstration outside the home of the CTA president, to demand restoration of Blue line services.

Studies conducted by the BLTT showed that, contrary to CTA claims of low rider numbers, the Blue Line carried a volume of passengers comparable to another commuter rail line which served a wealthy, white-majority suburb north of Chicago. The BLTT (2004: ii) concluded that the service cuts affecting Pilsen were 'discriminatory against the predominantly low income minority residents on the Southwest side of Chicago'.

After seven years of protests, on 1 January 2005 the Blue Line service was restored. Pilsen residents hailed it as a victory for community organization. Others, however, noted that the US real estate market was bubbling upwards, and Pilsen was primed for gentrification since it contained depreciated property yet was close to the city centre. Suspicions of CTA motives for restoring the service were increased when the route of the Blue Line was altered slightly, with the addition of a stretch of track to form a new Pink Line. This change in the services meant that commuters from Pilsen to major area institutions and employers, such as the University of Illinois and O'Hare Airport, would now need to change trains and increase their travel times (Little Village Environmental Justice Organization, n.d.). Many feared that the new Pink line was the first step in a much-discussed 'circle line' that would link Pilsen and gentrifying neighbourhoods to the north and south into a middle and upper class arc ringing the Loop, displacing poorer and immigrant communities westwards towards the city limits. The Pink line would then be a way of better integrating transport and regeneration strategies, albeit with negative impacts on local tenants.

Participatory planning

Following a series of disputes over economic development in Pilsen between 2001–2003, in March 2004 a non-binding referendum formulated by community groups such as the Pilsen Alliance asked local residents if they wanted a board of community members to review development proposals and submit advisory reports to the office of the alderman, the area's elected representative to the City Council. Just over 95 per cent of voters supported this measure, as did the alderman whose office subsequently established an advisory board consisting of local residents, business owners and non-profit community groups (Kim, 2004).

One of the first cases that this Pilsen Community Zoning Board (PCZB) assessed was the transformation of an industrial facility into housing. The Lerner cardboard box manufacturing factory had been bought in December 2004 by a local real estate company, Lipe Properties. Due to a historical anomaly in Chicago's zoning map, this industrial property was zoned for residential use and Lipe proposed converting it into around fifty luxury condominium flats called the Timber Lofts Apartments (Curran, 2006).

The PCZB's members were divided. Some, such as the local business lobby and a local business grouping, the Eighteenth Street Development Corporation, supported the Lipe proposal. Others, led by the Pilsen Alliance, opposed what they saw as gentrifying forces and suggested that the building would be better suited as a commercial property, that could provide jobs for local residents, such as a small business incubator or a warehouse for an area wholesaler.

As Pilsen residents learned of the development proposals, opinion polarized, culminating in a bilingual public meeting in February 2005. At this event, developer Steve Lipe stated that he had altered the plans in response to the local criticisms. He was changing the name to Chantico Lofts, after an Aztec goddess. The window frames would be red not black, to suit what he stated were Mexican tastes. He would restore murals on and near the site, and add others, including one of the Virgin of Guadalupe (Avila, 2005).

Thus the developer was consciously using Mexican imagery and design features as a form of negotiation with the local residents, though the prices would remain out of the reach of most of them. At the meeting, some favoured the housing development, arguing that it would bring opportunities for higher income people to reside in the area and act as role models for children. Following heated exchanges, it was revealed that a couple of months prior to buying the site, the developer had made financial contributions to the re-election campaign fund of the local alderman (albeit that these were legal). A similarly contentious City of Chicago Zoning Board meeting followed. Granting permission to build Chantico Lofts, elected officials derided those opposing the Chantico development and one alderman from a different part of the city told those giving testimony: 'We dictate the rules. We write the rules and you don't answer me. We tell you' (cited in E. Hague, 2006b; Hague *et al.*, 2008).

Forty-two new flats were constructed, with seven or eight of them reserved for sale at below market rates to people with lower incomes, although critics maintained that even this pricing was out of reach of local residents. They have Mexican-style orange painted balconies and Aztec symbols were painted on the side of the former factory building. A large mural of Chantico was emblazoned in the entrance.

After the Chantico Lofts debate the PCZB was disbanded and replaced by the Pilsen Planning Council (PPC). Former PCZB members received letters stating the new group was to be more 'objective' and 'professional' than its predecessor (Avila, 2005). The membership of the revised PPC comprised largely those community groups who had supported the Chantico Lofts development. Further, when the Chantico opponents spoke out on future development in Pilsen, they were often derided by the alderman's office and its supporters as mere rabble-rousers expressing uneducated opinions or pessimistic nay-sayers. This did not silence the critics who were next heard challenging a much larger development proposal.

Tax Increment Financing, industry and jobs

Pilsen was a focus for another major regeneration programme, Tax Increment Financing. In 2005, on one of Pilsen's major streets, 18th Street, a group of nineteenth-century warehouses and residences stood alongside disused rail tracks. By 2008, all that remained was rubble. The warehouses and houses had been demolished to make way for Centro18, a mixed-use 400-unit housing and retail development. Due to the subsequent recession, the project had not been constructed at the time of writing (mid-2010). The housing construction company had gone bankrupt and Pilsen was left with two blocks of vacant land from which, just a few years previously, fruit wholesalers had distributed watermelons.

What was most galling about this whole process was that the site was within a Tax Increment Financing (TIF) district that had been designated in 1998 as a 23-year commitment to encourage the development of commercial and light manufacturing in Pilsen. Groups like the Pilsen Alliance had formed in opposition to the TIF, fearing that the process would utilize public funds to stimulate private residential development that was out of reach of those with average incomes in Pilsen, a familiar criticism of property-led regeneration schemes.

Although the Centro18 proposal did not use public funds, it was located within the TIF which, when established, had been touted as an essential tool in the retention and creation of working-class jobs and promotion of local business (E. Hague, 2005). Now, with promises of a multimillion dollar housing and retail development, the earlier vision of economic development had been shelved as unworkable. Officials stated that properties on the site were obsolete and that unsuccessful efforts had been made to find new tenants for the warehouses. Anecdotal evidence, however, contradicted these statements as people reported that area food wholesalers, recently displaced from a site half a mile north which had been converted to high-end housing, were keen on the nearby Centro18 site.

The Centro18 site had been proposed for luxury residential development in 2003 but, at that time, a coalition of community groups had persuaded the alderman to publicly state that he opposed the housing development (Betancur, 2005). Now, just three years later, housing was again proposed for the site and this time the alderman's office, city officials and some of the organizations that had formed the PPC following the PCZB split, spoke out in favour of the proposals.

The architect promised integration of the buildings with the local area, not by refurbishing existing properties in an environmentally sustainable manner, but by designing the flats to supposedly look Mexican by invoking the step-backs of ancient Mayan pyramids. Green space was to be added in place of the rail tracks. Although residents agreed that parks were sorely needed in the area, the dimensions of this proposed park were more suited to a jogging track or dog run than games of soccer or baseball, leading to questions about the potential utility of the land for area families. Following a raucous community meeting, it was revealed that major stakeholders had made legal financial contributions to the alderman's re-election fund (Johnson, 2006).Opponents of the proposed development addressed a Chicago Plan Commission hearing, but their concerns were summarily dismissed. Permission was given to construct Centro18 and the existing buildings on the site were demolished in 2006. Yet, the site remained empty following the

2008 bankruptcy of the main developer and the housing market collapse (Podmolik, 2008). This illustrates a major problem with property-led regeneration. The market is volatile, and downward shifts will impact strongly on the kind of marginal sites that are the focus of regeneration projects.

One criticism of the proposed Centro18 project was its poor location in relation to area transit. It was approximately one mile away from Chicago's elevated rail-line network, and although it was alongside a commuter heavy rail station, this facility was rarely used. Further, as required by the City of Chicago, the development was to contain one car parking space per dwelling unit, and thus the prospect of adding four hundred cars to the nineteenth-century grid plan of streets seemed to be a recipe for traffic congestion and pollution. Thus the environmental dimension of development was weakly addressed in this case.

The lack of transit-oriented development, the size and scale of the project that was bigger than any other in Pilsen for over a century, and the cost of the proposed houses divided the community along different developmental visions. Indeed, such was the real estate speculation in Pilsen during the mid-2000s that architectural conservationists such as the Preservation Chicago (2005) group, for the first time identified a whole neighbourhood as under threat of demolition and redevelopment, with the consequent loss of century-old and often uniquely designed buildings.

Place branding and marketing

During the Blue Line transit dispute, the City of Chicago began to promote Pilsen as a destination for the consumption of ethnic Mexican culture. The city published brochures and laid on a free shuttle bus to ferry city visitors from the central business district Loop to Pilsen, and then on to the nearby Chinatown. This place marketing campaign aimed to rebrand Pilsen as an area of Mexican arts, culture, festivals, and cuisine. The alderman's office fully supported these efforts and spoke of the need to redevelop the area to become a Mexican equivalent to Chinatown or Greektown (Betancur, 2005: 28).

Local residents, once again, were divided. Many noted the dual irony of reduced commuter services for locals on the elevated rail lines at the same time as tourists were being given free rides to and from Pilsen at the city's expense. Others commented that another popular ethnic tourism destination in Chicago, Greektown, was replete with restaurants and a museum, but few if any residents were from Greece or of Greek descent. Pilsen, many feared, would become a Disneyfied Mexico-town without residents of Mexican descent who would be priced out of the area as it gentrified. What were once neighbourhood festivals that in the 1980s had helped to build community resistance to unwanted development proposals, were now marketed as authentic heritage events for tourists to enjoy (Betancur, 2005).

The character of the neighbourhood was already in transition. The Podmajersky artists' enclave had been nurtured since the 1960s when the Podmajersky family began to accumulate what was, by 2009, over 100 properties in a small area of Pilsen (Isaacs, 2003; Betancur, 2005; Chicago Art District, 2009). Now it was offering a range of studios and galleries, and an annual Arts Walk event to attract potential art buyers to Pilsen. The dispute again was about how Pilsen should develop economically and, just as importantly, whom this economic development was for – the local residents, regional property speculators, or international tourists?

In summary, this case study of Pilsen shows that the area was officially recognized as being in need to economic development, through the EZ designation. However, local residents were generally unsuccessful in their attempts to foster forms of development that were inclusive and would directly benefit the poor. Instead the regeneration model generally looked to capitalize on market potential, though the onset of the economic crisis from 2008 stalled this process. The governance approach within the regeneration paradigm was about projects and public–private partnerships, but this was regularly contested by local activists and NGOs.

The nature of the regulatory zoning regime was also important in shaping the outcomes. As is often the case, it contained contradictory elements: it was both open to local participation and objection yet also a force overriding local views, as was the case, for example, in the zoning of the Lerner factory for residential use. More participatory forms of governance came to the fore at times of crisis, but the underlying power remained with the city council and local aldermen and with those who could exercise power within land and property markets. There was scope for more environmentally oriented approaches to economic development, but these never developed, and the transit issue was addressed in ways that did not assist local livelihoods.

Cognitive skills

As well as demonstrating how economic development policies and practices play out in one area over time, the example of Pilsen also shows something of the kind of skills used by the various actors. Hague *et al.* (2006: 14) argued that 'generic' skills are needed that 'can be shared, transferred between, and learned from, all those with a stake in the sustainable development of settlements – planners, politicians, academics, community leaders and citizens'. They grouped these generic skills under the following headings: analytic and cognitive skills; communication, negotiation and inclusion; being strategic; management; and monitoring and learning. In regional and local economic development, the scope and application of each these sets of skills will vary from place to place, linked to the different typologies that we have used in previous chapters. However, these groupings provide a useful checklist for practitioners to address.

Cognitive skills are about understanding situations, and in particular the way that economic development initiatives always have to be fitted to a particular place at a particular time and within a particular governance context. The various examples in the numerous boxes in this book should not be seen like a catalogue from which a reader can select an initiative to implant in some very different place. Cognitive skills build a 'soft' appreciation of the uniqueness of the place, its people, institutions, codes and networks. Outsiders can all too easily be insensitive to the importance of such things, and alienate potential allies in the process. Equally, in economic development work there needs to be some understanding of how a business operates. This is an area that public officials and community activists may have little experience of. Internships, placements and secondments can help develop the necessary understanding.

In the Pilsen example, the practice of local economic development requires an understanding of Chicago as a global city, its politics and ethnic diversity, different cultural traditions, its legal codes and institutions, structures and agencies. For example, the local alderman is a powerful figure in a city long famous for the wheeler-dealing politics of the Democratic Party machine. In confronting the alderman, the Pilsen Alliance entered a battle they probably could not win. Pilsen also shows the need to understand how local regulatory systems work: who decides and how do they decide?

The exercise of cognitive skills in Pilsen also reveals an important point. It is that economic development agencies like the WBC or the board of the EZ are important but they are not the only players. Entrepreneurs and developers like Lipe and the Podmajersky family are vitally important, but so are bodies like the Pilsen Alliance, who have their own development agenda. Similarly, as in so many poor neighbourhoods around the world, informal business is important to livelihoods and in Pilsen during this period further disputes arose over the presence of day labourers waiting on the streets to be approached for casual work, a presence that was at odds with the new, gentrified, middle-class Pilsen that many stakeholders desired (Avila and Kapos, 2003).

Pilsen also shows the need to understand the relationships between different scales. Scale is an important concept in this field, yet many actors struggle to grasp the intricacies that connect different scales and the processes of mediating between conflicting priorities at different scales. Such processes will vary between different governance traditions, but the basic point as the Pilsen example shows is that global, national, regional/metropolitan and local scales and the relations between them are always likely to be present, and need to be understood. The empty Centro18 site is a local reminder of what happens when wrong assumptions are made about the global economy.

Awareness of gender and ethnicity are also needed. In Pilsen the name change from Timber Lofts to Chantico and the efforts to make the area a 'Mexican Chinatown' show that investors and policy-makers have sought in their own ways to recognize and exploit the area's Latino culture. Although this culture is often perceived to be patriarchal, many of Pilsen's community activists are women. One of them, Alejandra Ibañez, Executive Director of the Pilsen Alliance, explained that when giving testimony at City Hall in opposition to the Chantico development, she felt vulnerable: 'how are they going to treat a relatively young, Latina woman who works at a small non-profit agency?'. After an alderman addressed her saying, 'hey lady', Ibañez recalled, 'As much as I knew that their

The ability to analyse local property markets remains a valuable skill. The Pilsen example shows developers and the TIF board exercising such skills, though as the Centro18 case showed, a closer analysis of the needs of local wholesalers, and a better analysis of transit as a generator of possible customers could have been useful. Similarly, there needs to be analysis of labour markets, housing markets and the role of transport and communications in connecting them. The story of the Blue Line makes this point. How do people travel between work and home? Similarly, the need to understand livelihoods – how people likely to be impacted upon by an economic or environmental change earn their living – is fundamentally important for any economic development strategy aimed at poverty alleviation.

It is often said that knowledge is power, and as the Pilsen example is infused with multiple power relations, it is no surprise that the Pilsen Alliance recognized that it needed to gather and analyse evidence so as to strengthen its case. Since 2004 they have worked with DePaul University's Department of Geography on a Building Inventory Project. The Geography students are taught how to collect information about the area's buildings and use that to monitor change in the neighbourhood (Bush, 2005; Hague, 2006a). Such practical initiatives and forms of mutual learning can be very valuable; analytical skills can be taught and need to be practised.

Many analytical skills involve quantitative analysis. Absolute numbers and percentages have to be calculated, trends discerned with appropriate statistical caution, relationships need to be quantified. However, analysis is not just a technical matter; it is also about empowerment and capacity building. Similarly, analysis will not necessarily provide an unambiguous, 'right' answer. In Pilsen, there was evidence to support a number of contending positions on every one of the issues, though not necessarily the same evidence. Thus the identification of evidence to be collected and the interpretation of any piece of analysis also involves judgements. While policy decisions always have to be based on imperfect information – you can never get all the up-to-date information you might ideally need – policy-making and information should be informed by evidence and understanding, not prejudice or untested assumptions. Box 13.2 summarizes the analytical skills illustrated in the Pilsen example.

Box 13.2: Analytical skills in the Pilsen example

- analysis of local labour markets: types and locations of jobs, types of skills;
- analysis of land and property markets: supply and demand of different land uses and the impacts of regulatory regimes; building condition, intensity of use of land, vacant sites, accessibility;
- analysis of transport systems: access points; connectivity to wider networks and travel times and travel costs; journey to work patterns and modes of transport used; and
- analysis of availability and use of open space and comparison with standards elsewhere.

Communication, negotiation and inclusion skills

Communication is a two-way process. It involves giving out information but also receiving information from others – the skills of being able to listen attentively and understand a different viewpoint. Language evidently matters, for example in Pilsen, Spanish is the first tongue for many residents, especially more recent immigrants. However, not all communication is aural. Drawings, for example, are important where proposed developments will have visual impacts on an area. Similarly, the murals in the Pilsen example were powerful means of communication. Even in countries where government-led initiatives are less likely to be contested than in USA, two-way communication still matters. Exposing information to critical scrutiny is likely to strengthen the quality of the final output. Similarly, communication needs to be undertaken in a timely manner, so that the flow of information is in step with events and deadlines for decisions. Documents should be locally accessible – not everyone has access to the internet. Maps, drawings and diagrams need to be explained in terms that the readers can understand. Face-to-face communication requires a capacity to make effective use of eye contact, body language and facial expressions, the tone of voice and choice of words.

Hague *et al.* (2006: 28) argued that ways need to be created to allow 'stakeholders to validate claims, identify priorities and develop strategies collectively through interaction and debate, while creating the mechanisms for inclusion of differently empowered social groups'. Pilsen comes close to this, though interaction and debate do not necessarily mean a 'level playing field' on which all the stakeholders have an equal opportunity to shape the outcomes. Identification of potential stakeholders is a crucial first step. Again it requires some immersion in the place, and use of networking skills so that a wide range of contacts can be built simply by asking others who else *they* consider to be relevant stakeholders. Databases need to be built and maintained. This will not be easy in situations where there is a high level of mobility between jobs and addresses. Furthermore, stakeholders should be able to find out how they can get further information if they want it.

Existing local enterprises should always be one of the stakeholders. Through talking with them it is possible to get an understanding of their needs. Can they get the right type of labour, access credit to fund new investment, and does the supply of premises meet their needs? However, as Pilsen shows, local businesses are by no means the only stakeholders. There are city-wide needs to be met as well as local needs; outside investors can also have a legitimate interest in an area, but so do local residents, and transit companies operating services on a corridor that runs through an area.

It is always desirable to provide accurate and clear information to all stakeholders at the same time, though it is clear that in Pilsen as in many other situations there are 'insider groups' and 'outsider groups', that is to say those close to and trusted by official agencies on the one hand and others who are not granted such access. Indeed, as the conflict increased, one 'insider group', the PCZB was even disbanded and replaced by a different one, the PPC.

Skills of negotiation are also crucial, since there will often be situations like those in Pilsen where actors faced with disagreement and opposition had to seek compromise solutions. In the end a negotiated outcome is more likely to prove to be an acceptable and lasting solution than one that is imposed. The essence of a negotiating strategy should be to aim for a 'win-win' situation by identifying and satisfying shared interests amongst the parties to the negotiation. This means being able to understand the position of the other party and to imagine what might appeal to them and what are their likely sticking points. Similarly, in any negotiation it is important to be clear about the ground that can be conceded and what is, in effect, 'non-negotiable'.

Inclusion requires skills to achieve an equitable situation where even 'difficult to reach' stakeholders (such as marginalized minority groups) are heard. Such skills are more commonly associated with community development rather than economic development, but really need to be part of the toolkit for regional and local economic development. The Pilsen Alliance, for example, held community workshops on TIFs, zoning and housing development, went door to door canvassing opinions, and helped prepare residents to speak to officials at City Hall. As always, much depends on local circumstances and available resources, but a few general rules of thumb can be sketched out. For example, focus groups – essentially a structured and recorded discussion with a small group seen as representative of a wider stakeholder – can be used to collect opinions in more depth than can be done through questionnaires or public meetings. When and if public meetings are staged, as happened in Pilsen, then they should be held at different times of the day and in different venues so that they are accessible to different groups of the population. For example, evening meetings are likely to be difficult for parents with young children to attend. Questions and answers between an audience and a panel of local development 'experts' or officials are not likely to be effective means to allow everyone to be heard: there is too little time and some people lack confidence to speak in public. However, postcards can be completed by members of the audience to raise questions or make points, or small group discussions can be organized where people can talk more easily.

Thus regional and local economic development requires 'people skills' and an ability to build consensus. These entail personal qualities such as energy, honesty, confidence, responsiveness and patience. Some will be better endowed with these qualities than others. However, the basic skills of communication, negotiation and inclusion can be taught, learned and practised, with learning on the job likely. They include quick thinking, empathy for others and their views, a capacity for accurate recording and documenting of discussions and decisions, and an ability to keep calm in situations of conflict. Box 13.3 reviews communication and negotiation skills.

Box 13.3: Communication and negotiation skills in the Pilsen example

---

- stakeholder analysis (often analysed in terms of power and their ability to influence, and/or by whether they stand to gain or lose from the project);
- database development (details of contacts);
- language skills (especially in multilingual areas);
- written, oral and graphic communication skills (clarity, accuracy, interest, website design);
- storytelling (using short, accessible accounts of, e.g. the area's history and identities to engage people);
- listening skills (ability to pay attention to what others are saying, and so fully understand their concerns and priorities);
- engagement skills (running public meetings; focus groups; interactive workshops; outreach through going to stakeholders in places, at times and in ways that is convenient to them);
- negotiation skills (clarity at the outset on what is and is not negotiable; understanding of position and priorities of others, possible incentives and relative dispositions of power); and
- lobbying skills (targeting key decision-makers and presenting a good case in a way that will appeal to them).

Management skills

The practice of regional and local economic development will certainly involve the management of time and most likely will require management of other resources such as money, premises and people. It is important to recognize that management is not just something that is done by senior staff: everybody in the team is a manager in one way or another. A key part of management is the capacity to act in a strategic way, to keep a sense of what is important and what can be sacrificed. Similarly, a balance often has to be struck between long-term aims and short-term aspirations. In the Pilsen case, for example, it can be argued that groups that opposed the Chantico Lofts development made a strategic error. By getting into confrontation with officials and the alderman who supported the development they put at risk their ability to exert influence through these channels on future developments in the area, and became isolated from other stakeholders. Of course, it is easy to be wise afterwards, and in real situations difficult decisions have to be taken, but the skill of anticipating long-term consequences is a useful one to have.

Very often in economic development work budgets need to be managed. It is common for project funding to be time-limited and any unspent money at the end has to be returned. Typically budgets require spending under pre-set headings, with limited scope to shift money between the different categories. Therefore the ability to plan and monitor a budget is an important skill, even if the organization is able to call on specialist skills to provide management support in this area. A key part of budgeting is the ability to think through the whole project, including the implementation phase and make realistic estimates of likely costs and income. Once again, experience helps and skills can be acquired on the job, but there is also a role for training.

Skills in leadership and partnership working are also needed. Leadership involves bringing stakeholders together to deliver an agreed programme or project. In the end it is people who drive an organization and inspiring leaders can make a difference. They need to be nurtured and valued. In turn, a leader needs to ensure that everyone inside the organization and all key stakeholders know what the priorities and values of the organization are. Leaders also need to encourage and develop their staff, and plan for their own succession. Leadership involves having a vision but also attending to delivery, which in turn requires some assessment of the resources needed for delivery (including the skills available within the team), and setting in place practices that will deliver the resources when they are needed.

In a partnership it is necessary to agree and make transparent the contribution that each partner will make towards achieving the common goals. The anticipated benefits to each partner also need to be defined and endorsed. Good partnership work means building trust and creating synergies between partners, and these are things that need to be recognized as important and actively worked at. Team working is important in a partnership, where each partner plays a role that supports rather than duplicates that of others. Indeed, team working is a vital management skill that is needed in many situations. Box 13.4 presents a list of management skills that were needed in the Pilsen example.

Box 13.4: Management skills in the Pilsen example

- management of time (personal, the time of the team, the phasing of the project);
- management of premises and sites (maintenance, security, continuity of access);
- management of budgets (planning and budget allocation, clarity in criteria and responsibilities for spending; auditing of spending);
- management of people (recruitment, training, retention);
- strategic planning (clarity about priorities and relations between short and long-term aims);
- management of risks (anticipation of what might happen, what the impact would be and how to reduce/mitigate risk);
- management of partnerships (understanding of all partners' priorities and resources; ability to build consensus); and
- leadership skills (holding on to the overall vision, taking responsibility, listening to what others are saying).

Delivery, evaluation and monitoring

Last but not least, skills are needed in implementing projects and in monitoring and evaluation. Delivery is very important. The Pilsen example showed the weakness of delivery in the EZs, and the failure to develop the Centro18 site. This contrasts with the successful delivery of the Chantico Lofts project and the Podmajersky artists' enclave. In the end much delivery is linked to management, having a well thought through strategy and the ability to assemble the right resources at the right time and in the right place.

Monitoring and evaluation should infuse the whole process of regional and local economic development, and not be seen as an 'add-on' only to commence when a project is finished. The basis for evaluating performance of an agency, programme or project, or of measuring the performance of a regional or local economy should be agreed and transparent (though also subject to review as times change). Monitoring involves setting objectives and measurable targets. Targets need to be realistic and time-bound. Key indicators need to be chosen, which are relevant to the targets but also able to be collected and analysed. Long lists of indicators are rarely helpful, take time to compile and may make unrealistic demands on the availability and /or quality of the data available. There is an increasing trend is for regions and cities to benchmark themselves against the performance of those in other countries. Benchmarking means comparing your performance against that of others with similar characteristics to your own, and on the same measures. Monitoring and evaluation should be a shared and open process, not something buried away within a bureaucracy, or simply an exercise in ticking boxes to show that something has been done with little regard to its relevance.

In Pilsen, the most systematic monitoring is of land and buildings through the work of the students at DePaul University. There was monitoring of local jobs in the EZ project, but overall many proposals came forward and actions were taken without full evaluation and monitoring. For example, although there was reference to the examples of Chinatown and Greektown when the rebranding of Pilsen as a 'Mexican experience' tourist destination was being proposed, there does not appear to have been any systematic evaluation of the situation in those two places. Similarly, the CTA decisions on the Blue Line seem to have not addressed the full range of impacts and distribution of costs and benefits. None of this is very surprising. Pilsen shows just how strongly the political sphere is used to develop, contest and resolve issues of local economic development.

Ethics and transparency

Pilsen also shows how ethical challenges are integral to the process. Decisions can influence what happens to large amounts of money, some of which came from taxpayers. Honesty and integrity are essential. Decisions also impact on livelihoods and jobs and access to housing, not least of poor people and other marginalized groups. The demands of a client or employer need to be balanced with respect for the interests of other groups and the wider society. Commercial confidentiality will need to be respected, but at what point does it become an excuse to avoid the kind of transparency that is an integral part of good, accountable governance?

There are no easy or universal answers to such questions. One advantage of professional bodies is that they usually have a Code of Professional Conduct that is binding on their members, but so far such codes are little developed in the field of regional and local economic development. In the meantime we can only call for all those engaged in these endeavours to be self-aware, self-critical, trustworthy and passionate about doing a good job that benefits those people in a region, city or neighbourhood who are in the greatest need.

Topics for discussion

Assess your own abilities on each one of these key skills and consider how you might improve and develop them.

- ability to create a vision;
- leadership;
- communication;
- team working;
- project management;
- process re-engineering to secure speedier and more effective development
- understanding sustainable development;
- the economics of growth, business and development;
- the processes of making decisions; and
- effective financial management.

There were clearly many conflicts over development and regeneration in Pilsen. How might skills of communication, negotiation and inclusion have been applied to work towards consensus outcomes?

Related reading

J. Egan *et al.* (2004) *The Egan Review: Skills for Sustainable Communities* (London: Office of the Deputy Prime Minister).

C. Hague, P. Wakely, J. Crespin and C. Jasko (2006) *Making Planning Work: A guide to approaches and skills* (Rugby, UK: Intermediate Technology Publications Ltd), 28–41.

14 Conclusions

Previous chapters have demonstrated that there is a wide array of practices within the field of regional and local economic development. For much of the twentieth century regional development was mainly about provision of advanced factories for manufacturing companies, and the idea of local economic development scarcely existed. Today the scope, and also the diversity of actions is much greater. Chapter 1 proposed a typology to put some order on what otherwise could be a bewildering and arbitrary list of different things done in different places. The typology was structured around two simple questions. These concerned the degree of priority given to market efficiency as against social or environmental priorities, and secondly, the question of whether market processes were seen as delivering the kind of development that is wanted. From these combinations four approaches to regional and local economic development were hypothesized: pro-business competition to attract inward investment; sector targeting and area regeneration; eco-modernization, and finally, pro-poor local economic development.

In Chapter 4 the typology was replicated by one that sought to match its four ideal types with similarly simplified styles of governance. The four were the centralized development state, the project state, smart planning and regulation, and 'development despite the state'. In combination these two typologies amounted to a set of hypotheses. Would they be able to categorize and make sense of the actual examples? Would they provide a means of interpretation of practice as being defined by policy aims and conditions of governance? Our opinion is that the answers are positive. This final chapter therefore takes and develops each of these four basic approaches and refines it in the light of our findings.

Pro-business competition to attract inward investment

Competition for inward investment is not new, whether at national, regional or local scale. In US cities there is a long tradition of 'boosterism' for example, while in Europe the EU has created strong directives about fair competition in part to address practices in which different countries competed with each other in the inducements they would offer to foreign investors. Similarly, as we saw in the example of the growth of the industrial complex in Liaoning Province in China (Box 3.2) regional development under the centrally planned economy was very much about inward investment into a region, albeit the development was planned and directed rather than attracted there through market-based inducements. What is new is globalization, which has so increased markets and locational options that the competition has become more intense and all pervasive.

Place competition is played out using a variety of mechanisms, which have been illustrated in earlier chapters. In Asia the 'Development State' leads strongly in direct provision of big infrastructure, though now working in various forms of partnership with the private sector or other governments, and often involves forms of tax breaks to investors. The Special Economic Zones of China (Box 4.3), Singapore's Overseas Industrial Parks (Box 4.2), and Malaysia's Multi-Media Super Corridor (Box 6.3) are startling and successful examples of what this approach can achieve. However there are models from elsewhere too, for example the Øresund bridge connecting Copenhagen and Malmö (Chapter 6), an exercise in transnational governance from super-state to local government. Where urban local government has strong powers and the political will, there can be interventions to aid business through use of powers of eminent domain as in Detroit (Box 5.2). The Detroit example is also a reminder that there are losers in competitive approaches, a point also observed when Jamaica's Export Processing Zone lost out to Mexican competition (Box 4.4), while Nigeria's development of Abuja (Box 6.4) and the aspirations of Vinh (Box 12.3) have met problems.

Place marketing and branding have become important ways to attract investment. Chapter 12 reviewed examples, notably the Doo

Wop-themed Wildwoods (Box 12.7). It also noted the increasing use of iconic architecture and design of spectacular public spaces such as Millennium Park, Chicago (Box 12.5) to set a tone for a 'global city'. There are also 'softer' forms of support given to aid the competitiveness of businesses in the hope that they will then be able to compete more effectively, such as the T&E Centres in Finland (Box 8.1) or the work of angel investors and business angels (Box 8.3).

The underlying assumption in this approach is that market forces will create prosperity through economic efficiency. Barriers to competition need to be removed. The 'creative class' has to be attracted and retained. By growing the economy as a whole in the end there are more opportunities for everyone. However, the notion that the attraction of business is insensitive to gender issues and involves direct losses to poor and marginalized groups runs through many of the examples. The form of the losses varies: displacement is a common theme, perhaps most overt in the way that homeless people have been targeted in some US cities (Chapter 9) or those in informal housing have been evicted in Abuja. The story of China's urban villages (Box 9.2) remains fascinating, yet still paints a picture of deep inequalities. Similarly where urban competition has been to host sports and mega-events there is a history of displacement of poor resident and often petty traders also. UN–Habitat (2010: 129, 130) cited Manila (1976), Seoul (1995), Seville (1992), Osaka (2002), Seoul (2002) Beijing (2008) and New Delhi, Vancouver and Shanghai (all 2010) in this respect, saying that making the places attractive to middle- and high-income earners makes it 'less liveable for those who fall outside these categories'.

Similarly, pro-growth approaches were slow to address the environmental implications of development, for example the water problems in San Diego that were outlined in Chapter 6, or the environmental pollution in Hong Kong (Box 7.4) and the legacy of past industrial development in Trenton (Box 7.2) and the Ruhr (Box 7.3). However there are signs that care for the environment is now a part of the business case. It is part of the narrative about the beneficial impacts of the Øresund crossing (maritime transport is a significant producer of CO_2 emissions), and as noted in Chapter 13, Chicago's 'global city' promotion has a green tinge, to cite just two examples.

Sector targeting and area regeneration

This approach shares a lot of common ground with the pro-business competition approach. Both look to economic efficiency as the prime aim. The difference is that the regeneration approach is directly grappling with situations of market failure, whereas the pro-business competition stance implicitly assumes that the market is strong and the main challenge is to maximize market share. The acknowledgement of market failure is overt in area regeneration work. The name itself implies a restoration of some kind of market normality in the area concerned. The reasons for the market failure can be many and will vary in detail from place to place. They are likely to include imperfect information, frictions in the land market such as are caused by landowners unwilling to release sites or sites being polluted by previous users, or just general lack of business confidence in the area. Sector targeting shares some of these assumptions. For example, the market may be slow to grasp the opportunities that exist to cluster and gain agglomeration economies, or to provide the kind of premises needed by an emergent sector. Thus the essence of the approach is to deliver a short-term 'fix' by working closely with the private sector, often through some kind of partnership.

The temporary and conditional nature of the intervention thus fashions and then is tailored by 'the project state' as a form of governance. Projects are typically allocated through some form of competitive bidding. They then use incentives, soft loans or other subsidies to bring private sector (and maybe community representatives) into partnerships that have a start date and an 'exit strategy'. Projects are more likely to carry requirements for monitoring and evaluation than are mainstream spending programmes, and to be linked to a set of key indicators. The tone is pragmatic: what works? In theory there is a strong emphasis on delivery, and the involvement of the private sector is often partly to draw on its expertise in this work. However, the need to fit everything into a defined time period can complicate as well as encourage delivery.

The main sectors sought in our examples have been research and development, as in the Research Triangle (Box 5.1) or the creative industries as in the Creative Coast example from Savannah, Georgia (Chapter 12) and in cultural clusters (Chapter 11), though some of the eco-parks (Chapter 7) target 'green industries'. The obvious risk is that success in attracting the new industries fails to be matched by re-skilling those falling out of old industries in the area so that they can access to new jobs. This was the case in the Research Triangle, for example. The fit between the Manchester music scene and the growth of creative industry jobs in the city (Box 11.2) owed something to serendipity, though also something to the way the Central Manchester Development Corporation its managed vacant properties. Similarly, the training for retailing work provided in the Meadowhall shopping centre (Chapter 10) can be seen as a kind of sector targeting in relation to training.

Area regeneration is most evident in post-industrial urban areas such as those in North America and Europe. As Chapter 9 explained, there is a basic debate about this property-based approach, with critics arguing for targeting help at individuals and families rather than areas. However, the scale of run-down neighbourhoods, together with the benefits of the targeted approach and, not least, the potential returns in increased land and property values if successful, all combine to make this a very common economic development activity. Examples were noted in Austin, Texas (Box 2.3), the Custard Factory in Birmingham, England (Box 4.7), the Tax Increment Financing projects in Addison, Illinois (Box 9.3) and in Pilsen, Chicago (Chapter 13), the HOPE VI programme (Box 9.4) and Chicago's Renaissance2010 Schools (Box 9.7), as well as the Business Improvement Districts such as that in Milwaukee (Box 10.3). The stories of Pittsburgh (Box 12.1) and Atlantic City (Box 11.4) also fit this regeneration theme.

As with the pro-business competition approach there have been some clear successes in terms of the aims of the projects. However, there is again a common theme of displacement of local residents, lack of sensitivity to needs of existing small businesses and resistance to programmes from within the communities directly affected. The saga of Pilsen illustrated such disputes in some detail and over a long period of time. In principle the problems can be tackled by better outreach, negotiation and compromises. Albeit the 'Mexicanization' solution for the Chantico Lofts case in Pilsen can easily be dismissed as a cosmetic gesture to local opinion, it does illustrate that negotiated outcomes can remove obstacles to delivery. What is much harder to negotiate is the market, with the onset of an economic crisis in 2008 posing severe problems for regeneration schemes premised on the imminence of rising property values. Stalled developments such as that at the Centro18 site in Pilsen are mirrored in many other regeneration areas at the time of writing in mid-2010.

Eco-modernization

The idea of eco-modernization in its earlier forms strongly looked to the market rather than governments to deliver an economic future, just like the pro-business competition approach. However, unlike in that approach, economic efficiency was not seen as the overarching aim: rather it was the means to the end of environmental sustainability. Examples like NaturVärme making and selling its heat pumps (cited in Chapter 7) fit this mould. However, as noted in Chapter 7, by 2009 eco-modernization was seen by Kitchen and Marsden (2009: 276) as 'a broad-based amalgam of policy concerns that suggests more normative approaches for the practice of sustainable development through reform and transformation of social structures, governments, businesses and markets'.

In terms of our typology and the diagrams in Chapter 1 this may seem to pull eco-modernization down towards the lower half, that is the regeneration and pro-poor approaches both of which recognize weaknesses in markets as well as failures by governments. states where environmental concerns have become somewhat mainstreamed, as in Scandinavia, Netherlands and Germany, local governments in particular play a leading role in the ecological transformation. The Emscher Park project (Box 7.3), for example, while working with partnerships and the private sector was a state-led vision, while governments in China were important to the massive Chengdu water project (box 6.6), even if money came from the Asian Development Bank and the private sector. Development of eco-industrial parks (Box 7.1) is an obvious practice of eco-modernization, and as we saw in Chapter 7 there has been a transition from an unplanned development at Kalundborg in Denmark to a situation where there is conscious design and planning of eco-industrial parks, often with strong governmental involvement.

In the Rouboix example (Box 4.6) the partnerships driving change were amongst public sector agencies, and the public sector bodies are fundamental to the institutional thickness that underpins the innovative forms of partnership in the Stuttgart Verband Region (Box 4.5). Some might argue that such projects are rather broad-based in their aims and so should not be included as they 'dilute' the ecological thrust of eco-modernization. For example, Stuttgart Verban Region has among its other activities promoted clusters in micro-electronics and in new media: surely this is a case of 'sector targeting' not 'eco-modernization'? Roubaix was about integrating public investment in economic, physical and social regeneration, lacking the focus on ecology that eco-modernization requires. A case can be made therefore that these two initiatives better fit the 'regeneration' box of the typology. However, their governance style, seems closer to 'smart planning and regulation' than to the 'project state'.

The title 'smart planning and regulation' was devised in Chapter 4 in developing the typology of governance styles. Indeed the text there hypothesized that governments played a significant role in delivering environmental improvement and change, albeit not necessarily through direct provision but rather through 'planning and regulation'. Such a regime would work with multiple stakeholders and use private sector style management methods. It would be most effective in situations where the economy was strong enough to generate resources from the private sector to invest in greening of production and places. Similarly, the hand of a regulator is stronger if private investors are desperate to invest, than if they have reservations and/or other options.

So what made this form of planning and regulation 'smart', while others, by implication, were less clever? The use of the word 'smart' probably came from the concept of 'smart growth' which is used in the USA to signal that planning and regulation does not have to be 'anti-growth', while also trying to build in conservation of open space, transit accessibility and more compact forms of development than typical US suburbia. The notion that environmental conservation and an ecological approach to development are 'smart' also picks up on the idea that disregard of the environment and the threat of climate change is 'stupid' as in the 2009 Franny Armstrong film *The Age of Stupid*. The example of transit-oriented development in Arlington (Box 6.5) captures this sense of 'smart' action, while the example of Český Krumlov (Box 11.6) shows imaginative action and creative initiatives in developing new institutions, as a way to link conservation to market opportunities.

There are two sorts of basic challenges in the eco-modernization approach. First, while it is convenient to imagine that good environmental practices are mutually supporting and self-sustaining, the reality is that there can easily be conflicts within the environmental field. Development of wind power, while desirable to reduce reliance on fossil fuels and CO_2 emissions, is particularly controversial because of its impacts of birds and on landscapes (see Box 7.6). Also as Box 7.7 showed sustainable construction may mean less comfortable buildings in some countries.

The second set of questions is about what happens if the market does not provide the desired eco-modernization? In a sense that has already been answered: others, including governments, need to step in. Regulation is very important, and there is evidence of some learning to do this better in, for example, the case of Hong Kong (Box 7.4). However, regulation can be ineffective in situations where administrations are weak and corrupt, and the collective commitment of governments globally to facing up to ecological challenges remains low at the time of writing, a few months after the disappointing outcomes of the 2009 climate change summit in Copenhagen. The geography of our examples of eco-modernization approaches is stamped by northern and central Europe, with some representation in North America and in Asia, an eco-tourism project in Kenya (Box 11.5), and an eco-city project in Abu Dhabi (Chapter 12). This is not to suggest that this is a definitive picture, but it is also an indicative one.

Pro-poor approaches: 'development despite the state'

The fourth element in the typology was 'pro-poor approaches to local economic development' which in Chapter 4 was characterized in governance terms as 'development despite the state'. Like eco-modernization it does not see economic efficiency as an end in itself. Pro-poor approaches were seen as being people-based (in contrast to the place and property-based approaches that characterize area regeneration) and about livelihoods and mobilization for change and social inclusion. The fundamental point is that unequal access to opportunities results in a situation where poor and marginalized groups face an inter-related set of disadvantages in health, housing and education, not to mention employment, which impact adversely not just on them but on economic development. Illness and pre-mature death, poor education and lack of a home undermine productivity. An effective focus on improving maternal and child health could be a more powerful economic development approach than chasing footloose international companies. Gender aware-ness and gender auditing of development practices (systematically assessing their impact on women and on men) are valuable tools that should be mainstream.

Such practices are not necessarily confined to the developing world. The work of Social Compact (Box 8.4) and the land reclama-tion project in Trenton (Box 7.2) are in the USA, as is the Harlem Children's Zone (Box 9.6) and the alternative food supply system in Chicago (Box 10.5). However, these are all situations where the conventional government systems, strong ones in some cases, simply failed to address the problems faced by groups of poor people. Elsewhere the book has pointed to the role of home-based enter-prises in Kitwe (Box 5.3), basic water supply in Khurda District in India (Box 6.7), waste recycling in the Philippines (Box 7.5), com-munity enterprise in Chile (Box 8.2), micro-credit in Alexandria, Egypt (Box 8.5), re-housing of slum dwellers in Mumbai (Box 9.5), kiosks for petty traders in St. Petersburg (Box 10.1), and cultural festivals in Jaipur (Box 11.7) and the food strategy in Belo Hori-zonte (Box 10.6). In addition the endeavours to develop fair trade (Box 10.4) connect the rich and the poor worlds.

It is not just the diversity of the places that stands out, but also the range and innovativeness of the practices. Women appear to be in leadership roles and gender to be a much more central compo-nent of the practices than in any of the other more conventional economic development activities discussed above. Most of the actions are led by NGOs, and a number involve social enterprises or other means of interfacing with markets to secure benefits for the poor. Generally this is not the result of some coercion by inter-national donor agencies, though the enduring impact of the Struc-tural Adjustment Programmes should not be ignored. Rather it is a pragmatic attempt to solve problems that the state, central or local, does not, and probably never has tackled. For example, as Fern-andes (2007: 203) commented: 'Resulting from the combination of speculative land markets, clientelist political systems, elitist urban planning practices and exclusionary legal regimes – which have long affirmed individual ownership rights over the constitutional principle of the social function of property – for some time now Brazil's process of informal urban development has not been the exception, but the main socio-economic way to produce urban space in the country'.

The challenges facing this, our 'fourth way' are huge. Baker (2008: 3) focusing only on urban poverty reported that 'approximately 750 million people living in urban areas in developing countries were below the poverty line of $2/day in 2002, and 290 million using the $1/day line. This represents approximately one third of all urban residents ($2/day) or 13 percent ($1/day), and one quarter of the total poor in developing countries. For the same time period, 2002, almost half of the world's urban poor were in South Asia (46 percent) and another third in Sub-Saharan Africa (34 percent) for $1/day line. Using the $2/day line, these proportions were 40 per cent for Africa and 22 percent for South Asia'. There an urgent need to scale up the kind of pro-poor practices we have discussed in this book, and make them mainstream, always recognizing that practices must be shaped to fit local cultures and institutions.

Into the future

There are discernable shifts in the recent literature on regional and local development. While the book has focused on policy and practice, and justified this by the extent to which the field is practice led, it is also clear that there are bodies of theory that have shaped practice, whether practitioners have recognized that influence or not. These were reviewed in Part 1. The 'new institutional economics' was introduced in Chapter 1, and in many respects underpins the analysis in the book. The restructuring thesis and theories of innovation were used in Chapter 2, which also critically reviewed the concept of the 'creative class'. Chapter 3 looked at issues of scale and 'glocalization', the rescaling of economic governance with the rise of city regions, regional competitiveness, competitive advantage, clusters and agglomeration economies. Issues about governance were the theme in Chapter 4, which included ideas about the 'hollowing out of the state', transnational forms of governance, public–private partnerships and the concept of 'institutional thickness' Chapter 4 also introduced the issue of gender, a theme returned to several times thereafter. In addition, through discussion of eco-modernization strategies some basic concepts from environmental science have been drawn upon, particularly those concerned with ecological systems.

The relevant literature is as rich and diverse as the practices and like them continues to develop. Finally then, let us speculate about how in this globally connected world with many key resources that are finite, theories to inform practice might develop. The impacts of the 2008 economic crisis continue to be felt. Similarly, there is mounting concern over climate uncertainty and risk, though less grasp of the implications that it has for potential intra-national and international struggles over water, land, jobs and international migrations of environmental refugees. In addition, the scale and pace of urbanization, while not the same even among developing countries, is creating concentrations of poor people amidst afflu-ence on a scale never known before.

In this context, ideas of regional resilience (see Chapter 3) will challenge the paradigm of regional competitiveness that held sway through the closing decade of the last Century and the first dec-ade of this one. Similarly, there is the emergence of the idea of 'urban ecological security' (Hodson and Marvin 2007). This is con-cerned with the ecological resource flows (particularly food, water and energy, and waste disposal), infrastructure and services that underpin a city's economy, but which could be under threat from extreme weather events such as flooding or extreme heat, or from global shortages. Hodson and Marvin (2007: 435) suggested that this process is occurring and involves 'withdrawal from and the bypassing of national and regional infrastructure, leading to the development of new archipelagos of connected world cities'. Last but not least, the idea of the right to the city will become a rallying focus for social and political action, backed by attempts to better theorize it, not least in the context of regional resilience and urban ecological security. These possibilities make it more urgent than ever to remove the national, or at best Anglo-American cultural and economic blinkers (often implicit and unacknowledged) that have restricted so much of the discourse in regional and local eco-nomic development.

Bibliography

B. M. Aakre (2006) 'Entrepreneurship and Business Development', *Innovation Academy Pack 4* (Alytus, Lithuania: Innovation Circle).

P. A. Adams (1996) 'Protest and the Scale of Telecommunications', *Political Geography*, 15(5), 419–41.

J. A. Agnew (1997) 'The Dramaturgy of Horizons: Geographical Scale in the "Reconstruction of Italy" by the New Italian Political Parties, 1992–1995', *Political Geography*, 16(2), 99–121.

B. Alexander (1998) 'Between two West Coast Cities, a duel to the last drop', *New York Times*, 8 December, G9.

P. Allmendinger (1997) *Thatcherism and Planning: The Case of Simplified Planning Zones* (Aldershot: Ashgate).

Alternative Energy (2010) 'Abu Dhabi to Build First Full Eco City', www.alternative-energy-news.info/abu-dhabi-eco-city/, date accessed 3 July 2010.

A. Amin (2009) 'Extraordinarily Ordinary: Working in the Social Economy', *Social Enterprise Journal*, 5(1), 30–49.

A. Amin and N. Thrift (1992) 'Neo-Marshallian Nodes in Global Networks', *International Journal of Urban and Regional Research*, 16(4), 571–87.

A. Amin and N. Thrift (1995) 'Globalisation, Institutional "Thickness" and the Local Economy', in P. Healey, C. Cameron, S. Davoudi, S. Graham and A. Madani-Pour (eds.), *Managing Cities: The New Urban Context* (Chichester: Wiley).

A. B. Amundsen (2001) 'Articulations of Identity: A Methodological Essay and a Report on Askim and Tidaholm', *Noord XXI Report No. 19* (Aberdeen, UK: Noord XXI Foundation).

K. Andersson (2006) 'Pursuing Innovations through Projects – The Paradox of Project Management as a Tool for Regional Development', in S. Sjöblom, K. Andersson, E. Eklund and S. Godenhjelm (eds.), *Project Proliferation and Governance – The Case of Finland* (Helsinki: Research Institute, Swedish School of Social Science).

J. Antoniou (ed.) (2001) *Implementing the Habitat Agenda: In Search of Urban Sustainability* (London: Development Planning Unit, UCL).

A. Appadurai (2000) 'Grassroots Globalisation and the Research Imagination', *Public Culture*, 12(1), 1–19.

R. C. Archibold (2006) 'Appeals court bars arrest of homeless in Los Angeles', *New York Times*, 15 April.

R. Archibold (2008) 'From sewage, added water for drinking', *New York Times*, 27 November, www.nytimes.com/2007/11/27/us/27conserve.html?_r=1 &scp=7&sq=san%20diego%20water&st=cse, date accessed 17 June 2010.

F. Armstrong (dir.) (2009) *The Age of Stupid* (Spanner Films).

J. Arndorfer (2003 [1997]) 'McSploitation', in T. Frank and D. Mulcahey (eds.), *Boob Jubilee: The Cultural Politics of the New Economy* (London and New York: W. W. Norton).

G. J. Ashworth and H. Voogd (1994) 'Marketing and Place Promotion', in J. R. Gold and S. V. Ward (eds.), *Place Promotion: The Use of Publicity and Marketing to Sell Towns and Regions* (Chichester: Wiley).

Asian Development Bank (2002) *Handbook for Integration Risk Analysis into the Economic Analysis of Projects* (Manila: Asian Development Bank).

Asian Development Bank (2005) *Chengdu Water Supply Project: Effective Public–Private Partnership at the Municipal Level* (Private Sector Department, Asian Development Bank).

C. Aubrey (2007) 'On a roll', *Guardian* (Society section), www.guardian.co.uk/society/2007/jun/20/regeneration.energy, 20 June, 9.

O. Avila (2005) 'Hispanic condo buyers seen as Pilsen threat', *Chicago Tribune*, 22 April, 1.

O. Avila and S. Kapos (2003) 'Day laborers feel spurned by new Pilsen; they feel spurned as community's economy develops', *Chicago Tribune*, 19 January, 1.

K. E. Axenov, I. Brade and A. G. Papadopoulos (1997) 'Restructuring the Kiosk Trade in St. Petersburg – A New Retail Trade Model for the Post-Soviet Period', *GeoJournal*, 42(4), 419–32.

P. Bagguley, J. Mark-Lawson, D. Shapiro, J. Urry, S. Walby and A. Warde (1990) *Restructuring: Place, Class and Gender* (London: Sage).

N. Bailey with A. Barker and K. MacDonald (1995) *Partnership Agencies in British Urban Policy* (London: UCL Press).

J. L. Baker (2008) 'Urban Poverty: A Global View', *World Bank Group Urban Papers* UP-5 (Washington, DC: International Bank for Reconstruction and Development/ World Bank).

R. Ball and A. C. Pratt (eds.), (1994) *Industrial Property: Policy and Economic Development* (London: Routledge).

K. Barker (2004) *Review of Housing Supply – Delivering Stability: Securing Our Future Housing Needs. Final Report – Recommendations* (Norwich: HMSO).

M. Barlow ([1940] 1976) *Royal Commission on the Distribution of the Industrial Population: Report*, Cmnd 6153 (London: HMSO, repr.).

R. H. Bates (1997) *Open Economy Politics: The Politics and Economics of the International Coffee Market* (Princeton: University of Princeton Press).

R. H. Bates (2005) *Beyond the Miracle of the Market: The Political Economy of Agrarian Development in Kenya*, 2nd edn (Cambridge: Cambridge University Press).

I. Begg (1999) 'Cities and Competitiveness', *Urban Studies*, 36(5–6), 795–809.

I. Begg (ed.) (2002) 'Introduction', in I. Begg (ed.), *Urban Competitiveness: Policies for Dynamic Cities* (Bristol: Polity Press), 1–10.

I. Begg, B. Moore and Y. Altunbas (2002) 'Long-Run Trends in the Competitiveness of British Cities', in I. Begg (ed.), *Urban Competitiveness: Policies for Dynamic Cities* (Bristol: Polity Press), 101–32.

P. Belli, J. R. Anderson, H. N. Barnum, J. P. Dixon and J.-P. Tan (2001) *Economic Analysis of Investment Operations: Analytical Tools and Practical Applications* (Washington, DC: World Bank Institute Development Studies, World Bank).

A. Benjamin (2009) 'Small is powerful', *Guardian* (Society section), 7 January, 1–2.

L. Bennett, J. L. Smith and P. A. Wright (eds.), (2006) *Where Are Poor People to Live?: Transforming Public Housing Communities* (Armonk, NY: M. E. Sharpe).

M. Berman (1982) *All That is Solid Melts into Air* (New York: Simon & Schuster).

A. Berube (2005) *Transatlantic Perspectives on Mixed Communities* (York: Joseph Rowntree Foundation).

J. Betancur (2005) 'Gentrification Before Gentrification? The Plight of Pilsen in Chicago', *Nathalie P. Voorhees Center for Neighborhood and Community Improvement White Paper* (Chicago: University of Illinois).

R. Bist (2004) 'The great Indian mall boom', *Asia Times Online*, 24 July, www.atimes.com/atimes/South_Asia/FG24Df01.html, date accessed 9 June 2009.

S. Black (dir.) (2001) *Life and Debt* (Tuff Gong Pictures).

D. Block and J. Kouba (2006) 'A Comparison of the Availability and Affordability of a Market Basket in two Communities in the Chicago Area', *Public Health Nutrition*, 9, 837–45.

Blue Line Transit Taskforce (2004) *Out of the Loop: The Case for Reinstating Owl and Weekend Services on the Douglas Blue Line* (Chicago: Blue Line Transit Taskforce).

M. Boddy (1999) 'Geographical Economics and Urban Competitiveness: A Critique', *Urban Studies*, 36(5–6), 811–42.

R. Bohne, U. Dittfurth and C. Klatt (eds.), (1999) 'Sustainable Development: A Challenge for Europe's Urban Regions: 3rd Biennial of Towns and Town Planners in Europe', Herne/Ruhrgebiet, 14–17 September 1999 (Berlin: Vereinigung fur Stadt-, Regional- und Landesplanung e.V.).

P. Boland (2007) 'Unpacking the Theory–Practice Interface in Local Economic Development: An Analysis of Cardiff and Liverpool', *Urban Studies*, 44(5–6), 1019–39.

E. Bonacich and J. Modell (1980) *The Economic Basis of Ethnic Solidarity* (Berkeley: University of California Press).

S. Borrowman (2000) *Capital of Silicon Glen* (Bathgate, UK: Drumduff Publications).

N. Bosma and R. Harding (2007) *Global Entrepreneurship: GEM Summary Results 2006* (Massachusetts: Babson College and London: London Business School), www.esbri.se/pdf/gemsummary_2006.pdf, date accessed 9 January 2010.

G. Bramley, C. Hague, K. Kirk, A. Prior, J. Raemaekers and H. Smith, with A. Robinson and R. Bushnell (2004) *Review of Green Belt Policy in Scotland* (Edinburgh: Scottish Executive Social Research).

B. Brangwyn and R. Hopkins (2008) *Transition Initiatives Primer – Becoming a Transition Town, City, District, Village, Community, or Even Island*, available online at www.transitiontowns.org/TransitionNetwork/TransitionPrimer.

C. Breitbach (2007) 'The Geographies of a More Just Food System: Building Landscapes for Social Reproduction', *Landscape Research*, 32(5), 533–57.

T. Brindley, Y. Rydin and G. Stoker (1989) *Remaking Planning: The Politics of Urban Change in the Thatcher Years* (London: Unwin Hyman).

S. J. Brinegar (2000) 'Response to Homelessness in Tempe, Arizona: Public Opinion and Government Policy', *Urban Geography*, 21(6), 497–513.

G. Bristow (2005) 'Everyone's a "Winner": Problematising the Discourse of Regional Competitiveness', *Journal of Economic Geography*, 5, 285–304.

British Retail Consortium (2009) www.brc.org.uk (home page), date accessed 27 May 2009.

A. Brownlow (2009) 'Keeping up Appearances: Profiting from Patriarchy in the Nation's "Safest City"', *Urban Studies*, 46(8), 1681–1702.

E. Bryld (2003) 'Potentials, Problems and Policy Implications for Urban Agriculture in Developing Countries', *Agriculture and Human Values*, 20(1), 79–86.

T. Bunnel (2002) '(Re)positioning Malaysia: High-Tech Networks and the Multicultural Rescripting of National Identity', *Political Geography*, 21, 105–24.

H. Bush (2005) 'Mapping Pilsen: one student at a time', *Chicago Journal*, 14 September.

C. Cadell, N. Falk and F. King (2008) *Regeneration in European Cities: Making Connections* (York: Joseph Rowntree Foundation).

D. Cadman and R. Topping (1995) *Property Development*, 4th edn (London: E. and F. N. Spon).

R. Camagni (2002) 'On the Concept of Territorial Competitiveness: Sound or Misleading?', *Urban Studies*, 39, 2395–2411.

R. Camagni and R. Capello (1990) 'Towards a Definition of the Manoeuvring Space of Local Development Initiatives: Italian Success Stories of Local Development – Theoretical Considerations and Practical Experiences', in W. B. Stöhr (ed.), *Global Challenge and Local Response: Initiatives for Economic Regeneration in Contemporary Europe* (London and New York: United Nations University/Mansell), 328–53.

Cambridge Journal of Regions, Economy and Society (2010), 3(2).

Capital Economics Ltd (2002) *Property in Business – A Waste of Space?* (London: RICS).

M. Carley and J. R. Bautista (2001) 'Urban Management and Community Development in Metro Manila', in M. Carley, P. Jenkins and H. Smith (eds.), *Urban Development and Civil Society: The Role of Communities in Sustainable Cities* (London: Earthscan).

Y. Carlsson (2001) 'Somewhere Between Venice and Harry-town: Drammen – Identity, Image and Attributes', *Noord XXI Report No. 18* (Aberdeen: Noord XXI Foundation).

H. P. Carroll (2006) 'Where to Go after Kelo? Back to the Future!', *New England Law Review*, 29(75), 75–108.

M. Castells (1996) *The Rise of the Network Society* (Oxford: Blackwell).

M. Castells and P. Hall (1994) *Technopoles of the World: The Making of Twenty-First Century Industrial Complexes* (London: Routledge).

M. Castells and A. Portes (1989) 'World Underneath: The Origins, Dynamics, and Effects of the Informal Economy', in A. Portes, M. Castells, L.

A. Benton (eds.), *The Informal Economy: Studies in Advanced and Less Developed Countries* (Baltimore: Johns Hopkins University Press), 11–37.

Caux Round Table (2009) 'Moral Capitalism for a Better World', www.cauxroundtable.org/(home page), date accessed 30 November 2009.

CEC (2001) *Unity, Solidarity, Diversity for Europe, Its People and Its Territory. Second Report on Economic and Social Cohesion* (Luxembourg: Office for Official Publications of the European Communities).

CEC (2004a) *Facing the Challenge: The Lisbon Strategy for Growth and Employment. Report of the High Level Group Chaired by Wim Kok* (Luxembourg: Office for Official Publications of the European Communities).

CEC (2004b) *A New Partnership for Cohesion: Convergence, Competitiveness, Cooperation. Third Report on Economic and Social Cohesion* (Luxembourg: Office for Official Publications of the European Communities).

Centre on Housing Rights and Evictions/Social and Economic Rights Action Centre (2008) *The Myth of the Abuja Master Plan: Forced Evictions as Urban Planning in Abuja, Nigeria, Mission Report* (Geneva: Centre on Housing Rights and Evictions).

Channel News Asia (2010) '1st team of Tianjin eco-city executives complete Green Building Devt Training', www.channelnewsasia.com/stories/singaporelocalnews/view/1067259/1/.html, date accessed 3 July 2010.

P. Chatterjee (2004) *The Politics of the Governed: Reflections on Popular Politics in Most of the World* (New York: Columbia University Press).

P. Chatterton and R. Hollands (2002) 'Theorising Urban Playscapes: Producing, Regulating and Consuming Youthful Nightlife City Spaces', *Urban Studies*, 39(1), 95–116.

M. Chen, J. Vanek, F. Lund, J. Heintz, R. Jhabvala and C. Bonner (2005) *Progress of the World's Women 2005: Women, Work and Poverty* (New York: United Nations Development Fund for Women).

P. C. Cheshire (1979) 'Inner Areas as Spatial Labour Markets: A Critique of the Inner Area Studies', *Urban Studies*, 16(1), 29–43.

P. Cheshire (1999) 'Cities in Competition: Articulating the Gains from Integration', *Urban Studies*, 36(5–6), 843–64.

Chicago Art District (2009) www.chicagoartsdistrict.org/ (home page), date accessed 17 July 2009.

S. Christopherson, J. Michie and P. Tyler (2010) 'Regional Resilience: Theoretical and Empirical Perspectives', *Cambridge Journal of Regions, Economy and Society*, 3, 3–10.

A. Clark (2008) 'Running on empty, motor city where houses sell for £500', *Guardian*, 25 October 2008, 6.

A. Cochrane, J. Peck and A. Tickell (1996) 'Manchester Playing Games: Exploring the Local Politics of Globalisation', *Urban Studies*, 33(8), 1319–36.

S. Colby, N. Stone and P. Carttar (2004) *Zeroing in on Impact – In an Era of Declining Resources, Nonprofits Need to Clarify Their Intended Impact*, Stanford Social Innovation Review (Stanford: Stanford Graduate School of Business).

Congress for the New Urbanism (2009) www.cnu.org (home page), date accessed 4 July 2009.

P. Cooke (1986) 'Global Restructuring, Industrial Change and Local Adjustment', in P. Cooke (ed.), *Global Restructuring Local Response* (London: Economic and Social Research Council).

P. Cooke (1987) 'Individuals, Localities and Postmodernism', *Environment and Planning D: Society and Space*, 5(4): 408–12.

P. Cooke (ed.) (1989) *Localities: The Changing Face of Britain* (London: Unwin Hyman).

J. Cortright (2006) *Making Sense of Clusters: Regional Competitiveness and Economic Development* (Washington, DC: Brookings Institution, Metropolitan Policy Program).

K. Cox and A. Mair (1989) 'Urban Growth Machines and the Politics of Local Economic Development', *International Journal of Urban and Regional Research*, 13(1), 137–46.

G. T. Crane (1994) '"Special Things in Special Ways": National Economic Identity and China's Special Economic Zones', *Australian Journal of Chinese Affairs*, 32, 71–92.

R. Crane and M. Manville (2008) 'People or Place? Revisiting the Who Versus the Where of Urban Development', *Land Lines*, 20(3), 2–7.

Creative Coast Alliance (2010) www.thecreativecoast.org (home page), date accessed 2 July 2010.

D. Crilley (1993) 'Architecture as Advertising: Constructing the Image of Redevelopment', in G. Kearns and C. Philo (eds.), *Selling Places: The City as Cultural Capital, Past and Present* (Oxford: Pergamon Press).

J. Crompton (2001) 'Public Subsidies to Professional Team Sport Facilities in the USA', in C. Gratton and I. P. Henry (eds.), *Sport in the City: The Role of Sport in Economic and Social Regeneration* (London: Routledge).

H. Crummy (1992) *Let the People Sing! A Story of Craigmillar* (Newcraighall: Helen Crummy).

W. Curran (2006) 'Gentrification: A Case Study', in R. P. Greene, M. J. Bouman and D. Grammenos (eds.), *Chicago's Geographies – Metropolis for the Twenty-First Century* (Washington, DC: Association of American Geographers), 259–63.

W. Curran (2007) '"From the Frying Pan into the Oven": Gentrification and the Experience of Industrial Displacement in Williamsburg, Brooklyn', *Urban Studies*, 44(8), 1427–40.

W. Curran and S. Hanson (2005) 'Getting Globalized: Urban Policy and Industrial Displacement in Williamsburg, Brooklyn', *Urban Geography*, 26(6), 461–82.

J. Curran, R. Rutherford and S. L. Smith (2000) 'Is There a Local Business Community? Explaining the Non-Participation of Small Business in Local Economic Development', *Local Economy*, 15(2), 128–43.

Dean Clough (2007) www.deanclough.com (home page), date accessed 17 November 2009.

M. Dear (1986) 'Postmodernism and Planning', *Environment and Planning D: Society and Space*, 4(3), 367–84.

M. Dear (1987) 'Society, Politics, and Social Theory', *Environment and Planning D: Society and Space*, 5(4), 363–66.

J. De la Mothe and G. Pacquet (1998) 'National Innovation Systems and Instituted Processes', in Z. Acs (ed.), *Regional Innovation, Knowledge and Global Change* (London: Pinter).

Department of the Environment (1994) *Vital and Viable Town Centres: Meeting the Challenge* (London: HMSO).

Department of the Environment (1996) *Sustainable Settlements and Shelter: The United Kingdom National Report Habitat II* (London: HMSO).

Department of the Environment/PIEDA (1995) The Impact of Environmental Improvements on Urban Regeneration (London: HMSO).

Department for Environment, Transport and the Regions/Commission for Architecture and the Built Environment (DETR/CABE) (2001) *The Value of Urban Design* (London: Thomas Telford).

H. de Soto (2000) *The Mystery of Capital: Why Capitalism Triumphs in the West and Fails Everywhere Else* (New York: Basic Books).

P. Desrochers (2000) 'Eco-Industrial Parks – The Case for Private Planning', *PERC Research Studies*, 00–1 (Bozeman, MT: Property and Environment Research Center), www.perc.org/articles/article212.php, date accessed 25 June 2010.

P. Dicken (2003) *Global Shift: Reshaping the Global Economic Map in the Twenty-First Century*, 4th edn (London: Sage).

D. Dolowitz and D. Marsh (1996) 'Who Learns What from Whom: A Review of the Policy Transfer Literature', *Political Studies*, 44, 343–57.

Doo Wop Preservation League (DWPL) (2009) www.doowopusa.org (home page), date accessed 8 July 2009.

Y. Dranitsyna (2006) 'Kiosks to close to battle piracy', *St. Petersburg Times*, 6 June, www.sptimesrussia.com/index.php?action_id=2&story_id=17802, date accessed 12 January 2009.

J.-F. Drevet (2007) 'Chasing a Moving Target: Territorial Cohesion Policy in a Europe with Uncertain Borders', in A. Faludi (ed.), *Territorial Cohesion and the European Model of Society* (Cambridge: Lincoln Institute of Land Policy).

S. Duncan and M. Savage (1989) 'Space, Scale and Locality', *Antipode*, 21(3), 179–206.

K. J. Dunham (2007) 'The economics of transit-oriented development', *Wall Street Journal*, 11 June.

O. J. Dwyer and D. H. Alderman (2008) *Civil Rights Memorials and the Geography of Memory* (Chicago: Center for American Places at Columbia College).

ECOTEC Research and Consulting Ltd (2005) 'The Territorial Impact of EU Research and Development Policies', *Final Report of ESPON 2006 Project 2.1.2*, www.espon.eu (home page), date accessed 27 May 2009.

T. Edmonds (2000) 'Regional Competitiveness and the Role of the Knowledge Economy', *House of Commons Library Research Paper 00/73* (London).

J. Egan (2002) 'To be young and homeless', *New York Times Magazine*, 24 March, 32–7, 58–9.

J. Egan *et al.* (2004) *The Egan Review: Skills for Sustainable Communities* (London: Office of the Deputy Prime Minister).

B. Einhorn and S. Prasso (1999) 'Mahathir's high-tech folly', *Business Week*, 29 March, 3622, 83–6.

Environmental Protection Agency (2009) *International Brownfields Case Study: Emscher Park, Germany*, www.epa.gov/brownfields/partners/emscher.htm, date accessed 14 April 2009.

L. Etter (2010) 'Food for thought: do you need farmers for a farmers market?', *Wall Street Journal*, 29 April, http://online.wsj.com/article/SB10001424052748703404004575198270918567074.html, date accessed 16 June 2010.

A. W. Evans and R. Richardson (1981) 'Urban Unemployment: Interpretation and Additional Evidence', *Scottish Journal of Political Economy*, 28(2), 107–24.

Fado Irish Pub (2009) www.fadoirishpub.com (home page), date accessed 2 February 2010.

Fairtrade Labelling Organizations Limited (FLO) (2010) www.fairtrade.net/ (home page), date accessed 7 July 2010.

S. Fan and K. Sheng (2007) 'Analysis on Economic Basis of City Cluster in Central Liaoning Province', *China City Planning Review*, 16(2), 49–55.

E. Fernandes (2007) 'Constructing the "Right to the City" in Brazil', *Social Legal Studies* 16 (2) 201–19.

M. P. Fernández-Kelly (1997) 'Maquiladoras: The View from Inside', in N. Visvanathan, L. Duggan, L. Nisonoff and N. Wiegersma (eds.), *The Women, Gender and Development Reader* (London: Zed Books).

D. Finegold (1999) 'Creating Self-sustaining, High Skill Ecosystems', *Oxford Review of Economic Policy*, 15(1), 60–81.

C. Fishman (2003) 'The Walmart you don't know', *Fast Company*, 1 December, www.fastcompany.com/magazine/77/walmart.html, date accessed 15 July 2010.

R. Florida (2002) *The Rise of the Creative Class: And How It's Transforming Work, Leisure, Community and Everyday Life* (New York: Basic Books).

R. Florida (2005) *Cities and the Creative Class* (New York and London: Routledge).

R. Florida (2007) 'Creative Class Communities', www.creativeclass.com/creative_class/2007/05/06/creative-class-communities, date accessed 9 December 2009.

R. Florida (2008) *Who's Your City? How the Creative Economy Is Making Where You Live the Most Important Decision of Your Life* (New York: Basic Books).

S. Fothergill, S. Monk and M. Perry (1987) *Property and Industrial Development* (London: Hutchinson).

A. Friedberg (2002) 'Window Shopping: Cinema and the Postmodern', in M. J. Dear and S. Flusty (eds.), *The Spaces of Postmodernity: Readings in Human Geography* (Oxford and Malden, MA: Blackwell).

J. Froelich (2010) 'Farmers market to stay in Gillett Park', *Tomah Journal*, 14 May, www.tomahjournal.com/articles/2010/05/14/news/00lead.txt, date accessed 16 June 2010.

C. Fudge and J. Rowe (2001) 'Ecological Modernization as a Framework for Sustainable Development: A Case Study in Sweden', *Environment and Planning A*, 33, 1527–46.

J. Gardiner (2006) 'Hope Springs Eternal', *Regeneration and Renewal*, 1 December, 20–1.

J. Garreau (1991) *Edge City: Life on the New Frontier* (New York: Anchor Doubleday).

W. Ge (1999) 'Special Economic Zones and the Opening of the Chinese Economy: Some Lessons for Economic Liberalization', *World Development*, 27(7), 1267–85.

D. Gibbs (2003) 'Ecological Modernisation and Local Economic Development: The Growth of Eco-Industrial Development Initiatives', *International Journal of Environment and Sustainable Development*, 2(3), 250–66.

T. J. Gilfoyle (2006) *Millennium Park: Creating a Chicago Landmark* (Chicago and London: University of Chicago Press).

M. Gittell, K. Newman, J. Bockmeyer and R. Lindsay (1998) 'Expanding Civic Opportunity: Urban Empowerment Zones', *Urban Affairs Review*, 33(4), 530–58.

R. Goodman (1995) *The Luck Business: The Devastating Consequences and Broken Promises of America's Gambling Explosion* (New York, London, Sydney and Tokyo: Martin Kessler Books).

I. Gordon (1999) 'Internationalisation and Urban Competition', *Urban Studies*, 36(5–6), 1001–16.

A. Gouldson, P. Hills and R. Welford (2008) 'Ecological Modernisation and Policy Learning in Hong Kong', *Geoform*, 39, 319–30.

S. Graham and S. Marvin (2001) *Splintering Urbanism: Network Infrastructures, Technological Mobilities and the Urban Condition* (London and New York: Routledge).

D. Grammenos (2006) 'Latino Chicago', in R. P. Greene, M. J. Bouman and D. Grammenos (eds.), *Chicago's Geographies – Metropolis for the Twenty-First Century* (Washington, DC: Association of American Geographers), 205–16.

J. Grant (2006) *Planning the Good Community: New Urbanism in Theory and Practice* (London and New York: Routledge).

C. Grasland and P. Beckouche (2007) *Europe in the World: Territorial Evidence And Visions* (Luxembourg: ESPON).

C. Gratton, N. Dobson and S. Shibli (2000) 'The Economic Importance of Major Sports Events: A Case Study of Six Events', *Managing Leisure*, 5(1), 17–28.

C. Gratton, N. Dobson and S. Shibli (2001) 'The Role of Major Sports Events in the Economic Regeneration of Cities: Lessons from Six World or European Championships', in C. Gratton and I. P. Henry (eds.), *Sport in the City: The Role of Sport in Economic and Social Regeneration* (London: Routledge).

S. Gray (2009a) 'Can America's urban food deserts bloom?', *Time Magazine*, 26 May, www.time.com/time/nation/article/0,8599,1900947,00.html, date accessed 16 June 2010.

S. Gray (2009b) 'Community Service 2009 – LaDonna Redmond', *Time Magazine*, 10 September, http://205.188.238.181/time/specials/packages/article/0,28804,1921165_1921239_1921216,00.html, date accessed 16 June 2010.

A. Green (2008) 'Attacks on the homeless rise, with youths mostly to blame', *New York Times*, 15 February, 12.

F. J. Greene, P. Tracey and M. Cowling (2007) 'Recasting the City into City-Regions: Place Promotion, Competitiveness Benchmarking and the Quest for Urban Supremacy', *Growth and Change*, 38(1), 1–22.

G. Greff (2008) 'Enchanted Highway', www.enchantedhighway.net (home page), date accessed 10 November 2009.

M. Griffin and E. Frongillo (2003) 'Experiences and Perspectives of Farmers from Upstate New York Farmers' Markets', *Agriculture and Human Values*, 20, 189–203.

R. Griffiths (1998) 'Making Sameness: Place Marketing and the New Urban Entrepreneurialism', in N. Oatley (ed.), *Cities, Economic Competition and Urban Policy* (London: Paul Chapman).

Growing Home (2009) A non-profit organic agriculture business, www.growinghomeinc.org (home page), date accessed 30 November 2009.

C. Guy (1994) *The Retail Development Process: Location, Property and Planning* (London: Routledge).

S. Guy (2009) 'Walmart eyes 12 Chicago "food desert" sites', *Chicago Sun-Times*, 7 February.

C. Hague (2001) 'The Swedish Recipe for Rural Renewal', *Regeneration and Renewal*, 27 April, 18–20.

C. Hague (2005a) 'Planning and Place Identity', in C. Hague and P. Jenkins (eds.), *Place Identity, Participation and Planning* (London and New York: Routledge), 3–17.

C. Hague (2005b) 'Identity, Sustainability and Settlement Patterns', in C. Hague and P. Jenkins (eds.). *Place Identity, Participation and Planning* (London and New York: Routledge), 159–82.

C. Hague (2007) 'Urban Containment: European Experience of Planning for the Compact City', in G.-J. Knaap, H. A. Haccou, K. J. Clifton and J. W. Frece (eds.), *Incentives, Regulations and Plans: The Role of States and Nation-states in Smart Growth Planning* (Cheltenham, UK and Northampton, MA: Edward Elgar).

C. Hague (2009) 'Territorial Ambitions', *Planning*, 1 May, 14–15.

C. Hague, P. Wakely, J. Crespin and C. Jasko (2006) *Making Planning Work: A Guide to Approaches and Skills* (Rugby, UK: Intermediate Technology Publications Ltd).

E. Hague, C. Thomas and S. Williams (2000a) 'Equity or Exclusion? Contemporary Experiences in Post-industrial Urban Leisure', in C. Brackenridge, D. Howe and F. Jordan (eds.), *Just Leisure: Equity, Social Exclusion and Identity* (University of Brighton: Leisure Studies Association), 17–33.

E. Hague, C. Thomas and S. Williams (2000b) 'Political Constructions and Social Realities of Exclusion in Urban Leisure: The Case of Elderly Women in Stoke-on-Trent, England', *World Leisure Journal*, 42(4), 4–13.

E. Hague (2001) 'The Great Regeneration Gamble', *Regeneration and Renewal*, 25 May, 20–1.

E. Hague (2005) 'Tax Increment Financing – An Ongoing Contest over Urban Land Use in Pilsen, Chicago', *Urban News: Newsletter for the Urban Geography Specialty Group*, Association of American Geographers, 26(3), 7–9.

E. Hague (2006a) 'Service Learning in Pilsen, Chicago', in R. P. Greene, M. J. Bouman and D. Grammenos (eds.), *Chicago's Geographies – Metropolis for the Twenty-First century* (Washington, DC: Association of American Geographers), 264–7.

E. Hague (2006b) '"We Dictate the Rules" – Community Activism, Emotional Authority and Land-Use Zoning in Chicago', Association of American Geographers Annual Meeting, Chicago.

E. Hague, W. Curran and Pilsen Alliance (2008) *Contested Chicago: Pilsen and Gentrification/Pilsen y el aburguesamineto: Una lucha para conserver nuestra Comunidad* (available from www.lulu.com).

Haile, F. (2008) interview by E. Hague with Fritz Haile, of the Creative Coast Alliance, conducted on 24 July.

Hakka Tung Blossom Festival (2009) http://tung.hakka.gov.tw (home page), date accessed 13 June 2009.

S. Handy (1996) 'Understanding the Link between Urban Form and Non-Work Travel Behavior', *Journal of Planning Education and Research*, 15 (3), 183–198.

K. B. Hankins (2007) 'The Final Frontier: Charter Schools as New Community Institutions of Gentrification', *Urban Geography*, 28(2), 113–28.

K. T. Hansen (2002) 'Who Rules the Streets?', in K. T. Hansen and M. Vaa (eds.), *Reconsidering Informality: Perspectives from Urban Africa* (Uppsala: Nordiska Afrikainstitutet).

K. T. Hansen and M. Vaa (2004) 'Introduction', in K. T. Hansen and M. Vaa (eds.), *Reconsidering Informality: Perspectives from Urban Africa* (Uppsala: Nordiska Afrikainstitutet).

Harlem Children's Zone (2008) 'The Harlem Children's Zone Project Model', www.hcz.org/images/white_paper-edit_exsum12_12_08.pdf, date accessed 17 January 2009.

D. Harvey (1989) *The Condition of Postmodernity: An Enquiry into the Origins of Cultural Change* (Oxford and New York: Blackwell).

D. Harvey (2000) *Spaces of Hope* (Edinburgh: Edinburgh University Press).

D. Harvey (2005) *A Brief History of Neoliberalism* (Oxford, Oxford University Press).

R. Hassink (2010) 'Regional Resilience: A Promising Concept to Explain Differences in Regional Economic Adaptability?', *Cambridge Journal of Regions, Economy and Society*, 3, 45–58.

D. Havlick and S. Kirsch (2004) 'A Production Utopia? RTP and the North Carolina Research Triangle', *Southeastern Geographer*, 44(2), 263–77.

P. Healey (2006) 'On Learning from Situated Experiences', *Planning Theory and Practice*, 7(4), 475–8.

D. Held, A. McGrew, D. Goldblatt and J. Perraton (1999) *Global Transformations: Politics, Economics and Culture* (Cambridge: Polity Press).

J. Helyar (1988) 'Split-level south: sun belt's economy booms in many cities, but rural regions lag', *Wall Street Journal*, 15 January.

C. High and G. Nemes (2007) 'Social learning in LEADER: Exogenous, endogenous and hybrid evaluation in rural development', *Sociologia Ruralis*, 47(2), 103–19.

M. K. Hingley, A. Lindgreen and M. B. Beverland (2010) 'Barriers to Network Innovation in UK Ethnic Fresh Produce Supply', *Entrepreneurship and Regional Development*, 22(1), 77–96.

M. Hirsch (2008) 'How to Doo Wop: 1997–2008', Society for Commercial Archaeology Conference, Albuquerque, New Mexico, 12 September.

P. Hirst and J. Zeitlin (1991) 'Flexible Specialisation vs. Post-Fordism: Theory, Evidence and Policy Implications', *Economy and Society*, 20, 1–56.

P. Q. Hirst and G. Thompson (1999) *Globalization in Question: The International Economy and the Possibilities of Governance*, 2nd edn (Cambridge: Polity Press).

B. Hochleutner (2003) 'Bids Fare Well: The Democratic Accountability of Business Improvement Districts', *New York University Law Review*, 78, 374–404.

M. Hodson and S. Marvin (2007) 'Urban Ecological Security – The New Urban Paradigm?', *Town and Country Planning*, 76(12), 433–5.

B. Holcomb (1993) 'Revisioning Place: De- and Re-constructing the Image of the Industrial City', in G. Kearns and C. Philo (eds.), *Selling Places: The City as Cultural Capital, Past and Present* (Oxford: Pergamon Press).

B. Holcomb (1994) 'City Make-overs: Marketing the Post-industrial City', in J. R. Gold and S. V. Ward (eds.), *Place Promotion: The Use of Publicity and Marketing to Sell Towns and Regions* (Chichester: Wiley).

A. Hoogvelt (2001) *Globalization and the Post-colonial World: The New Political Economy of Development* (Basingstoke: Palgrave).

Housing and Urban Development (HUD) (2008) HOPE VI, www.hud.gov/offices/pih/programs/ph/hope6/, date accessed 15 October 2008.

Housing and Urban Development (2009) *Chicago, Illinois Empowerment Zone Annual Report*, www5.hud.gov/urban/perms/printReport.asp?report=1048, date accessed 15 July 2009.

G. Howe (1978) 'A zone of enterprise to make all systems "go"', speech to the Bow Group, 26 June (London: Conservative Central Office).

Y. Huang (2003) 'Renters' Housing Behaviour in Transitional China', *Housing Studies*, 18(1), 103–126.

J. Huber (1982) *Die verlorene Unschuld der Ökologie* ['The Lost Innocence of Ecology: New Technologies and Superindustrialized Development'] (Frankfurt am Main: S. Fischer Verlag).

J. Huber (1985) *Die regenbogengesellschaft: Ökologie und Sozialpolitik* ['The Rainbow Society: Ecology and Social Politics'] (Frankfurt am Main: S. Fischer Verlag).

Innobasque (2009) 'Regions at risk of energy poverty', *Interim Report of the ESPON Re-Risk project*, www.espon.eu (home page), date accessed 26 May 2009.

Institut für Regionalforschung, Christian–Albrechts–Universität Kiel, Germany *et al.* (2005) 'Territorial Impact of EU Transport and TEN Policies', *Final Report of ESPON Project 2.1.1*, www.espon.eu (home page), date accessed 30 November 2009.

International Planning Studies (2009), 14(4).

D. Isaacs (2003) 'East Pilsen's makeover', *Chicago Reader*, 12 December.

Isles (2009) www.isles.org (home page) date accessed 14 April 2009.

T. Jackson and B. Illsley (2006) 'Designed to last', *New Start*, 15 December, 16–17.

Jaipur Virasat Foundation (2009) www.jaipurvirastfoundation.org (home page), date accessed 13 June 2009.

S. James and T. Lahti (2004) *The Natural Step for Communities: How Cities and Towns Can Change to Sustainable Practices* (Gabriola Island, Canada: New Society Publishers).

M. Jänicke (1985) *Preventive Environmental Policy as Ecological Modernization And Structural Policy*, Discussion Paper IIUG dp 85–2, Internationales Institut Für Umwelt und Gesellschaft, Wissenschaftszentrum Berlin Für Sozialforschung (WZB).

Y. C. Jao, C. K. Leung and C. H. Chai (eds.), (1986) *China's Special Economic Zones: Policies, Problems, and Prospects* (Oxford: Oxford University Press).

P. Jenkins, H. Smith and Y. P. Wang (2007) *Planning and Housing in the Rapidly Urbanising World* (London and New York: Routledge).

C. Jensen-Butler (1999) 'Cities in Competition: Equity Issues', *Urban Studies*, 36(5–6), 865–91.

J. Johnson (2006) 'Pilsen community speaks out', www.Chicago.Indymedia. org (home page), date accessed 2 February 2006.

A. Jones and M. Munday (2001) 'Blaenavon and United Nations World Heritage Site Status: Is Conservation of Historical Heritage a Road to Local Economic Development?', *Regional Studies*, 35(6), 585–90.

F. T. Kalabamu (1987) 'Rickshaws and the Traffic problems of Dhaka', *Habitat International*, 11(2), 123–31.

A. Y. Kamete (2004) 'Home Industries and the Formal City in Harare, Zimbabwe', in K. T. Hansen and M. Vaa (eds.), *Reconsidering Informality: Perspectives from Urban Africa* (Uppsala: Nordiska Afrikainstitutet).

D. Kampus (2008) 'Integrated planning of a shopping-center in Graz/Austria', *European Local Transport Information Service*, www.eltis.org/study_sheet.phtml?study_id=1775, date accessed 30 June 2010.

B. M. Kazimbaya-Senkwe (2004) 'Home-Based Enterprises in a Period of Economic Restructuring in Zambia', in K. T. Hansen and M. Vaa (eds.), *Reconsidering Informality: Perspectives from Urban Africa* (Uppsala: Nordiska Afrikainstitutet).

G. Kearns (1993) 'The City as Spectacle: Paris and the Bicentenary of the French Revolution', in G. Kearns and C. Philo (eds.), *Selling Places: The City as Cultural Capital, Past and Present* (Oxford: Pergamon Press).

G. Kearns and C. Philo (1993) 'Culture, History, Capital: A Critical Introduction to the Selling of Places', in G. Kearns and C. Philo (eds.), *Selling Places: The City as Cultural Capital, Past and Present* (Oxford: Pergamon Press).

M. Keating (2001) 'Governing Cities and Regions: Territorial Restructuring', in A. J. Scott (ed.), *Global City-Regions: Trends, Theory, Policy* (Oxford: Oxford University Press), 371–90.

W. D. Keating and N. Krumholz (eds.), (1999) *Rebuilding Urban Neighborhoods: Achievements, Opportunities, and Limits* (Thousand Oaks, CA: Sage).

D. Keeble (1976) *Industrial Location and Planning in the United Kingdom* (London: Methuen).

P. Kellett and A. G. Tipple (1997) 'The home as workplace: a study of in-come-generating activities within the domestic setting', paper presented to the International Symposium on Culture and Space in Home Environments: Critical Evaluations and New Paradigms (Istanbul: Istanbul Technical University and IAPS).

Kelo et al. v. *City of New London et al.*, 545 US 469, 2005.

G. Kim (2004) 'Pilsen residents win vote on zoning', *Chicago Tribune*, 17 March.

J. W. Kindt (1998) 'Legalized Gambling Is Bad for Business', in R. L. Evans and M. Hance (eds.), *Legalized Gambling: For and Against* (Chicago and La Salle, IL: Open Court).

King Sturge/Business in the Community (2006) *The Contribution of the Retail Sector to the Economy, Employment and Regeneration* (London: King Sturge).

Kipepeo (2009) Kipepeo Butterfly Project, www.kipepeo.org (home page), date accessed 26 May 2009.

R. J. R. Kirby and T. Cannon (1989) 'Introduction', in D. S. G. Goodman (ed.), *China's Regional Development* (London: Routledge).

L. Kitchen and T. Marsden (2009) 'Creating Sustainable Rural Development through Stimulating the Eco-Economy: Beyond the Eco-Economic Paradox', *Sociologica Ruralis*, 49(3), 273–94.

M. Kitson, R. Martin and P. Tyler (2004) 'Regional Competitiveness – An Elusive Yet Key Concept?', *Regional Studies*, 38(9), 991–9.

M. Koljatic and M. Silva (2006) 'Adding Value to Wild Fruits: A Chilean Experience', *ReVista, Harvard Review of Latin America*, fall 2006, 20–22.

Korea National Cleaner Production Center (2010) 'Eco-Industrial Parks', at www.kncpc.re.kr/eng/topics/EcoIndustParks.asp, date accessed 25 June 2010.

P. K. Kresl (1995) 'The Determinants of Urban Competitiveness', in P. K. Kresl and G. Gappert (eds.), *North American Cities and the Global Economy: Challenges and Opportunities – Urban Affairs Annual Review* (Sage Publications).

P. Krugman (1995) *Development, Geography and Economic Theory* (Cambridge, MA: MIT Press).

P. Krugman (1996a) 'Urban Concentration: the Role of Increasing Returns and Transport Costs', *International Regional Science Review*, 19, 5–48.

P. Krugman (1996b) 'Making Sense of the Competitiveness Debate', *Oxford Review of Economic Policy*, 12, 483–499.

P. Krugman (1997) *Pop Internationalism* (Cambridge, MA: MIT Press).

G. Krumme (1969) 'Towards a Geography of Enterprise', *Geography*, 45, 30–40.

C. Landry (2000) *The Creative City: A Toolkit for Urban Innovators* (London: Comedia/Earthscan).

F. M. Lappé (2009) 'The city that ended hunger', *Yes!* magazine, spring 2009, www.yesmagazine.org/issues/food-for-everyone/the-city-that-ended-hunger, date accessed 1 July 2010.

C. Leadbeater (2005) 'Design your own revolution', *Observer*, 19 June, 15.

C. Leadbeater and P. Miller (2004) *The Pro-Am Revolution* (London: Demos).

G. C. Leef (2005) '*Kelo* v. *City of New London*: Do We Need Eminent Domain for Economic Growth?', *The Freeman*, 55(9), 13–16.

H. Lefebvre (1968) *Le droit à la ville* (Paris: Anthropos).

H. Lefebvre (1973) *Espace et politique* (Paris: Anthropos).

H. Lefebvre (1990) *Du contrat de citoyenneté* (Paris: Sylleps/Périscope).

A. Lehavi and A. N. Licht (2007) 'Squaring the Eminent Domain Circle: A New Approach to Land Assembly Problems', *Land Lines*, 19(1), 14–19.

S. Leitham, R. W. McQuaid and J. D. Nelson (2000) 'The Influence of Transport on Industrial Location Choice: A Stated Preference Experiment', *Transportation Research A*, 34, 515–35.

H. Leitner, C. Pavlik and E. Sheppard (2002) 'Networks, Governance and the Politics of Scale: Inter-Urban Networks and the European Union', in A. Herod and M. Wright (eds.), *Geographies of Power: Placing Scale* (Oxford: Blackwell).

J. Lepawsky (2005) 'Stories of Space and Subjectivity in Planning the Multimedia Super Corridor', *Geoforum*, 36(6), 705–19.

K. C. Leung (2004) *The Essence of Asset Management – A Guide* (Kuala Lumpur: UNDP–TUGI in association with the Eastern Regional Organization for Planning and Housing and the Asia Pacific Institute for Good Asset Management).

W. Lever and I. Turok (1999) 'Competitive Cities: Introduction to the Review', *Urban Studies*, 36(5–6), 791–3.

C. Leys (1996) *The Rise and Fall of Development Theory* (London: James Currey).

M. Lezama, B. Webber and C. Dagher (2004) *Sourcing Practices in the Apparel Industry: Implications for Garment Exporters in Commonwealth Developing Countries* (London: Special Advisory Services Division of the Commonwealth Secretariat).

N. Lichtenstein (2009) *The Retail Revolution: How Walmart Created a Brave New World of Business* (New York: Metropolitan Books).

I. Light (1972) *Ethnic Enterprise in America* (Berkeley: University of California Press).

C. E. Lindblom (1959) 'The Science of "Muddling Through"', *Public Administration Review*, spring 1959, reproduced in A. Faludi (ed.) (1973), *A Reader in Planning Theory* (Oxford and New York: Pergamon Press).

A. N. Link and J. T. Scott (2003) 'The Growth of Research Triangle Park', *Small Business Economics*, 20, 167–75.

P. Lipman and N. Haines (2007) 'From Education Accountability to Privatization and African American Exclusion – Chicago Public Schools' "Renaissance 2010"', *Educational Policy*, 21(3), 471–502.

Little Village Environmental Justice Organization (n.d.) 'The Pink Link: A Closer Look', available from: LVEJO, 2856 S. Millard Ave, Chicago, IL 60623; www.lvejo.org

K. B. Liu (1982) Speech at the Conference of Territory Planning of Southern Provinces and autonomous Regions, in Local Bureau of Planning Commission of Shaanxi Province (ed.) (1984) *Reference Materials for Territory Planning*, Vol.1 (Mimeo).

318   *Bibliography*

X. Liu, G. K. Heilig, J. Chen and M. Heino (2007) 'Interactions Between Economic Growth and Environmental Quality in Shenzhen, China's First Special Economic Zone', *Ecological Economics*, 62, 559–70.

P. Loftman and B. Nevin (2003) 'Prestige Projects, City Centre Restructuring and Social Exclusion: Taking the Long-Term View', in M. Miles and T. Hall (eds.), *Urban Futures: Critical Commentaries on Shaping the City* (London and New York: Routledge).

J. R. Logan and H. L. Molotch (1987) *Urban Fortunes: The Political Economy of Space* (Berkeley: University of California Press).

M. Lorenzen (2007) 'Social Capital and Localised Learning: Proximity and Place in Technological and Institutional Dynamics', *Urban Studies*, 44(4), 799–817.

J. Lovering (2001) 'The Coming Regional Crisis (And How to Avoid It)', *Regional Studies*, 35(4), 349–54.

E. A. Lowe (2001) *Eco-Industrial Park Handbook for Asian Developing Countries*, Report to the Asian Development Bank, Environment Department (Oakland, CA: Indigo Development). Available online: www.indigdev.com/Handbook.html, date accessed 25 June 2010.

E. McCann (2008) 'Livable city/unequal city; The politics of policy-making in a "creative" boomtown', *Interventions Economiques*, 37, http://benhur.teluq.uquebec.ca/rie/2008001/doss_2_McCann.html, date accessed 15 July 2008.

J. McCarthy (1998) 'US Urban Empowerment Zones', *Land Use Policy*, 15(4), 319–30.

R. MacDonald (1995) 'IBA Emscher Park', *Urban Design*, 56 (October), 28–31.

S. Macdonald (2006) 'Mock shop trains unemployed for work', *Regeneration and Renewal*, 1 December, 25.

P. Macnaughten, R. Grove-White, M. Jacobs and B. Wynne (1995) *Public Perceptions and Sustainability in Lancashire: Indicators, Institutions, Participation*, report to Lancashire County Council.

C. Maganda (2005) 'Collateral Damage: How the San Diego–Imperial Valley Water Agreement Affects the Mexican Side of the Border', *Journal of Environment and Development*, 14(4), 486–506.

B. McKenna (2006) 'Detroit's other Super Bowl', *Free Press*, 8 March.

D. Maclennan (1994) *A Competitive UK Economy: The Challenges for Housing Policy* (York: Joseph Rowntree Foundation).

R. McLeod and D. Hughes (2006) 'This house believes that the private finance market will never fund major slum upgrading', in R. McLeod and K. Mullard (eds.), *Bridging the Finance Gap in Housing and Infrastructure* (Rugby: ITDG Publishing), 137–48.

C. Marrs (2006) 'Olympic Legacy Guru', *Planning*, 28 July, 13.

T. Marsden and R. Sonnino (2005) 'Setting up and Management of Public Policies with Multifunctional Purpose: Connecting Agriculture with New Markets and Services and Rural SMEs', Multagri project – UK national report, WP5 (Cardiff: School of City and Regional Planning, University of Cardiff).

A. Marshall (1890) *Principles of Economics* (Basingstoke: Macmillan).

R. Martin and P. Sunley (1996) 'Paul Krugman's Geographical Economics and Its Implications for Regional Development Theory: A Critical Assessment', *Economic Geography*, 72, 259–92.

D. Massey (1981) 'The UK Electrical Engineering and Electronics Industries: The Implications of the Crisis for the Restructuring of Capital and Locational Change', in M. Dear and A. J. Scott (eds.), *Urbanisation and Urban Planning in Capitalist Society* (London: Methuen).

D. Massey (1995) *Spatial Divisions of Labor: Social Structures and the Geography of Production*, 2nd edn (New York: Routledge).

D. Massey and R. Meegan (1982) *The Anatomy of Job Loss* (Andover, UK: Methuen).

J. Mead (2007) 'Pilsen: 150 Years of Struggle', presentation at DePaul University, Chicago, 5 November.

P. Merrion (2006) 'Dead zone: a $100–mil. dud', *Crain's Chicago Business*, 23 October, 29(43), 3.

D. Mitchell (1997) 'The Annihilation of Space by Law: The Roots and Implications of Anti-Homeless Laws in United States', *Antipode*, 29(3), 303–35.

D. Mitchell (2003) *The Right to the City: Social Justice and the Fight For Public Space* (New York: Guilford Press).

A. Mol and G. Spaargaren (1993) 'Environment, Modernity and the Risk-Society: The Apocalyptic Horizon of Environmental Reform', *International Sociology*, 8(4), 431–59.

J. H. Mollenkopf and M. Castells (eds.), (1992) *Dual City: Restructuring New York* (New York: Russell Sage Foundation).

J. Montgomery (2007) *The New Wealth of Cities: City Dynamics and the Fifth Wave* (Aldershot, UK and Burlington, VT: Ashgate), 299–358.

A. Mountz and W. Curran (2009) 'Policing in Drag: Giuliani Goes Global with the Illusion of Control', *Geoforum*, 40(6), 1033–40.

MSC Malaysia (2009) www.mscmalaysia.my (home page), date accessed 19 February.

B. Mullings (1995) 'Telecommunications restructuring and the development of export information processing services in Jamaica', in H. Dunn (ed.), *Globalization, Communications and Caribbean Identity* (New York: St Martin's Press), 163–84.

B. Mullings (1998) 'Jamaica's Information Processing Services: Neoliberal niche or structural limitation?', in T. Klak (ed.), *Globalization and Neoliberalism: The Caribbean Context* (Lanham: Rowman & Littlefield), 135–54.

M. Munday and A. Roberts (2006) 'Developing Approaches to Measuring and Monitoring Sustainable Development in Wales: A Review', *Regional Studies*, 40(5), 535–554.

K. Murakami and D. M. Wood (2006) 'Becoming the City of Trees: Spatial Planning in Japan and the Feelings of Place', *Planning Theory and Practice*, 7(4), 445–48.

G. Myrdal (1957) *Economic Theory and the Underdeveloped Regions* (London: Duckworth).

W. J. V. Neill (2003) *Urban Planning and Cultural Identity* (London and New York: Routledge).

E. Nel and C. M. Rogerson (2005) 'Setting the Scene: Local Economic Development in Southern Africa', in E. L. Nel and C. M. Rogerson (eds.), *Local Economic Development in the Developing World* (New Brunswick, NJ: Transaction Publishers), 1–16.

K. Nelson (2009) 'Conn. land vacant 4 years after court OK'd seizure', *Associated Press*, 25 September.

NEPAD (2008) NEPAD in brief, www.nepad.org/2005/files/inbrief/php, date accessed 23 August 2008.

P. Newman and A. Thornley (2005) *Planning World Cities: Globalization and Urban Politics* (Basingstoke and New York: Palgrave Macmillan).

M. Newson (1992) *Managing the Human Impact on the Environment* (London: Belhaven).

Q. Nguyen (2008) 'How to combat urban sprawl: a case study of Arlington, Virginia', unpublished M.Sc. thesis (Glasgow: University of Glasgow).

S. W. Nicholas, B. Jean-Louis, B. Ortiz, M. Northridge, K. Shoemaker, R. Vaughan, M. Rome, G. Canada and V. Hutchinson (2005) 'Addressing the Childhood Asthma Crisis in Harlem: The Harlem Children's Zone Asthma Initiative', *American Journal of Public Health*, 95(2), 245–49.

NMSDC (2009) National Minority Supplier Development Council, Inc., www.nmsdcus.org (home page), date accessed 17 November 2009.

J. Nolan (2000) 'Auto plant vs. neighborhood: The Poletown battle', *Detroit News*, 27 January.

I. Nonaka and H. Takeuchi (1995) *The Knowledge-creating Company* (Oxford: Oxford University Press).

D. Noon, J. Smith-Canham and M. Eagland (2000) 'Economic Regeneration and Funding', in P. Roberts and H. Sykes (eds.), *Urban Regeneration: A Handbook* (London, Thousand Oaks, CA and New Delhi: Sage).

D. C. North (1990) *Institutions, Institutional Change and Economic Performance* (Cambridge: Cambridge University Press).

D. Oakley and H.-S. Tsao (2006) 'A New Way of Revitalizing Distressed Urban Communities? Assessing the Impact of the Federal Empowerment Zone Program', *Journal of Urban Affairs*, 28(5), 443–71.

D. Oakley and H-S. Tsao (2007) 'The Bottom-Up Mandate: Fostering Community Partnerships and Combating Economic Distress in Chicago's Empowerment Zone', *Urban Studies*, 44(4), 819–43.

N. Oatley (1998) 'Cities, Economic Competition and Urban Policy', in N. Oatley (ed.), *Cities, Economic Competition and Urban Policy* (London: Paul Chapman).

N. Oatley and C. Lambert (1997) 'Local capacity in Bristol: tentative steps towards institutional thickness', paper delivered to Bristol/Hanover Symposium, Bristol, May.

K. Ohmae (1995) *The End of the Nation State: The Rise of Regional Economies* (London: HarperCollins).

Øresundbro Konsortiet (2008) Facts worth knowing about the Øresund Bridge, www.ooresundbro.com/library/?obj=6196, date accessed 13 April 2009.

Organisation for Economic Co-operation and Development (OECD) (2001) *Local Partnerships for Better Governance* (Paris: OECD).

PA Cambridge Economic Consultants (1987) *An Evaluation of the Enterprise Zone Experiment* (London: Inner Cities Directorate, Department of the Environment, HMSO).

B. Page (1993) 'Agro-industrialization and rural transformation: the restructuring of Midwestern meat production', unpublished Ph.D. dissertation (Berkeley: University of California).

J. Pallot and D. J. B. Shaw (1981) *Planning in the Soviet Union* (London: Croom Helm).

M. Parkinson, M. Hutchins, J. Simmie *et al.* (2004) 'Competitive European Cities: Where Do the Core Cities Stand?', *Urban Research Summary No.13* (London: Office of the Deputy Prime Minister).

J. Peck (2005) 'Struggling with the Creative Class', *International Journal of Urban and Regional Research*, 29(4), 740–70.

D. Pellow (2002) *Garbage Wars: The Struggle for Environmental Justice in Chicago* (Cambridge, MA: MIT Press).

A. A. Pereira (2004) 'State Entrepreneurship and Regional Development: Singapore's Industrial Parks in Batam and Suzhou', *Entrepreneurship and Regional Development*, 16, 129–44.

A. A. Pereira (2007) 'Transnational State Entrepreneurship? Assessing Singapore's Suzhou Industrial Park Project (1994–2004)', *Asia Pacific Viewpoint*, 48(3), 287–98.

F. Perroux (1950) 'Economic Space, Theory and Applications', *Quarterly Journal of Economics*, 64, 89–104.

M. Pezzini (2003) *Cultivating Regional Development: Main Trends and Policy Challenges in OECD Regions*, www.oecd.org;dataoecd/44/20/2489826. pdf, date accessed 3 December 2009.

A. Pike, S. Dawley and J. Tomaney (2010) 'Resilience, Adaptation and Adaptability', *Cambridge Journal of Regions, Economy and Society*, 3, 59–70.

D. A. Pines (2005) 'Thriving in the Zone', *US News and World Report*, 31 October.

M. E. Podmolik (2008) 'Foundation Crumbles on Kimball Hill', *Chicago Tribune*, 7 December, 1.

Poletown Neighborhood Council v. *City of Detroit* (1981) 410 Mich. 616; 304 NW 2d 455; 1981 Mich. LEXIS 250: Docket No. 66294.

S. Popkin, B. Katz, M. K. Cunningham, K. D. Brown, J. Gustafson, and M. A. Turner (2004) *A Decade of HOPE VI* (Washington, DC: Urban Institute), www.urban.org/UploadedPDF/411002_HOPEVI.pdf, date accessed 24 June 2009.

M. E. Porter (1990) *The Competitive Advantage of Nations* (New York: Free Press).

M. E. Porter (1995) 'The Competitive Advantage of the Inner City', *Harvard Business Review*, May/June, 55–71.

M. E. Porter (1996) 'Competitive Advantage, Agglomeration Economies and Regional Policy', *International Regional Science Review*, 19, 85–90.

M. E. Porter (2000) 'Location, Competition and Economic Development: Local Clusters in the Global Economy', *Economic Development Quarterly*, 14, 15–31.

M. E. Porter (2001) *Clusters of Innovation: Regional Foundations of US Competitiveness* (Washington, DC: Council on Competitiveness).

M. E. Porter (2003) 'The Economic Performance of Regions', *Regional Studies* 37, 549–78.

K. Pothukuchi (2009) 'Community and Regional Food Planning: Building Institutional Support in the United States', *International Planning Studies*, 14(4), 349–67.

H. Prates (2007) Brazilian Beats, www.i-genius.org/member/profile.pho/id/235, date accessed 30 November 2009.

A. Pred (1966) *The Spatial Dynamics of Urban Growth in the United States, 1840–60* (Cambridge: MIT Press).

V. Prescott (2009) 'Word of Mouth', New Hampshire Public Radio, 8 April. www.nhpr.org/node/24278, date accessed 13 September 2009.

Preservation Chicago (2005) *Chicago's Seven Most Threatened Buildings 2006: Pilsen* (Chicago: Preservation Chicago).

ProLogis (2008) 'China's Special Economic Zones and National Industrial Parks–Door Openers to Economic Reform', *ProLogis Research Bulletin*, spring 2008, www.prologisresearch.com/supplychain/docs/China_Research_Final.pdf, date accessed 25 August 2008.

PRZOOM (2007) '£6.4 million boost for Birmingham's custard factory', www.przoom.com/news/15503, date accessed 1 September 2008.

G. Raagmaa (2002) 'Regional Identity in Regional Development and Planning', *European Planning Studies*, 10(1), 55–76.

J. Raemaekers (2000) 'Planning for Minerals, Waste and Contaminated Land', in P. Allmendinger, A. Prior and J. Raemaekers (eds.), *Introduction to Planning Practice* (Chichester: Wiley).

M. Ram and T. Jones (2007) 'Ethnic minority business in the UK: a review of research and policy development', paper to the ESRC/CRE/DTI/EMDA Ethnic Minority Business Workshop.

B. Ramasamy, A. Chakrabarty and M. Cheah (2004) 'Malaysia's Leap into the Future: an Evaluation of the Multimedia Super Corridor', *Technovation*, 24(11), 871–83.

D. Ransom (2008) 'Starting up: funding your social venture', *Wall Street Journal*, http://online.wsj.com/article/SB122124827514029295.html, date accessed 12 September 2008.

J. Ratcliffe, M. Stubbs, and M. Shepherd (2004) *Urban Planning and Real Estate Development*, 2nd edn (London and New York: Spon Press).

Real ND (2009) 'The Enchanted Highway – Regent, North Dakota', www.realnd.com/enchantedhighwayindex.htm, date accessed 20 July 2009.

M. R. Redclift (1987) *Sustainable Development: Exploring the Contradictions* (London: Routledge).

D. A. Reingold (2001) 'Are TIFs Being Misused to Alter Patterns of Residential Segregation? The Case of Addison and Chicago, Illinois', in C. L. Johnson and J. Y. Man (eds.), *Tax Increment Financing and Economic Development: Uses, Structures and Impact* (Albany: State University of New York Press).

M. Reisner (1986) *Cadillac Desert: The American West and Its Disappearing Water* (New York: Hudson Books).

R. Renstrom (2004) 'San Diego promotes recycled water usage', *Waste News*, 1 March, 13.

ReVista, Harvard Review of Latin America (2006), fall, 6–31.

M. Richardson and A. Wilson (2008) *Wales Fair Trade Nation Report*, Fforwm Masnach Deg Cymru/Wales Fair Trade Forum, Cardiff. Available online: www.fairtradewales.com/fileserve/fileserve/741, date accessed 27 April 2010.

T. J. Rickard (2003) 'Jamaica's Response to Marginalization within the Global Economy', in W. Leimgruber, R. Majoral and C-W. Lee (eds.), *Policies and Strategies in Marginal Regions: Summary and Evaluations* (Aldershot: Ashgate), 81–96.

S. D. Ricketts (2002) 'Free Zone Garment Workers: How Do They Cope?', *Social and Economic Studies*, 51(4), 127–52.

M. Ringer (1989) 'Is the Shopper Really King?', *Estates Gazette*, 8945, 109–12.

Roadside America (2009) 'Enchanted Highway', www.roadsideamerica.com/story/2155, date accessed 20 July 2009.

E. Robbins (2003) 'Winning the Water Wars', *Planning*, 69(6), 28–33.

J. Robert (2007) 'The Origins of Territorial Cohesion and the Vagaries of its Trajectory', in A. Faludi (ed.), *Territorial Cohesion and the European Model of Society* (Cambridge, MA: Lincoln Institute of Land Policy).

P. Roberts (1995) *Environmentally Sustainable Business: A Local and Regional Perspective* (London: Paul Chapman).

C. Rocha and I. Lessa (2009) 'Urban Governance for Food Security: The Alternative Food System in Belo Horizonte, Brazil', *International Planning Studies*, 14(4), 389–400.

R. J. Rogerson (1999) 'Quality of Life and City Competitiveness', *Urban Studies* 36(5–6), 969–85.

S. Rozario (2007) 'The dark side of micro-credit', www.opendemocracy.net (home page), date accessed 30 November 2009.

D. Rose (2008) 'Within the embers of the garment', *Jamaica Gleaner*, 4 July.

C. F. Sabel (1992) 'Studied trust', discussion paper, Science Centre, Berlin.

C. Sadovi (2009) 'No school honeymoon – angry parents, frustrated teachers heckle Huberman', *Chicago Tribune*, 29 January, 13.

R. Salais and M. Storper (1992) 'The Four "Worlds" of Contemporary Industry', *Cambridge Journal of Economics*, 16, 169–93.

J. Sanderson and S. M. N. Islam (2007) *Climate Change and Economic Development: SEA Regional Modelling and Analysis* (Basingstoke: Palgrave Macmillan).

A. Sapir, P. Aghion, G. Bertola, M. Hellwig, J. Pisani-Ferry, D. Rosati, J. Viñals and H. Wallace, with M. Butti, M. Nava, and P. M. Smith (2004) *An Agenda for a Growing Europe: The Sapir Report* (Oxford: Oxford University Press).

N. Sato (2006) 'City Planning of Sendai: Now and for the Future', *Planning Theory and Practice*, 7(4), 461–69.

T. Saunders and L. McGovern (1993) *The Bottom Line of Green Is Black: Strategies for Creating Profitable and Environmentally Sound Businesses* (San Francisco: Harper).

H. V. Savitch (2002) 'What is New about Globalization and What Does It Portend for Cities?', *International Social Science Journal*, 54(172), 179–89.

Lord Scarman (1986) *The Brixton Disorders 10–12 April 1981*, Cmnd 8427 (London: HMSO).

H.-R. Schalcher (2008) *Office Building in India: Development Alternatives World Headquarters* (Zurich: Holcim Foundation for Sustainable Construction), www.holcimfoundation.org (home page), date accessed 27 May 2009.

H. S. Schell (1968) *History of South Dakota* (Lincoln: University of Nebraska Press).

M. Scott (2010) 'Not only Russia and Qatar who are rubbing hands after Zurich', *Guardian*, 8 December, Sports Guardian, 8.

Scottish Office (1998) *Travel Choices for Scotland: White Paper* (Edinburgh: Stationery Office), www.archive.official-documents.co.uk/document/cm40/4010/tc-xc.htm, date accessed 12 December 2009.

J. Seager (2003) *The Penguin Atlas of Women in the World* (New York: Penguin).

P. Selman (1996) *Local Sustainability: Managing and Planning Ecologically Sound Places* (London: Paul Chapman).

K. Shannon and A. Loeckx (2004) 'Vinh – Rising from the Ashes', in A. Loeckx, K. Shannon, R. Tuts and H. Verschure (eds.), *Urban Trialogues: Visions_Projects_Co-productions Localising Agenda 21* (Nairobi: UN–Habitat).

J. Simmie (2001) 'Innovation and Agglomeration Theory', in J. Simmie (ed.), *Innovative Cities* (London and New York: Spon Press), 11–52.

D. E. Simpson (dir.) (2009) *Milking the Rhino* (Kartemquin Films).

F. Singh (2009) 'Chowkri Modikhana, Jaipur, India', presentation at the Prince's Foundation for the Built Environment 6th Annual Conference, St James's Palace, London, 5 February.

N. Smith (1984) *Uneven Development: Nature, Capital and the Production of Space* (Oxford: Blackwell).

N. Smith (1998) 'Antinomies of space and nature in Henri Lefebvre's The Production of Space', in A. Light and J. Smith (eds.), *The Production of Public Space* (Lanham, MA: Rowman & Littlefield).

N. Smith (2004) 'Scale Bending and the Fate of the National', in R. McMaster and E. Sheppard (eds.), *Scale and Geographic Inquiry: Nature, Society, and Method* (Oxford: Blackwell).

N. Smith and W. Dennis (1987) 'The Restructuring of Geographical Scale: Coalescence and Fragmentation of the Northern Core Region', *Economic Geography*, 63(2), 160–82.

M. Smith, J. Whitelegg and N. Williams (1998) *Greening the Built Environment* (London: Earthscan).

A. Y. So, N. Lin and D. Poston (2001) *The Chinese Triangle of Mainland China, Taiwan and Hong Kong: Comparative Institutional Analyses* (Westport, CT: Greenwood Press).

Social Compact (2007) *Detroit Neighborhood Market DrillDown: Catalyzing Business Investment in Inner City Neighborhoods* (Washington, DC: Social Compact, Inc.).

D. Sonnenfeld and A. Mol (2006) 'Environmental Reform in Asia', *Journal of Environment and Development*, 15(2), 112–37.

R. Sonnino (2009) 'Feeding the City: Towards a New Research and Planning Agenda', *International Planning Studies*, 14(4), 425–35.

S. Sood and H. Pattinson (2006) 'Urban Renewal in Asia-Pacific: A Comparative Analysis of Brainports for Sydney and Kuala Lumpur', *Journal of Business Research*, 59(6), 701–8.

S. Stagl (2002) 'Local Organic Food Markets: Potentials and Limitations for Contributing to Sustainable Development', *Empirica*, 29(2), 145–62.

Standing Advisory Committee on Trunk Road Appraisal (1999) *Transport and the Economy: Full Report (SACTRA)* (London: Department for Environment, Transport and the Regions).

C. Steel (2008) *Hungry City: How food shapes our lives* (London: Chatto & Windus).

N. Stern (2006) *Stern Review: The Economics of Climate Change* (London: HM Treasury).

G. Sternlieb and J. W. Hughes (1983) *The Atlantic City Gamble* (Cambridge, MA: Harvard University Press).

Stop Heathrow Expansion (2007) Campaign, www.stopheathrowexpansion.com (home page), date accessed 12 November 2009.

D. J. Storey (2003) 'Entrepreneurship, Small and Medium Sized Enterprises and Public Policies', in Z. J. Acs and D. B. Audretsch (eds.), *Handbook of Entrepreneurship Research: An Interdisciplinary Survey and Introduction* (Dordrecht: Kluwer Academic Publishers), 473–514.

W. B. Stöhr (1990) 'Introduction', in W. B. Stöhr (ed.), *Global Challenge and Local Response: Initiatives for Economic Regeneration in Contemporary Europe* (London and New York: United Nations University/Mansell), 20–34.

M. Storper (1995) 'The Resurgence of Regional Economies, Ten Years Later: The Region as a Nexus of Untraded Interdependencies', *European Urban and Regional Studies*, 2(3), 191–221.

M. Storper (1997) *The Regional World: Territorial Development in a Global Economy* (New York: Guilford Press).

S. Strambach with A. D'Lorio and C. Steinlein (2001) 'Innovative Clusters and Innovation Processes in the Stuttgart Region', in J. Simmie (ed.), *Innovative Cities* (London and New York: Spon Press).

D. Stull and M. Broadway (2004) *Slaughterhouse Blues: The Meat and Poultry Industry in North America* (Toronto: Thomson Wadsworth).

E. Swyngedouw (1997) 'Neither Global nor Local: "Glocalization"' and the Politics of Scale', in K. Cox (ed.), *Spaces of Globalization: Reasserting the Power of the Local* (New York: Guilford).

Talking History (2005) 'Enchanted Highway', internet radio programme, www.talkinghistory.org/radio.html, date accessed 20 July 2009.

S. Tanaka and K. Murakami (2006) '"The City of Trees": The Role of a Grand Concept for Sendai Spatial Planning', *Planning Theory and Practice*, 7(4), 449–60.

T&E Centres (2009) Employment and Economic Development Centres, www.te-keskus.fi (home page), date accessed 17 November 2009.

I. Taylor, K. Evans and P. Fraser (1996) *A Tale of Two Cities: Global Change, Local Feeling and Everyday Life in the North of England. A Study in Manchester and Sheffield* (London: Routledge).

Thames Town (2009) www.thamestown.com/english/ (home page), date accessed 8 July 2009.

A. K. Thas (2007) *Gender Assessment of Selected E-Business and Strategies in Asia: The Case Studies of Malaysia, the Philippines, the Republic of Korea and Thailand*, Economic and Social Commission for Asia and the Pacific, Gender and Development Discussion Paper Series No. 19.

C. Thomas and E. Hague (2000) 'Steel Blooms – Exploring the Symbolic Landscape of Etruria', in T. Edensor (ed.), *Reclaiming Stoke-on-Trent: Identity, Leisure and Space in the Potteries* (Stoke-on-Trent: Staffordshire University Press), 105–30.

W. N. Thompson (1997) *Legalized Gambling: A Reference Handbook*, 2nd edn (Santa Barbara: ABC–CLIO).

A. Thornley (1991) *Urban Planning Under Thatcherism: The Challenge of the Market* (London: Routledge).

S. Thottathil (2008) 'Fair Trade or Food Miles?', *Geography Review*, 21(3), 18–19.

R. Tolley and B. Turton (1995) *Transport Systems, Policy, and Planning* (Harlow: Longman Scientific & Technical).

S. Tomic (2003) 'Hamilton Urban Braille System: Urban Design for an Aging Society', *Plan Canada*, 43 (1), 41–43.

P. Tough (2004) 'The Harlem Project', *New York Times Magazine*, 20 June, 44.

P. Tough (2008) *Whatever It Takes: Geoffrey Canada's Quest to Change Harlem and America* (Boston: Houghton Mifflin).

J. Townley (2009) 'Policy Changes for Fair Trade in Wales', *Journal of International Development*, 21, 1027–30.

Transition Network (2010) www.transitionnetwork.org (home page), date accessed 2 July 2010.

UN–Habitat (2001) *Cities in a Globalizing World: Global Report on Human Settlements 2001* (London and Sterling, VA: Earthscan), 146–58.

UN–Habitat (2006) *State of the World's Cities 2006–2007: The Millennium Development Goals and Urban Sustainability: 30 Years of Shaping the Habitat Agenda* (London: Earthscan).

UN–Habitat (2008) *State of the World's Cities 2008/2009: Harmonious Cities* (London and Sterling, VA: Earthscan).

UN–Habitat (2010) *State of the World's Cities 2010/2011: Bridging the Urban Divide* (London: Earthscan).

UNESCO (2009) http://whc.unesco.org (home page), date accessed 12 June 2009.

United Nations (1998) *Role of Micro-Credit in the Eradication of Poverty: Report of the Secretary General*, A/53/223 (New York: United Nations).

United Nations Centre for Human Settlements (2001) *Cities in a Globalizing World: Global Report on Human Settlements 2001* (London: Earthscan).

United Nations Centre for Human Settlements (HABITAT) (1996) *An Urbanizing World: Global Report on Human Settlements, 1996* (Oxford: Oxford University Press).

Urban and Economic Development, Ltd. (URBED) (1987) *Re-using Redundant Buildings: Case Studies of Good Practice in Urban Regeneration* (London: Department of the Environment, Inner Cities Directorate, HMSO).

Urban Task Force ([1999] 2005) *Towards an Urban Renaissance: Final Report* (London: Department of the Environment, Transport and the Regions).

US Department of Agriculture (2009a) 'Farmers markets and local food retailing', *Agricultural Marketing Service*, www.ams.usda.gov/AMSv1.0/ FARMERSMARKETS, date accessed 16 June 2010.

US Department of Agriculture (2009b) 'Access to affordable and nutritious food', *Economic Research Service Report Summary*, www.ers.usda.gov (home page), date accessed 1 June 2010.

P. van Doren (1995) 'Adopting the Innovative Environment Approach: A Programme of Regional Development for Charleroi', in C. Demaziere and P. A. Wilson (eds.), *Local Economic Development in Europe and the Americas* (London: Mansell), 92–111.

T. Veblen (1912) *The Theory of the Leisure Class* (New York: Macmillan).

Verslo Angelas (2009) www.versloangelas.lt (home page), date accessed 30 November 2009.

I. Vojnovic; C. Jackson-Elmoore, J. Holtrop and S. Bruch (2006) 'The Renewed Interest in Urban Form and Public Health: Promoting Physical Activity in Michigan', *Cities*, 23(1), 1–17.

A. Wajda (dir.) (1977) *Man of Marble* (Film Polski Film Agency).

P. Wakely and N. You (2001) *Implementing the Habitat Agenda: In Search of Urban Sustainability* (London: Development Planning Unit, UCL).

Y. P. Wang (2004) *Urban Poverty, Housing and Social Change in China* (London and New York: Routledge).

Y. P. Wang and A. Murie (1999) *Housing Policy and Practice in China* (Basingstoke and London: Macmillan Press).

Y. P. Wang, Y. Wang and J. Wu (2009) 'Urbanisation and Informal Development in China', *International Journal of Urban and Regional Research*, 33(4), 957–73.

Y. P. Wang, Y. Wang and J. Wu (2010) 'Housing Migrant Workers in Rapidly Urbanizing Regions: A Study of the Chinese Model In Shenzhen', *Housing Studies*, 25(1), 83–100.

K. Ward (2006) '"Policies in Motion", Urban Management and State Restructuring: The Trans-Local Expansion of Business Improvement Districts', *International Journal or Urban and Regional Research*, 30(1), 54–75.

K. Ward (2007) '"Creating a Personality for Downtown": Business Improvement Districts in Milwaukee', *Urban Geography*, 28(9), 781–808.

R. Ward (1985) 'Minority Settlement and the Local Economy', in B. Roberts, R. Finnegan and D. Gallie (eds.), *New Approaches to Economic Life* (Manchester: Manchester University Press).

R. Ward and R. Jenkins (eds.), (1984) *Ethnic Communities in Business* (Cambridge: Cambridge University Press).

S. V. Ward and J. R. Gold (1994) 'Introduction', in J. R. Gold and S. V. Ward (eds.), *Place Promotion: The Use of Publicity and Marketing to Sell Towns and Regions* (Chichester: Wiley).

WaterAid (2008) 'Small Yet Significant: Network Approach to Total Sanitation', *Water and Sanitation Perspective 02* (New Delhi: WaterAid India).

B. Waterhout (2008) *The Institutionalisation of European Spatial Planning* (Delft: Delft University of Technology).

J. Watts (2009) 'China puts its faith in solar power with huge investment', *Guardian*, 27 May, 1.

S. Wearing and J. Neil (2009) *Ecotourism: Impacts, Potentials and Possibilities*, 2nd edn (Oxford, UK: Butterworth-Heinemann).

A. Weber (1929) *Theory of the Location of Industries*, trans. C. J. Friedrich (Chicago: University of Chicago Press).

C. L. Weber and H. S. Matthews (2008) 'Food-Miles and the Relative Climate Impact of Food Choices in the United States', *Environmental Science and Technology*, 42(10), 3508–13.

R. Weber (2002) 'Extracting Value from the City: Neoliberalism and Urban Redevelopment', *Antipode*, 34(3), 519–40.

R. Weber (2003) 'Equity and Entrepreneurialism: The Impact of Tax Increment Financing on School Finance', *Urban Affairs Review*, 38(5), 619–44.

R. Weber, S. D. Bhatta and D. Merriman (2003) 'Does Tax Increment Financing Raise Urban Industrial Property Values?', *Urban Studies*, 40(10), 2001–21.

WIEGO (2009) www.wiego.org (home page), date accessed 8 June 2009.

P. Wilbourn (1997) 'Final Touches to the Ground Rules', *Planning*, 29 August, 8–9.

S. Wilkinson and R. Reed (2008) *Property Development*, 5th edn (London and New York: Routledge).

R. H. Williams (1996) *European Union Spatial Policy and Planning* (London: Paul Chapman Publishing).

J. S. C. Wiskerke (2009) 'On Places Lost and Places Regained', *International Planning Studies*, 14(4), 369–87.

K.-Y. Wong (1987) 'China's Special Economic Zone Experiment: An Appraisal', *Geografiska Annaler B*, 69(1), 27–40.

K.-Y. Wong and D. K. Y. Chu (eds.), (1985) *Modernization in China: The Case of the Shenzhen Special Economic Zone* (Oxford and New York: Oxford University Press).

S.-W. Wong and B. Tang (2005) 'Challenges to the Sustainability of "Development Zones": A Case Study of Guangzhou Development District, China', *Cities*, 22(4), 303–16.

World Bank (1997) *World Development Report 1997: The State in a Changing World* (Oxford: Oxford University Press).

World Bank (2009) World Development Report 2009: Reshaping Economic Geography (Washington, DC: World Bank).

World Bank (2010a) www.worldbank.org/EA784ZB3F0, date accessed 15 January 2010.

World Bank (2010b) www.worldbank.org/XC74PWPTZ0, date accessed 15 January 2010.

World Bank (2010c) 'Local Economic Development', www.worldbank.org/urban/led, date accessed 7 July 2010.

World Business Chicago (2009a) www.worldbusinesschicago.com/press/TopGroup-fDi-May09pdf, date accessed 14 July 2009.

World Business Chicago (2009b) www.worldbusinesschicago.com/wbc-2008-Annual-Report-Web.pdf, date accessed 14 July 2009.

World Commission on Environment and Development (1987) *Our Common Future* (Oxford: Oxford University Press).

World Water Council (2009) www.worldwatercouncil.org/fileadmin/ Financing_water_for_all/Gurria_Task_Force_ActionCases/Japan_ Case_Studies_on_Financing_December_2005_.doc, date accessed 18 February 2009.

J. Worthington (1982) 'Changing Industrial Environments', *Architects Journal*, 175(16), 80–2.

J. Wylie (1989) *Poletown: Community Betrayed* (Urbana and Chicago: University of Illinois Press).

C. Yeoh, W. P. N. How and A. L. Leong (2005) '"Created" Enclaves for Enterprise: An Empirical Study of Singapore's Industrial Parks in Indonesia, Vietnam and China', *Entrepreneurship and Regional Development*, 17(6), 479–99.

C. Yeoh, V. Sim, W. How (2007) 'Transborder Industrialization in the Framework of Singapore's Regionalization Strategy: The Case of Singapore's Gambit in Vietnam', *Journal of Asia-Pacific Business*, 8(3), 63–90.

J. Zhu (1994) 'Changing Land Policy and its Impact on Local Growth: The Experience of the Shenzhen Special Economic Zone, China, in the 1980s', *Urban Studies*, 31(10), 1611–23.

S. Zukin (1995) *The Cultures of Cities* (Malden: Blackwell).

Index